LAKE CHAMPLAIN

BOOKS BY RALPH NADING HILL

The Winooski
(Rivers of America series)

Contrary Country

Sidewheeler Saga

Window in the Sea

Yankee Kingdom: Vermont and New Hampshire
(Regions of America series)

The College on the Hill: A Dartmouth Chronicle

Vermont: A Special World
(co-editor)

Vermont Album

Lake Champlain: Key to Liberty

For Younger Readers:

Robert Fulton and the Steamboat

The Doctors Who Conquered Yellow Fever
(Landmark Books)

Fiction:

The Voyages of Brian Seaworthy

LAKE CHAMPLAIN

KEY TO LIBERTY

by Ralph Nading Hill

Epilogue by Arthur B. Cohn

The Countryman Press

WOODSTOCK, VERMONT

Twentieth Anniversary Edition, 1995

Published by
The Countryman Press, Inc.,
PO Box 175, Woodstock, Vermont 05091-0175

ISBN 0-88150-354-1

Original design by Linda Dean Paradee
Printed in Canada

Contents

Foreword

Remembering Ralph Nading Hill.

RALPH Nading Hill was "Vermont's memory," said Thomas Slayton, editor of *Vermont Life,* when Hill died on December 11, 1988, at the age of 70.

"We're gaining on it!" was the late author's favorite expression; in a life full of challenges, he used it often, from his first book, *The Winooski,* for The Rivers of America Series in 1949, during the herculean overland transfer of the *Ticonderoga* from Lake Champlain to its berth at the Shelburne Museum, to his final, persistent campaign to establish the Ethan Allen Homestead in Burlington's intervale.

Hill loved the lake in all its capricious moods, observed daily from the wheelhouse atmosphere of his Oakledge lakeshore home or over the gunwales of his boat, and would have cheered both the discoveries described in this edition by Arthur Cohn and the environmental protective measures organized by the Lake Champlain Basin coalition undertaken since his death.

A high level of creative energy, outspoken opinions, and a wry—sometimes acerbic—sense of humor characterized this bachelor historian *engagé* who never suffered fools willingly or in silence. A tall, lean *bon vivant,* Hill had a taste for antiques, maritime art, and classic cars.

Born in Burlington in 1917, Hill was educated at Burlington High School and Dartmouth College, and served as a special agent in the army's counterintelligence corps during the Second World War. *The Winooski* was followed by a dozen more books, including *Contrary Country* in 1950, *Yankee Kingdom: Vermont & New Hampshire* in 1960, and, for younger readers, *Robert Fulton and the Steamboat* and *The Doctors Who Conquered Yellow Fever.* He wrote as gracefully as he lived, with uncommon flair, fashioning the facts of the past into seamless, entertaining narratives.

In the early 1950s, he closed the colorful century of steam transportation on the lake as president of the Shelburne Steamboat Company, operating the 220-foot sidewheeler *Ticonderoga* for the last four years of its life afloat. Unwilling to see it scrapped, he persuaded Electra Havemeyer Webb to preserve the ship and move it to a permanent berth in her Shelburne Museum as the last survivor of the walking-beam sidewheeler passenger packet so familiar to generations of travelers on the lakes, sounds, and rivers of America. The ensuing saga of the *Ticonderoga*'s two-mile overland portage during the fall and winter of 1954–55 is described in dramatic detail in this book.

The museum, Mrs. Webb's great "collection of collections" of Americana, was one of Hill's consuming interests. He served as trustee for more than twenty years; to it, he willed his Oakledge house and the copyrights to his books.

His death was a professional as well as personal loss, for he gave the fledgling Countryman Press a major boost by choosing us to publish this book in 1977, when we were only four years old, rather than one of his major New York publishers. Such encouragement of Vermontiana was also demonstrated by his decades of involvement with *Vermont Life* as a senior editor on the magazine's advisory board. This text was commissioned and first serialized by the *Burlington Free Press* as part of its commemoration of America's Bicentennial. All the copies of the first clothbound edition—elegantly designed by Linda Paradee—were sold within a year, many through *Vermont Life*, which published two more printings. In 1987, we brought out the first paperback edition, which has been reprinted twice.

Lake Champlain was widely praised. Writing in *Vermont History*, John H.G. Pell, president of the Fort Ticonderoga Foundation, commented: "The great American novel has waited in vain for an author but the saga of Lake Champlain has found one, the only person who could do it justice . . . Combining extensive historical knowledge with careful research, spending a good part of his life on the lake, and bringing the literary skill of a professional writer and poet to the undertaking, [Hill] has produced a superbly interesting and informative book. It is a joy to read as well as to behold."

Hill's enduring passion during the last decade of his life was the Ethan Allen Homestead on a low promontory overlooking the Winooski River's floodplain outside of Burlington, not far from his brother Ira's sawmill on the lower falls. Allen settled there in 1787 and built a post-and-beam clapboard dwelling, one step up from a log house. In 1814, many years after Ethan Allen's sudden death, the farm and homestead were sold. Their provenance was ignored until Hill rediscovered the place while exploring the area for *Lake Champlain*.

As a result of his indefatigable efforts, the house was placed on the state and national registers of historic places, and in 1981 the Ethan Allen Homestead Trust was established to restore the dwelling to its original condition and create the visitors center which, today, serves as a living memorial to both Allen and Hill.

Seldom have a popular historian and an active preservationist been so perfectly embodied in one person with so much foresight and energy. These accomplishments in bringing New England history to life for generations of Americans were widely recognized during his lifetime: He was awarded the Preservation Trust of Vermont Award, an Award of Merit from the American Association for State and Local History, and other honors from the state of Vermont, and Dartmouth and Champlain Colleges.

"Lake Champlain is a living body, not a passive witness to history," H. Nicholas Muller III, then a professor of history at the University of Vermont and now director of the Wisconsin Historical Society, wrote in his foreword to the first edition of this book. "It became the meeting place of empires . . . The future of the United States rested precariously in a balance that could have been tipped by a change of wind in 1776 at Valcour Island or in 1814 at Plattsburgh Bay. Lake Champlain was the 'key to liberty' that shaped the destinies of the men and empires that used it. Now, in many ways, it has become their hostage . . . As Hill learned from his long study [of the lake], 'A present without a past is unthinkable: If we had not fathomed where we were, we could not reckon where we are. Nor have the least inkling of where we are bound.' *Lake Champlain: Key to Liberty* makes an important contribution to our understanding of the lake as the twenty-first century approaches."

Hill's lifelong career as a writer and historian and his genial personality gave him "an immense knowledge of Vermont history, politics, and society," Thomas

Slayton wrote in a *Vermont Life* postmortem. "But more than that, Ralph had an instructive, bred-in-the-bone understanding of the indefinable something that makes Vermont what it is . . . It was that instinctive sense that helped him write accurately and with great insight about his consuming passion, Lake Champlain."

—Peter S. Jennison

For Anthony H. Shaw
The sixth generation to
know and love Lake Champlain

LAKE CHAMPLAIN

I

The Making of the Lake.

᪥᪥᪥

Its Early Peoples.

O N a tour of America in the spring of 1835, Tyrone Power (the first) boarded the *Phoenix* at Whitehall, the lively southernmost port of Lake Champlain. As the steamboat left the tiny basin, the eye of the long needle of the Narrows, he wrote in his journal of richly green meadow slopes and cliffs clothed in flowering shrubs:

At last the lake expanded gloriously, reminding me, at a first glimpse, of the Trossachs, save that here was less grandeur and deep shadow, the outlines of the mountains were softer and the valleys more fertile.

The Green Mountains of the state of Vermont now bounded the lake upon the north, and on the south rose the giant mountains of the state of New York. These were forever changing in form as we crossed and recrossed the lake in order to land or receive passengers. . . .

Had these beauties been given to England or to Scotland, they would each and all have been berhymed and bepainted until every point of real or imaginable loveliness had been exhausted: for myself I have looked on many lakes, and by none have been more delightfully beguiled than by a contemplation of this during some nine hours of sunshine, sunset, and twilight.

Such hyperbole was unusual for Englishmen confronted by such relics of the King's misfortunes as the forts at Ticonderoga and Crown Point. But nineteenth century travelers were enchanted with wild vistas of the new world and were eager to report their discoveries to their countrymen, whose homelands' familiar beauty had been "berhymed and bepainted" for centuries.

The compliment of all compliments, foreign and domestic, was bestowed by the American author, William Dean Howells, frequently a guest of his publisher, Henry Holt, from whose splendid house in Burlington could be seen the Green Mountains, the lake, and the entire sweep of Adirondacks. He declared no view in the world to be its equal. Inhabitants of the Champlain Valley who cannot believe their eyes or who take their surroundings for granted must therefore be persuaded that compared even to the Swiss Alps, the fjords of Norway, or the misty Scottish lakes, the gifts of nature have nowhere been more generous; and that if Champlain were the possession of other countries or continents, its virtues would be proclaimed from the mountain tops.

If another superlative may be added, it would be that Lake Champlain is the most historic body of water in the western hemisphere: a silver dagger from Canada to the heartland of the American colonies that forged the destiny of France and England in America, and of the United States. Liberated from war and the threat of war early in the nineteenth century, it became a thriving thoroughfare of trade and travel. Having since escaped the lacerations of other famous waterways that have fallen prey to industry, commerce, and an excess of tourism, the lake remains surprisingly well preserved. The reasons for this — that it is frozen several months of the year, that it has been deemed impractical to widen the canals that lead to tidewater north and south, that the stream of commerce has cut new channels elsewhere and that the shores of the lake have for one reason or another remained largely protected — account for its survival in a nearly natural state. Thus it has retained those qualities which give special places spirit and meaning: beauty and a rich body of traditions. While the latter are man-made, we have the accidents or designs of nature to thank for the lake's beauty.

If all the gigantic contortions that created the Champlain Valley and its bordering mountains during the past half-billion years could be compressed into a day, any lake-dweller would gladly trade that much of his life for a chair in the sky to witness the creation of today's remarkable tableau of land and water. As geologists have reconstructed it, the scene would open on a lunar landscape beneath a formidable range of mountains, among the oldest on earth, the Adirondacks. East of their sharp and lofty crests some great stirring within the earth compresses its crust so that it folds downward into a trough. This is invaded from the north and south by the ocean, which washes mud and clay from the mountains and deposits it in layers thousands of feet deep. These sediments are compressed into rock which first rises above, then sinks back into the sea.

Presently a profound subterranean upheaval again forces back the ocean, tilts these layers of rock and thrusts them upward to create, to the east, towering new peaks: the Green Mountains and the long chain of Taconics. Fiery intrusions of granite force their way upward. New crests are now built up by deep forces inside the earth, and again worn down by the elements until only stumps of the highest of them, the present Mount Mansfield, Camel's Hump, and the lesser peaks are left. A new series of convulsions create the Rocky Mountains in the far West, and by this time a stream has eroded a path through the Champlain Valley. A lush mantle of plants and trees presently appears. These at length perish in an age of cold, ushering an enormous wall of ice from the north which carries everything before it, scouring even the tops of the mountains.

The stream in the valley is buried under mile-high ice, irresistible in its southward journey to its ultimate destruction under the sun. Melting as it slowly retreats it creates Lake Vermont, which submerges most of the land in the Champlain Valley west of the Green Mountains. Having sunk once more under this incalculable burden, the floor of the valley is now below the level of the ocean, which rushes in from the north to displace the waters of the

1. *Adirondacks, among the oldest ranges on earth, descend steeply to Champlain's west shore.*

2. *Older strata above younger at Burlington's Rock Point compose a famous geological landmark.*

melting glacier. But the so-called Champlain Sea, an arm of the Atlantic, also gradually drains away when its bed, relieved of the weight of ice, slowly rises. Mountain rivers and streams fill the basin and the contours of the present lake, after thousands of sunsets in the making, gradually appear.

This chronicle of rocks and water is read in tiny marine fossils embedded in the shores, in the skeleton of a whale discovered far above them during a railroad excavation; in the red sandstone of Burlington Harbor's southern ledges (a vestige of the sea's original sedimentation) and in the far-famed overthrust just beyond the harbor's northern point where, as the result of contortions during the birth of the Green Mountains, older rocks were thrust over the younger. Something is to be learned from the configuration and substance of every mile of shoreline from the basin at Whitehall to a point 118 miles to the north in Quebec, where the lake becomes more properly the Richelieu River, a tributary of the St. Lawrence. But Champlain did not always drain north. During the ice age it emptied south into the Hudson, and may at times have submerged the rivers on the west slopes of the Green Mountains to pour over the height of land into the Connecticut. It has been observed that if the floor of the Champlain Valley continues to rise as it has, a further uplift of only four-tenths of an inch per mile would reverse its flow into the Hudson. It will take another twelve hundred centuries for this to happen, the final effect of an age of ice a million years in the making, but a mere pinpoint on the scale of our geological history.

The largest body of deep fresh water in the United States other than the Great Lakes, Champlain encompasses some 490 square miles, of which 55 are islands. It sets Vermont and northern New England apart from New York as irrevocably as the North Sea separates Britain and France. Although it is technically a federal waterway, Vermont "owns" 322 of its square miles. New York, 151, and Canada, 17. The lake's greatest width is 12 miles and its deepest point, two miles north of Split Rock, is 399 feet. Fed from the western slopes of the Green Mountains by the Missisquoi, Lamoille, Winooski, and Otter Creek; in the south by the Poultney, the Mettowee, Wood Creek and Lake George; and in the west from the wild eastern ridges and ravines of the Adirondacks by the Big and Little Chazy, the Saranac, Ausable, Salmon, and Bouquet — Champlain drains some 8,277 square miles of mountain wilder-

3. Lying in the path of prevailing winds, the lake's ancient trough became a portal to the country.

ness, rolling hills, and fertile flatlands. Since the lake at its highest in the spring is only 100 feet above sea level, the Adirondack crests rising a mile above the water afford a spectacle much like that of the Rockies from the western plateau, where the viewer already stands a mile above sea level.

The lake's location between chains of mountains in a valley leading north and south to the two great valleys of the St. Lawrence and Hudson, must have had as much to do with man's arrival perhaps 8,000 years ago as it has with his aggressions and wanderings during the last three centuries. From the southern end of the lake, access to the Hudson could be gained by passing over Wood Creek or Lake George. Early nomads and later conquerors were then afforded a continuing journey by water to the midwest by way of the Mohawk, or to the Atlantic seaboard by way of the Hudson itself. The destiny of an inland waterway that nearly makes an island of New England was obviously preordained. "By far the most important inland water in North America," a returned prisoner from Quebec wrote on an early English map, "because it is . . . a canal leading from New England and New York to the very Bowels of Canada."

The early peoples who occupied the Champlain Valley unfortunately left fewer clues of their origins than the rocks. The campsite of Paleo-Indians dating back to the retreat of the glacier some 8,000 years ago has been found in Franklin County. These people presumably crossed the land bridge then connecting Siberia and Alaska and migrated south the length of North America, across the Isthmus of Panama and into South America. One branch that left the trunkline of this migration at approximately "Ohio" led southeast to "Florida," and another turned northeast to the shores of the Champlain Sea.

After several thousand years, these pioneers were succeeded by the Archaic People — hunters and fishermen who may have arrived with the evergreen forests and who used spears tipped with chipped slate points, stones to anchor their fishnets, bone implements, wooden vessels, and bowls of soapstone. They in turn were replaced by the Woodland Peoples, forebears of the Algonquin and Iroquois tribes whom the white explorers and settlers first encountered in the seventeenth century. Much more is known of their presence, since the white pioneers recorded what they learned first-hand of their culture. Ordinarily, their artifacts are much nearer the surface of the ground, but sometimes very old Woodland burials also are discovered not very far down.

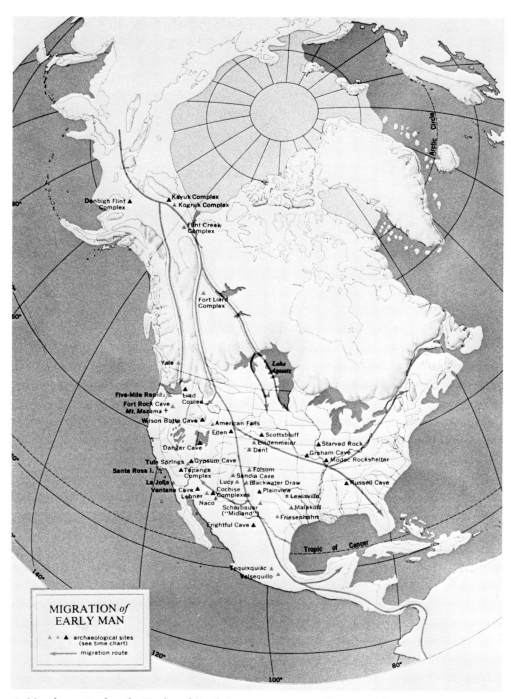

MIGRATION *of* EARLY MAN

▲ ▲ ▲ archaeological sites (see time chart)

← migration route

4. *Man first arrived on the North and South American continents by way of the land-bridge connecting Siberia and Alaska in glacial times. One branch of this migration led to the shores of the much enlarged Champlain Sea left by the melting glacier.*

The late Professor George H. Perkins of the University of Vermont described bowl-shaped early Woodland graves found under the stumps of Norway pines on a ridge in East Swanton. Surrounded by belongings, the skeletons lay in a flexed position in sand stained a deep red-brown, apparently signifying burial rites wherein water mixed with hematite (a piece of which was found in one of the graves) was poured over the remains. Hence they were called the Red Paint People, who lived both in Archaic and early Woodland times.

In 1934, a task force sent to Lake Champlain from the Museum of the American Indian in New York excavated a knoll at the mouth of East Creek, which enters the Lake at Mount Independence. Beneath a layer containing Revolutionary musket balls and clay pipes were found shards of Iroquois pottery and triangular arrowpoints. Under this layer Algonquin pottery and notched arrow-points appeared. Seven feet down were unearthed 45 early Woodland graves disclosing the artifacts of the forgotten race: fifteen-inch stone spearheads, strings of copper beads, and in one grave alone, six dozen finely chiseled arrowheads that probably belonged to the long-departed hunter.

The presence of this site may have had much to do with the flint quarries

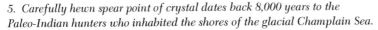

5. *Carefully hewn spear point of crystal dates back 8,000 years to the Paleo-Indian hunters who inhabited the shores of the glacial Champlain Sea.*

on the slopes of Mount Independence and Ticonderoga from which generations of Indians cut blocks of stone to be made into implements or for barter
with other tribes. An Iroquois legend about this place, recounted by Jesuit
priests, explains the Indians' custom of stopping there to gather flints:

They never fail to halt at this place to pay homage to a race of invisible men who
dwell there at the bottom of the lake. These beings occupy themselves in preparing
flints nearly all cut for the passerby, provided the latter pay their respects to them by
giving them tobacco. If they give these beings much of it, the latter give them a
liberal supply of stones. These water men travel in canoes, as do the Iroquois; and
when their great captain proceeds to throw himself into the water to enter this place,
he makes so loud a noise that he fills with fear the minds of those who have no
knowledge of this great spirit and of these little men.

Far to the north on the shores of St. Albans Bay a similar outcropping of
flint was worked extensively by Indians who obviously used it for trade,
since blocks of it were found on the shore far from the site where the outcropping occurs.

There are references to numbers of implements found near the mouths of
the larger rivers — a great many on the Otter Creek where a heavy copper
celt weighing 38 pounds, eight inches long, two wide, and apparently cast,

*6. Purpose of the exquisitely ground and polished artifact called a
boatstone was probably either ornamental or ceremonial.*

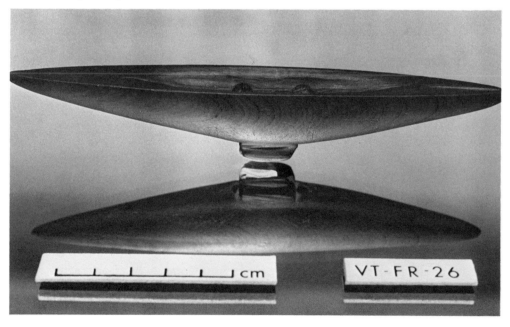

7. *Beads of shells (bottom and top right) and copper (center) were found in graves dating to first millennium B.C.*

8. *Early Woodland Peoples' awl of Great Lakes copper was obviously imported; whetstone served to sharpen implements.*

not hammered, was discovered. All the way from Colchester Point to Williston, the Winooski abounded in wrought flints, celts and chippings. A large settlement or gathering place containing many artifacts was unearthed in a sand ridge on the west shore near Plattsburg. The New York historian David Kellogg, described the Ticonderoga promontory as "black with flints."

In 1938 Dr. John H. Bailey, reporting for the Champlain Archaeological Society, described a site at Chipman's Point below an overhanging cliff where from time immemorial a shelter had existed for at least two types of Indians. In the ashes of their campfires on a floor made from chips of limestone that had fallen from the cliff were found a polished bone dagger made from a large animal and the graves of a young child surrounded by large clam shells and of a pet dog under limestone slabs. Long after these people had departed, perhaps several hundred years, another group with arrow-tips of triangular points, and pottery jars moved in, spreading fallen rock over the old habitation to make a new floor. Along with stone arrowpoints they used awls and fishhooks of bone. They, too, lost a child whose remains were unearthed near the wall. And they were cannibals, for the bones of a woman, perhaps a captive, were buried in a pile with her skull placed on top.

An important discovery of some 90 graves of early Woodland People of all ages buried on the banks of the Missisquoi over 2,000 years ago was made in 1973 when a backhoe, digging the foundation for a house, uncovered a skull. Digging ceased while the Vermont Archaeological Society and the anthropology department of the University of Vermont enlisted student volunteers in the removal of earth in sections. Several skulls, together with remnants of burial cloth remarkably well preserved by the chemical action of copper beads, were transported undisturbed to the University laboratory with the earth in which they lay. A large assortment of very fine "Adena-style" arrow and spear points of many sizes, and meticuously finished pieces of tubular sandstone, used apparently for smoking, and native to Ohio, were also recovered.

During a lifetime of investigating sites on and near the northeast shores of the lake L. B. Truax of St. Albans collected thousands of artifacts. For every such serious student of our stone age, there are scores of others whose finds have been collected by accident or at random. These do little to solve the puzzle, but at least attest to the widespread and longstanding Indian occupation of the Champlain Valley. How could it have been otherwise? Past discoveries must represent the smallest fragment of what has been plowed under or buried in gravel or silt along the shores of the lake or its tributaries.

Scattered references in the histories of the first white settlers demonstrate that the last Indians in the valley left more than artifacts to prove their presence. At the mouth of the LaPlatte River, which empties into the bay at Shelburne, a history of the town in one of *Hemenway's* gazeteers describes:

... a field of about 25 acres, on the east side of the river near the mouth which had been cleared and cultivated for a length of time, as there were no stumps of the original timber. This clearing was in a square form with a heavy growth of timber on all sides, and two large trees of the original growth left standing in the clearing. There were numerous heaps or small piles of stones in this field which must have been carried there, probably for campfires, as there were no stones in the soil. This field was evidently abandoned by the savages several years before any settlement was made by the whites, as it was covered with a thick growth of small trees unlike the surrounding timber. Arrowheads, flints, and other articles were to be found on this field in considerable numbers, which was conclusive evidence of its having been occupied by savages for many years.

Among the intervales where resident or nomadic Indians raised their corn were the floodplains of the Winooski. Near its mouth white explorers found several hundred acres entirely cleared of trees.

However baffling the larger mystery of where and in what order which tribes or nations occupied the shores of Lake Champlain, it at least is clear that a large Indian village long stood near the mouth of the Missisquoi on its right bank in what is now West Swanton. In a speech to the governor of Quebec in 1776, a late generation of Abnakis said so. "We, the Missisquoi Indians of the St. Francis or Abnaki tribe, have inhabited that part of Lake Champlain known by the name of Missisquoi from time unknown to any of us here present." The site of their village appears on early maps. Moreover, it is written that for fifteen miles from the lake almost every field on the river showed evidence of Indian occupation. From some 1,000 relics dug up from about two feet below the surface, L. B. Truax concluded that the place had not only been occupied by the Abnakis, but previously by the Iroquois, and long before them by a much more ancient people.

9. Unearthed on a bank of the Missisquoi, an early Woodland Indian skull dates back 2500 years.

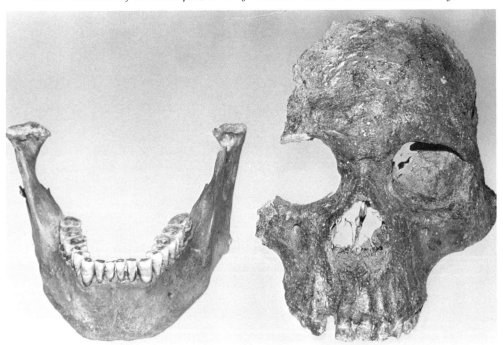

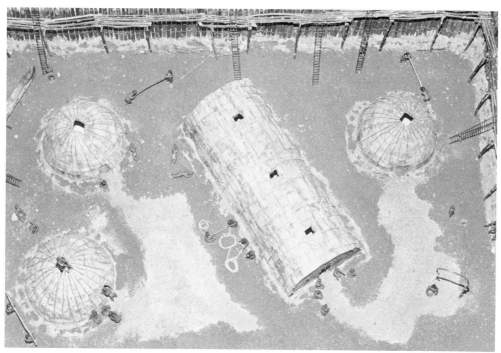

10. Model of an Abnaki village demonstrates construction of elm and birch bark.

One hundred eighty warriors are said to have lived in the Abnaki "castle" in 1736, indicating a total population of 800. A raging sickness appears to have wiped out the village a few years previously. In order to escape evil spirits, the remaining inhabitants temporarily abandoned their fine fields and took refuge in Quebec on the river St. Francis.

Although some of the pieces of the Algonquin-Iroquois puzzle are in place, much of it remains sky and water with nary a cloud nor a ripple to help fill the empty spaces. Yet this much is established: that long before Europeans had arrived the lake had become the boundary between two great nations of Indians, the Algonquins holding the "Vermont" shore and everything east, southeast, and north of it — all that became New England and southeastern Canada. The Abnakis, joined by other eastern Algonquins, occupied an area roughly between the Kennebec River and Lake Champlain. The Iroquois claimed the "New York" shore and all the land west to the Great Lakes and south even to parts of Virginia and the Carolinas. Among the five nations of the Iroquois, the Mohawks were, of course, masters of the Adirondack wilderness.

In his monograph, *The Eastern Border of the Iroquois*, Gordon M. Day

11. One of the finest specimens of pottery unearthed in New England, this jar found in Colchester in 1825 bears characteristic St. Lawrence Iroquois markings.

emphasizes that place names on the west shore of the lake were Iroquois, and those on the east shore, Algonquin, thus confirming the lake as the boundary. The dark forests of the Green Mountains were the Abnakis' hunting ground, through which they crossed eastward to the *Quinatucquet*, "The Great River," mainly by way of two of the lake's tributaries, the *Winooski-took*, "Onion land River" and *Pecouk-took*, "Crooked River," Otter Creek.

Abnaki names preserved and interpreted by Day, Rowland Robinson, Walter Crockett, John Huden, and others, include that of the lake, *Petoubouque*, "The Waters that Lie Between" (the Iroquois called it *Caniaderi-Guarunte*, "The Door to the Country"); *Mississiak* or *Missisquoi*, "People at the Marshy Grassy Place;" *Quineaska*, the La Platte River; *Quineaska-took*, "The Long Joint," Shelburne Point; *Wujahose* (also *Odziozo*) for the spirit guarding Rock Dunder; *Tobapsqua*, "The Pass Through the Rock," Split Rock; *Sungahnee*, "Fish-weir River," Lewis Creek;

K'chenamehau, "The Great Island," Grand Isle; and *Moze-o-de-be-wadso,* "The Moose Head Mountain," Mount Mansfield.

The importance that the Indians attached to place names is highlighted by Day's description of the origin of Rock Dunder, considered by the Abnakis the most prominent feature of their mythology (and by the Iroquois, some sources affirm, as the northeast cornerstone of their empire). The great Abnaki Transformer, or Creator of land, water, and life was named *Odziozo:*

It was Odziozo who laid out the river channels and lake basins and shaped the hills and mountains. Just how long he took is a subject which Abnakis, only recently deceased, used to discuss over their campfires. At last he was finished, and like Jehovah in *Genesis,* he surveyed his handiwork and found it was good. The last work he made was Lake Champlain and this he found especially good. It was his master-piece. He liked it so much that he climbed on to a rock in Burlington Bay and changed himself into stone so that he could better sit there and enjoy the spectacle through the ages. He still likes it, because he is still there and used to be given offerings of tobacco as long as Abnakis went this way by canoe, a practice which continued until about 1940. The rock is also called *Odziozo,* since it is the Trans-former himself. It is the one called Rock Dunder on modern maps.

Noting that the Mohawk name for Rock Dunder, *Rotsio,* is similar to the *Odziozo* of the Abnaki, Day suggests that the Mohawks may have borrowed it. He believes that their traditions about the rock somehow became con-fused with the drowning south of the rock in 1667 of their friend, Arendt Van Corlaer, a popular Dutch official in New York. In early accounts the lake was thus sometimes called Corlaer.

"What bearing does all this have on the questions of who occupied the eastern shore of the Lake?" Day concludes. "Simply this; by placing their Transformer and other cosmological tales in this region, the St. Francis Abnakis show that they regard it as their original homeland."

II

The Arrival of Samuel de Champlain and His Fateful Encounter with the Iroquois.

HAD it not been for the compulsion of Samuel de Champlain to write down what he saw and heard, the beginning of the recorded history of Lake Champlain might have been indefinitely postponed. Although Columbus long had preceded him, little knowledge about the interior of North America had accumulated. When Champlain's canoe emerged from the Richelieu on to the shining lake in July 1609, the only European settlements on the continent other than Port Royal and his own at Quebec were those of the Spaniards in Florida and Mexico and Britain's two-year-old colony at Jamestown.

Ever hopeful of finding the fabled northwest passage to China, other explorers came and saw. But too often they did not write, at least in very much detail. Champlain, the discoverer, adventurer, and empire builder, earned his place in history because of Champlain, the map-maker and journalist. Although Jacques Cartier had climbed Quebec's Mount Royal 74 years before Champlain, we are treated merely to a glimpse of vague seas to the south through the eyes of his guide, an Algonquin chief.

Little is known of Champlain's early life in the French fishing port of Brouage other than that he was a sea captain's son and the nephew of an officer in the Spanish navy. This accounts for his later confessions that "the art of navigation has long been my love, and has impelled me to expose myself nearly all my life to the impetuous waves of the ocean." Before he was 30,

Champlain had himself become captain of a ship bound for a two-year expedition to the West Indies and New Spain, during which he became the first to visualize a canal through the Isthmus of Panama. His attention then was drawn to the North. For three years beginning in 1603 he scouted and mapped the Atlantic coast all the way from Nova Scotia to Massachusetts. After an interval in France he set forth again in 1608, this time on a voyage up the broad St. Lawrence where, during the cruelest of winters, he laid the foundations of the settlement at Quebec. The next spring he agreed to join a war party of Algonquins who were anxious to engage their enemies in battle on the "Sea of the Iroquois" to the south.

Although the expedition left Quebec on June 18 in high spirits after a week of feasts and war games, a dispute divided the Indians at the mouth of the Richelieu and some of them departed. Champlain became further discouraged to find rocky rapids at Chambly where a portage would be necessary. Determined at all costs to see the great lake "full of fair islands

12. Although the lake appears distorted in relation to the Atlantic coast and a swollen St. Lawrence River, Champlain was an expert cartographer for his time.

and of fine countries" the party of three Frenchmen and 60 Indians carried 24 canoes and all their supplies around the rapids. Skirting low-lying islands with lush fields and pine forests filled with deer and other animals, they entered the lake early in July.

Historians have been unable to agree on some of the finer points of what happened next. Champlain's biographer, Morris Bishop, finds his chronology "often sadly at fault," and certain descriptive details confusing if not questionable. The Indians described a *Chaousarou* 8 or 10 feet long, which must have been the original Champlain monster. Champlain writes that he saw one five feet in length as thick as a man's thigh with silver-gray scales a dagger could not pierce and two-and-a-half-foot jaws filled with sharp and dangerous teeth:

The point of the snout is like that of a hog. This fish makes war on all others in the lakes and rivers and possesses, as these people assure me, a wonderful instinct; which is, that when it wants to catch any birds, it goes among the rushes or reeds bordering the lake in many places, keeping the beak out of water without budging, so that when the birds perch on his beak, imagining it a limb of a tree, it is so subtle that closing the jaws which it keeps half open, it draws the birds under water by the feet. The Indians gave me a head of it, which they prize highly saying, when they have a headache they let blood with the teeth of this fish at the seat of the pain which immediately goes away.

Since the largest muskellunge or northern pike would never reach ten feet, the identity of the *Chaousarou* must forever remain a mystery.

The snow Champlain wrote that he saw on the peaks of the Green Mountains must have been some kind of mirage, unless 1609 was an earlier version of 1816 when there was frost every month all summer. Or perhaps he became disoriented and reported the rocky escarpment on Whiteface, the Adirondack peak, as being on the eastern side of the lake. Whatever the discrepancies, it is unjust to find fault with a journal that is obviously accurate in so many respects. Champlain could hardly have recorded his observations with a quill pen while tossing among the waves. He probably trusted his memory, making periodic entries whenever he had an opportunity. Everything that he reported but did not see was, of course, subject to the lively imaginations of his Indian interpreters. (Loose quotations from his journal account for some of the confusion, and students would do well to check the translation by A. N. Bourne.)

After entering the lake he passed four beautiful islands, obviously Isle La Motte, Long Island (Grand Isle), and Valcour. His guides said these islands had formerly been inhabited by Indians but had been abandoned for a long time because of war between the Algonquins and Iroquois. As the islands receded and the broad lake opened before them, Champlain's interpreter told him that it extended close to the eastern mountains (by way of rivers). When he asked if they were inhabited "they told me that they were — by the Iroquois — and that in these places there were beautiful valleys and other stretches fertile in grain such as I had eaten in this country, with a great many other fruits."

Since his guides previously had reported that the Iroquois and Algonquins had abandoned the area, we are faced with a contradiction. Purely on the basis of the Indians' statement to Champlain that the Iroquois occupied the eastern shore, the Dutch spread the name *Irocoisia* across the Green Mountains on a 1614 map. If his Indians wanted to fight the Iroquois, and they then were living on the intervales of the Winooski, why didn't they seek them there instead of on the Adirondack shores far to the southwest? For it was there, they told him, that they were to go to find their enemies. Gordon Day thinks that Champlain misunderstood them. If Indians were living on the "Vermont" shore, and they must have been if their fields were full of corn, they were Algonquins. John Huden, however, citing the mixture of Algonquin and Iroquois artifacts unearthed on the eastern shore (of which the Iroquois jar found in Colchester is the foremost example) suggests that there may have been Iroquois outposts at Shoreham, Addison, Colchester, Milton, and Swanton. Yet Swanton was also an Algonquin site where the previously described Abnaki village was later found. These are some of the reasons why statements about which groups of Indians occupied the Champlain Valley remain speculative.

A grove of chestnut trees, the only one Champlain had seen since his previous voyage to America, caught the attention of historical detectives. They found them to have grown in only one place in the Champlain Valley, on the hill in Burlington above the intervale farm of a later pioneer, Ethan Allen. In the mid-nineteenth century their ancient stumps were still in evidence, some of them three centuries old. A professor and later president of

13. *Dutch map of 1614, largely a copy of Champlain's, labels the east side of the lake as
Iroquois country, based on a statement of the discoverer's Algonquin guides.*

the University of Vermont (Joseph Torrey) searched both shores of the lake for others like them but found none. The implication is clear: after leaving the islands in the north, Champlain crossed to the eastern shore and paddled a short distance up the river that they told him led to the mountains. The problem here is that since Champlain says he continued his course on the west side, he could not have seen the chestnuts on the east side. Since two to three weeks elapsed from the time he entered the lake until he met the Iroquois on July 29, he must, however, have done considerable exploring. As he neared Iroquois country the Indians, he wrote:

. . . often came to me to ask if I had dreamed, and if I had seen their enemies. I answered them "no," and told them to be of good courage and to keep up hope. When night came we pursued our journey until daylight, when we withdrew into the thickest part of the woods and passed the rest of the day there. About ten or eleven o'clock, after having taken a little walk around our encampment, I went to rest and I dreamed that I saw the Iroquois, our enemies, in the lake near a mountain, drowning within our sight; and when I wished to help them our savage allies told me that we must let them all die, and that they were worthless. When I woke up they did not fail to ask me, as is their custom, if I had dreamed anything. I told them the substance of what I had dreamed. This gave them so much faith that they no longer doubted that good was to befall them.

When evening came we embarked in our canoes to continue on our way; and, as we were going along very quietly, and without making any noise, on the twenty-ninth of the month we met the Iroquois at the end of a cape that projects into the lake on the west side, and they were coming to war. We both began to make loud cries, each getting his arms ready. We withdrew toward the water and the Iroquois went ashore and arranged their canoes in line, and began to cut down trees with poor axes which they get in war sometimes, and also with others of stone; and they barricaded themselves very well.

Our men also passed the whole night with their canoes drawn up close together fastened to poles so that they might not get scattered . . . we were on the water within arrow range of the side where their barricades were.

When they were armed and in array, they sent two canoes . . . to learn from their enemies if they wanted to fight. They replied that they desired nothing else, but that . . . they must wait for the daylight to recognize each other, and that as soon as the sun rose they would open the battle. This was accepted by our men and while we waited, the whole night was passed in dances and songs, as much on one side as on the other, with endless insults and other talk, such as the little courage they had, their feebleness and inability to make resistance against their arms . . . Our men also were not lacking in retort, telling them that they should see such power of arms as never before. . . . After plenty of singing, dancing and parleying with one another, daylight came. My companions and I remained concealed for fear that the enemy should see us preparing our arms. . . . After arming ourselves with light armor, each of us took an arquebus and went ashore. I saw the enemy come out of their barricade, nearly 200 men, strong and robust to look at, coming slowly toward us with a dignity and assurance that pleased me very much. At their head there were three chiefs. Our men also went forth in the same order, and they told me that those who wore three large plumes were the chiefs . . . and that I should do all I could to kill them. I promised them to do all in my power and said that I was very sorry that they could not understand me well, so that I might give order and system to their attack of the enemy. . . .

As soon as we were ashore they began to run about 200 paces toward their enemy, who were standing firmly and had not yet noticed my companions, who went into the woods with some savages. Our men began to call me with loud cries and, to give me a passageway, they divided into two parts and put me at their head, where I marched about twenty paces in front of them until I was thirty paces from the enemy. They, at once saw me and halted, looking at me, and I at them. When I saw them making a move to shoot at us, I rested my arquebus against my cheek and aimed directly at one of the three chiefs. With the same shot two of them fell to the ground, and one of their companions, who was wounded and afterward died. I put four balls into my arquebus. When our men saw this shot so favorable for them, they began to make cries so loud that one could not have heard it thunder. Meanwhile the

14. *Champlain fires his arquebus in the fateful battle between Canadian Algonquins and Iroquois.*

arrows did not fail to fly from both sides. The Iroquois were much astonished that two men had been so quickly killed, although they were provided with armor woven from cotton thread and from wood, proof against their arrows. This disturbed them greatly. As I was loading again one of my companions fired a shot from the woods, which astonished them again to such a degree that, seeing their chiefs dead, they lost courage, took to flight and abandoned the field and their fort, fleeing into the depths of the woods. Pursuing them thither I killed some more of them. Our savages also killed several of them and took ten or twelve of them prisoners. The rest escaped with the wounded. There were fifteen or sixteen of our men wounded by arrow shots, who were soon healed.

After we had gained the victory they amused themselves by taking a great quantity of Indian corn and meal from their enemies, and also their arms, which they had left in order to run better. And having made good cheer, danced and sung, we returned three hours afterward with the prisoners.

This place, where this charge was made, is in latitude 43 degrees and some minutes, and I named the lake Lake Champlain. He fought for the lake

The journal proceeds to describe the torture of one of the prisoners; he was roasted by degrees and while still alive literally torn apart limb by limb. Champlain begged them to stop so he could put the poor wretch out of his misery with a shot from his arquebus, which they finally permitted him to do. His habitual reference to the Indians as savages was in this respect most apt (but there was nothing civilized about an arquebus, either).

Of all the questions raised by the lake journal, which ends with the return of the war party to Canada, the location of the battle has touched off the most salvos. The fix of Champlain's astrolabe was not precise enough to designate either Ticonderoga or Crown Point as the place. Champlain says he saw the "rapid" at the foot of Lake George "afterward," obviously after the conflict. Furthermore, he marks Lake George on his map of 1632, and shows by a number keyed to a legend that the battle was fought on the peninsula at the north side of the stream. If, as he implies, the party started back to Canada three hours afterward, it is hard to see how Crown Point could have been the site, since it is fourteen miles to the north. He could scarcely have gone from there to Ticonderoga, seen the outlet of Lake George, and returned within three hours after the battle.

However, Champlain also describes it as being waged at the end of a cape that extended into the lake from the western shore, which more aptly describes Chimney Point at the lake's narrowest crossing, where the French later built their first fortifications. Yet the claim of Ticonderoga seems much stronger — one of these places decreed by nature to smell of blood, as one historian has put it.

Although many adventures awaited Champlain in the northern wilderness, he never returned to his lake. But his image in stone, on canvas, and in ink, a fleshy man with moustaches, confidently striding forward or peering into distant waters from the prow of a canoe, will always be with us. Unfortunately, this image is false and his true one will probably never be known. The likeness we have came from a nineteenth-century lithograph, the work of an artist named Ducornet, who was born without arms and with only one leg and painted historical works with a brush held between his toes. He claimed that his likeness of Champlain was copied from the seventeenth-century portrait by Moncornet, but no such original has ever appeared. There is a portrait by the latter, identical to Ducornet's in every detail, of a rogue named Particelli, financial administrator of Louis XIV, and it is this man's face that has been foisted on us all these years.

As Morris Bishop has pointed out, Champlain would have had to be small and wiry in stature to have endured such hardships; no over-stuffed figure could have kept pace with the Indians or, having been wounded as was Champlain in 1615, have been carried sixty miles on their backs through the forests of central New York.

III

A Fifteen-Decade Struggle for Empire: French and Algonquin against British and Iroquois.

C HAMPLAIN'S arquebus echoed throughout the eastern forests and as far across the sea as the courts of London and Paris. From that day on, the Iroquois became the sworn enemies of France and the inseparable allies of the Dutch and English, who had thunder-sticks as powerful as those of the French friends of the Algonquins. Bishop writes:

This new weapon was to transform completely the wars of red men and white, and red men and red. The battle of Ticonderoga was fought by two massed groups in close order. We shall not see such another. The Indians soon threw away their useless shields, revised their tactics, and resorted to a strategy of raids and surprises.

What we have seen was a Stone Age battle, half war, half sport. It was a noble dance of death, a bloody ballet performed according to accepted rules. Champlain, with his new weapon, violated the rules.

But the alliances of English and Iroquois, French and Algonquin were also created by another mighty force — the lowly beaver. Since European fashion dictated that every gentleman must wear a beaver hat, the search for pelts had to be extended across the Atlantic. As early as 1534, on the occasion of Cartier's arrival on the coast of New Brunswick, the Indians held up beaver pelts on their paddles. They had become North America's ultimate treasure by the time Champlain arrived on the lake and (almost simultaneously) Henry Hudson, to the south, sailed his *Half Moon* up his broad river. A mere four years later the Dutch had engaged in a treaty with the Iroquois and built a trading post at Albany for the exchange of guns for beavers. (Arendt Van Corlaer, the Dutchman who, it will be recalled, drowned in Lake Champlain and for whom it was briefly named, traveled to Mohawk villages smashing barrels of rum the Indians had received from unscrupulous traders. Hence the esteem in which he was held by the sachems of the Iroquois.)

Meanwhile the Algonquins were ranging north and west from the St. Lawrence to find furs to be traded to the French at Quebec. When the Iroquois had exhausted the supply of beavers in the Mohawk Valley and the Adirondacks, they began foraging further north and west into the Algonquin forests of the St. Lawrence Valley. Coveted but not yet occupied by the French, Lake Champlain became the avenue of a struggle that was to last over two centuries.

The future of the valley was foretold in the sufferings of Father Isaac Jogues, a French Jesuit missionary who tried to convert the Iroquois to Christianity. Arriving at the bleak promontory of Quebec in 1636, he managed to survive the first of his perilous forays into Iroquois country despite an epidemic among the Indians which they blamed on the French clergy. Though his accomplishments failed to match his ardor, he persevered for six years, until he and two comrades were captured in an Iroquois ambush in an area of the St. Lawrence known as Lake St. Peter. In a doleful journey up the Richelieu and south through Lakes Champlain and George (Jogues called the latter St. Sacrement) to the Mohawk Valley, they were subjected to fiendish tortures. On Jogues Island (near Westport) its namesake was knocked senseless while running the gauntlet, which he called "the narrow road to Paradise." Later his hair, beard, and fingernails were torn out, and his fingers chewed until they were deformed.

Ransomed by Arendt Van Corlaer and a Lutheran clergyman after fourteen months in captivity, he returned to France where he received a special dispensation from the Pope to celebrate Mass despite his mutilated hands. In 1644 he returned to Canada, to Lake Champlain, and to the scene of his sufferings as an emissary during a brief interval of peace with the Iroquois. A box of religious articles he left with them on this mission proved fatal, for they came to regard it as occupied by evil spirits. Despite warnings that the Indians also blamed the Jesuits for crop failures, he returned once more in 1646. Subjected to new tortures, he was spared a lingering death with the blow of a tomahawk. Cutting off his head as a warning to future

15. The sufferings of Father Isaac Jogues, a French Jesuit missionary, were without parallel in the crusade to bring Christianity to the Iroquois.

missionaries, the Indians mounted it on a palisade picket facing north to the place beyond the waters whence the hated "Black Robes" had come.

Convinced that their path to the Champlain Valley was endangered by the failures of their missionaries and by daring Iroquois raids into Quebec, the French started building forts. The first, a palisaded stockade at the mouth of the Richelieu, was named in honor of the powerful Cardinal who, as the leader of the French Company of One Hundred Associates, had supported Champlain's voyage into the lake. The founding in 1642 of Montreal, much closer than Quebec to the avenue of terror to the south, prompted further fort building at Chambly, Sainte-Therese and, in 1666, Sainte Anne, at the foot of Lake Champlain and the tip of Isle La Motte — the first settlement in what was to become Vermont. Dedicated on July 26 of that year, the fort was 144 feet long by 96 feet wide with a double log palisade and a bastion at each corner. There were several buildings inside, at least one of them with a brick oven.

Fortunately, we have a glimpse of the first desperate winter at St. Anne through the eyes of Francois Dollier de Casson, a Sulpician monk who went there on snowshoes not long after his arrival in Canada from France. His knee was swollen from an injury during a recent Mohawk campaign, he had never been on snowshoes before, and the struggle of the last few miles almost overwhelmed even his vigorous physique. With their diet of salted

16. In the absence of an authentic likeness of Champlain, tercentenary of his discovery was memorialized by Rodin in this bust depicting the spirit of France.

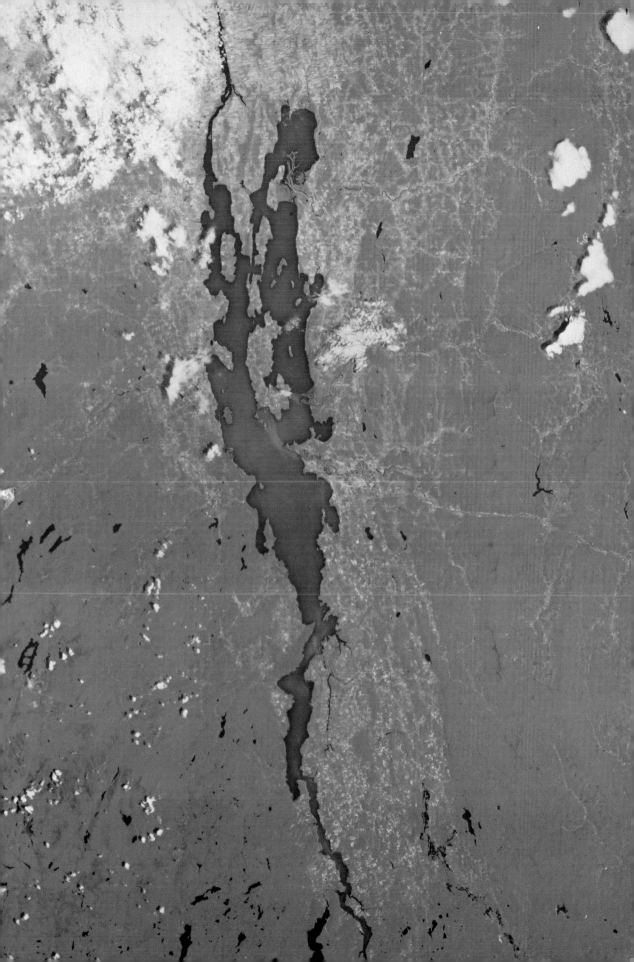

In an amiable but austere mood the lake coats the Vermont shore with ice. By Clyde H. Smith.

In the eye of a satellite 560 miles above the earth, Lake Champlain trails like an aquatic vine through the infra-red mountains (overleaf, courtesy Heath Riggs). More than responding to weather, the lake makes its own, as when it fills the winter sky with steam. Finally it is tamed by ice but not without a struggle. Right: Reflections from the escarpments of Whiteface present a year-round illusion of snow. By Clyde H. Smith.

Lake is viewed in a rare moment of serenity from the summit of Mansfield. By Clyde H. Smith.

Winter ice. By Stuart Perry.

Old lighthouse and modern beacon guide ships past Split Rock.
Mt. Philo overlooks a vast and variegated tableau. By R.N. Hill.

meat and bread, he found 40 of the 60 soldiers sick with scurvy. Two, he wrote, had died:

. . . one of them asking for a priest for eight whole days without being able to have him before he died lamenting. Several others near death likewise were appealing to Heaven, when God at that very moment sent one to help them. So intent were they, with sighs and longings, that as soon as they saw us, far off on Lake Champlain, which surrounds the fort, they sent word to M. La Motte, the commander.

He immediately rushed out with all the officers and men not absolutely needed to guard the fort and came to meet me with unspeakable joy, embracing me with so tender an affection I cannot describe it. "Welcome!" they all said. "What a pity you did not arrive a little earlier! How the two soldiers who have just died longed for you! What joy your coming will bring to all our sick. How the news of your coming cheers them! How grateful we are to you for coming!" While they greeted me, one unburdened me of my knapsack, another took my altar service. Thus relieved, I was led to the fort. After saying some prayers, I visited many sick in their cabins, and then went to eat with M. L Motte and Durantaye and all the junior officers.

It was high time I came, for of the sixty soldiers in the fort, forty had scurvy, and seemed near death. The well were afraid of the contagion, especially as they had no vegetables — only bacon and bread made of flour damaged in ocean transit. Until the end of the autumn they had planned to abandon this place. They decided to man it after the oncoming winter prevented the Intendant from sending better provisions. Thus they had to subsist on what little could be hurried in. Unfortunately, the flour was spoiled and the sailors on the voyage from France had tapped the brandy kegs and refilled them with sea water. They also had a cask of vinegar that would have been excellent for their malady, but unluckily it all leaked out.

Finally things got into such a state that everyone would have died if La Motte, wanting at all costs to save the life of one of his juniors, had not sent him to Montreal with some men. They came back well supplied, because M. Souart and Mlle. Mance, alarmed that I should die, sent me several sleighs loaded with all kinds of foods, such as purslane, salt pork, onions, poultry, and a lot of Touraine prunes. When M. La Motte saw all these provisions come into his fort, while his friends had sent him very little, as they could not obtain more, he very nearly had a little quarrel with his missionary. True, as we were good friends, the trouble was not very serious. He said to me, "Since we eat together, I'll take charge of the supplies." I answered, "I do a good deal of work for the soldiers. The king will maintain me well enough. I shall not touch these supplies. They are all for the sick, for I am well enough to do without."

With that he had everything brought into his room, and he began to distribute every morning to all the sick, soup made by himself, in which he placed bits of pork and fowl. In the evening he gave everyone twelve or fifteen stewed prunes. Thus he saved many soldiers' lives until they could be taken to Montreal on sleighs, in turn. This was the only way to cure them, for the air was so infected at St. Anne not one who stayed recovered.

This sickness lasted three whole months. The death agony lasted eight days, during which the stench was so great that it reached almost to the center of the fort, although the patients were shut up in their rooms. The dying were so far gone that no one dared so much as go near them, except the priest and a surgeon named Forestier. As I spent all my time with the sick, I can bear witness that by day or night he came very promptly whenever called. True, seeing how exhausted he was, and fearing that he would completely collapse, toward the end I called him as little as possible.

The neglected sick hit upon a successful way to get help from some comrade. They set about making elaborate wills, as if they had been very rich, saying "I give so much to so and so because he helped me in my last illness, and when I was forsaken." Every day saw such wills made. Those who saw through the device smiled at the resource of these poor fellows, who did not have a cent in the world.

What can be said of the whole epidemic is that if the body was worn out, there was balm to the spirit in the devout lives men began to lead. Well or ill, the soldiers behaved as if they took communion daily — in fact they did very frequently. The hours of mass and prayers were set, and each was careful to go. Oaths and indecent language were hardly heard at all. Devotion was so widespread that I felt amply repaid for my work. I was present at the deaths of eleven soldiers, who were apparently so well prepared as one could wish.

Every arrival from Montreal brought me fresh provisions, which reinforced my bedside prayers. If I were not in the sickrooms, or in mine getting a little rest, I went to the place between the bastions of the fort where the snow was tramped down, to take the air and run back and forth, in order to avoid the disease, which bothered some. Anyone who saw me would have thought me crazy, had he not known how essential such violent exercise was to keep off the illness. It was certainly funny to watch me say my breviary on the run, but I had no other time, and believed I should use it well in saying my office — without casuists' finding fault. If my room had been larger I could have done it more properly there. But it was such a small narrow hole — so dark the sunlight never reached it, and so low I could not stand straight in it.

One day M. La Motte, realizing how few men he had fit for combat, and how far in enemy country he was, said jokingly to me, "Look, sir, I will never surrender. As it has been in your line, I'll give you a bastion to hold."

Falling in with his banter, I replied, "Sir, my company consists of the sick, with the doctor as lieutenant. Prepare me some wheeled stretchers and we'll take them to whatever bastion you say. They are brave now; they won't run away as they did from you and Durantaye's companies to join mine.

In the spring of 1668 news reached Fort St. Anne that it would be honored with a visit by Msgr. de Laval, Bishop of New France. Carrying only a wooden cross and a simple mitre, he arrived with one ecclesiastic in a bark canoe paddled by two peasants and is thought to have stayed for several days. An interval of peace with the Iroquois had begun; they were

figures des montaignais *figure des sauvages abnouchicois*

David pelleter fecit

17. *Champlain decorated his map of 1613 with figures of Indians, presumably Algonquins.*

requesting and welcoming French missionaries, and the bishop may at this time have confirmed some of them who had been converted. Thereafter little is written of life at the fort. Captain de la Motte soon went to Montreal as its governor, and his troops seem to have gone with him. Others may have replaced them for the next two years. But with the valley temporarily at peace, the fort was abandoned in 1671.

Having acquired New York in a treaty with the Dutch in 1665, the British were anything but ignorant of events in the north. In 1687 the governor of New York proposed to the King that a fort be built at the "pass in the lake" at what the French called Pointe a la Chevelure, where the two points come very close together. The name Chevelure, or scalp, applied to the east, or Vermont point, and may have been derived from Iroquois scalps taken by Champlain's Algonquins when they stopped there after the battle to torture their prisoners. Crown and Chimney Points, as they later were named, must have long served as a crossing by the Indians (as they did later for whites) and as a camping place for French and English war parties on their way up and down the lake. In 1690 a small stone fort or trading post seems to have been constructed at Chimney Point under the aegis of a Dutchman named Jacobus de Warm, sent there with twelve English and twenty Mohawks to watch the French. Chimney Point thus became the first outpost of the British in Vermont, 34 years before the building of Fort Dummer across the Green Mountains on the Connecticut.

We are now at the threshold of the French and Indian Wars, a titanic struggle of seven-and-a-half decades by England and France for the control of North America. Scholars, not to mention laymen, have tended to bog down in the incessant marching and counter-marching in this bloody drama, but a review at least of the high points is necessary for an understanding of Lake Champlain's lofty role. The rising struggle was, of course, heightened by the unresolved question of ownership of the lake. The French claimed it because they discovered it. The English claimed it because the Iroquois had always considered it theirs, and they had made the British their protectors.

During the four wars: King William's (1689-97), Queen Anne's (1702-13), King George's (1744-48), and the French and Indian War (1755-63) the mere frown of a European monarch was enough to stir up the wilderness 3,000 miles away; maps of the world were drawn and redrawn, and the destinies of England, France, Spain, Portugal, and even of Austria, Prussia, Russia, and India were rising and falling with the tides of battles. For the purpose of this narrative, it is enough to say that the French had begun to back their claims in the Champlain Valley with force, and the British in New York and southern New England were just as actively opposing them. What started out as a series of small raids from north to south and south to north culminated eventually in the clash of great armies.

1666.   Sieur de Courcelles, whom Louis XIV had named governor of the royal colony of New France the previous year, decided to repay the Mohawks for their raids with a winter attack by way of frozen Lake Champlain. The governor himself commanded a force of 500 men wearing snowshoes they did not know how to use. Carrying heavy packs of blankets, biscuits, and other provisions, suffering from frost bite and "snow-shoe sickness," they left the lake at Crown Point, stumbled through the mountains to the southwest and lost eleven men in an Iroquois ambush near Schenectady before the magnanimous Van Corlaer, protecting them from the Mohawks they had come to destroy, provided them with food for the return trip to Canada. (Profoundly grateful, Courcelles invited Van Corlaer to Canada and it was on his way there the next year that the latter drowned in the lake near Otter Creek.) Pursued part of the way north by the Iroquois, Courcelles ran out of food at Chimney Point and lost 60 soldiers from cold and starvation. The remainder, barely subsisting on wild game and suffering from snow-blindness, straggled back to Canada.

Efforts to make peace with the Iroquois were now shattered near Fort Sainte Anne by the death of M. de Chazy (a nephew of the Canadian Viceroy, Sieur de Tracy) at the hands of the Mohawks. The chief who had killed him was hanged by Tracy, and the war on the Iroquois resumed the following September. This time 1,300 troops set forth from Sainte Anne in 300 canoes and bateaux, the regulars in shining armor, and the naked Algonquins fiercely painted for battle. Although the enemy eluded them, they succeeded in burning four Mohawk villages and destroying all their grain. During the return trip a severe storm on the lake swamped two canoes and eight men were drowned. Except for Captain La Motte, on the way back left to guard Sainte Anne (with troops whose hardships during the ensuing winter have previously been described), the rest of M. de Tracy's force triumphantly returned to Quebec. Their villages destroyed, the Mohawks in 1672 engaged in a treaty with the new Canadian governor, the Count of Frontenac, and peace reigned for a decade.

1689. The Iroquois again went on the warpath following unsuccessful expeditions against them by the two Canadian governors who succeeded Frontenac. Starting in 1687 with a raid on the Richelieu River settlement of Chambly, the Mohawks dashed north 900 strong and nearly destroyed Montreal two years later. Remaining several weeks to plunder, they even ate some of the inhabitants.

1690. Another winter expedition of 114 French and Indians, with the object of destroying Fort Orange (Albany), set forth from Canada on snowshoes but instead laid waste to the village of Schenectady, killing 60 men, women, and children and taking 80 prisoners. Major Peter Schuyler pursued them with 150 Mohawks but gave up the chase at Crown Point. When their food gave out the French were obliged to eat some of their horses and to boil and eat shoe leather. Six died of starvation; others, wandering off into the wilderness, never reached Canada. The British retaliated with an attack on La Prairie, burning sixteen houses and slaughtering some of the inhabitants and 150 cattle.

1691. Leading 250 Indians and whites down the lake to Canada, Major Schuyler met a larger force of French and Indians. A fierce battle raged without much advantage to either side.

1693. The Count of Frontenac, having been reappointed Royal Governor of Canada, organized a force of about 700 French and Indians who set forth over the ice of Lakes Champlain and George and destroyed the lower Mohawk villages. Schuyler pursued them north with a force almost as large which, however, suffered from a lack of food and shoes. A blizzard covered the tracks of the French, the Indians refused to proceed, and Schuyler retreated. The French were no better off; the ice in the lakes was honeycombed, rain had spoiled the cache of food they had left at Chimney Point,

18. *Section of "A New and Exact Map of the Dominions of the King of Great Britain on ye Continent of North America" (Herman Moll, geographer, 1715) shows an exaggerated St. Lawrence River, a bloated Lake Champlain and contested territory north of the English colonies.*

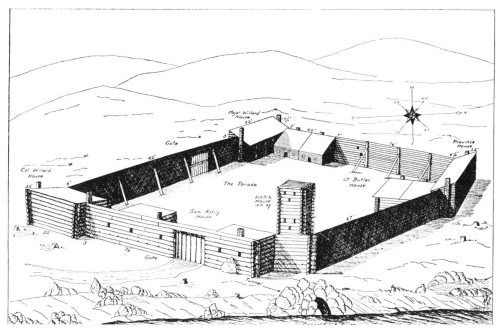

19. *Except for the short-lived Lake Champlain outpost built at Chimney Point in 1690, Fort Dummer in what became the town of Brattleboro was the first English bastion in "Vermont."*

and they were forced to subsist on boiled moccasins and water (the Indians ate their dead prisoners).

1704. The French attacked Deerfield, Massachusetts, by way of the lake and the Winooski River, returning the same way and carrying with them inhabitants they had not killed, among them the Reverend John Williams, who survived the death march to Canada over the melting ice of the river and lake.

1724. From his stronghold or fort on Missisquoi Bay near the Abnaki village, Chief Gray Lock, the Algonquin scourge of New England, preyed on Connecticut River towns with sudden raids from the forests. Since he always eluded expeditions sent north to rout him out of his lair, the southern settlements were never safe as long as he lived (he apparently died of old age). One of the main reasons for the building this year of Fort Dummer on the southeastern tip of what became Vermont is said to have been fear of the stealthy Gray Lock and his shadowy band of Abnaki warriors.

1731. Having fallen into the hands of the French, the small stone fort or trading post built at Chimney Point by the British in 1690 was rebuilt and/or enlarged with a stockade 100 feet square and bastions at each corner.

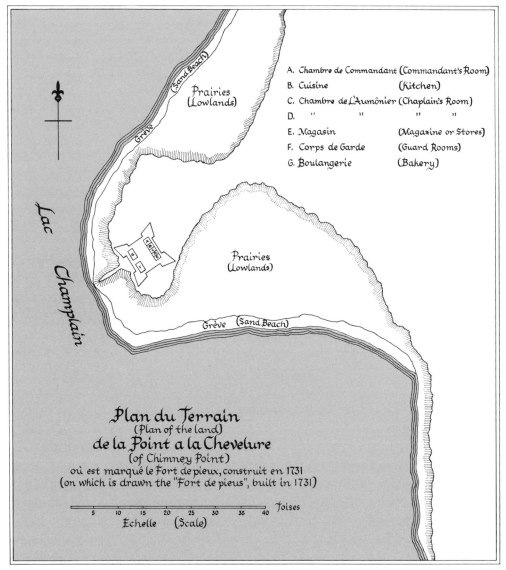

A. Chambre de Commandant (Commandant's Room)
B. Cuisine (Kitchen)
C. Chambre de L'Aumônier (Chaplain's Room)
D.   "   "   "   "
E. Magasin (Magazine or Stores)
F. Corps de Garde (Guard Rooms)
G. Boulangerie (Bakery)

Plan du Terrain
(Plan of the land)
de la Point a la Chevelure
(of Chimney Point)
où est marqué le Fort de pieux, construit en 1731
(on which is drawn the "Fort de pieus", built in 1731)

Toises
5   10   15   20   25   30   35   40
Echelle   (Scale)

20. *The French built a little-known fort at Chimney Point before Fort St. Frederic at Crown Point.*

Called the Fort at Pointe a la Chevelure, or de Pieux, it was garrisoned by two officers and thirty men and became the center of a small French community on the nearby shores and on "les Isles aux Boiteaux," an island between Chimney Point and Hospital Creek that has since disappeared. (Twenty-five years later some 300 men were reported by Robert Rogers to be living in the area.) The settlement was later destroyed, leaving blackened chimneys from which the point received its English name.

1734.   The King and the governor-general of New France directed that construction begin of a new fort, later called St. Frederic, on the tip of Crown Point, directly across the narrow neck of water from Chimney Point — a much more ambitious effort than anything the French had previously undertaken to enforce their claims to the lake and valley. (The building of this fort generally is supposed to have begun several years earlier, having been confused with the 1731 fort at Chimney Point.) In 1735, a priest who was serving as chaplain wrote that the building in which he stayed was not yet finished, so that he was only partly sheltered from the rain.

Touring the new fort in 1740, the Chevalier de Beauharnois, nephew of the Canadian governor, reported to his uncle that he had inspected the soldiers' armament and found it in poor condition. Although the fort was very much to his liking he criticized:

... an inner court in which one's foot sinks 6 inches when it rains, and which would be worth the trouble to have paved; in the second place, a well which gives no water and which might be deepened with advantage; fortifications without ditches and without ramparts — simply curtained on the inner side with clay, upon which one cannot walk when it has rained; no barracks, guard-rooms on the third floor, no cells, no prison, the environs of the fort not sufficiently cleared; that, my dear uncle, is about all that I should criticize.

Improvements and additions of the stone barracks for the officers and men, the church within the enclosure, a drawbridge with a subterranean passage under it leading to the lake, and the four-story stone citadel in the northeast corner with walls ten feet thick and containing 20 cannon, had produced a fort whose strategic importance followed only those of Quebec and Louisbourg (although French commanders found little about it to admire).

Sailing between forested shores broken only by the fort and the set-tlements within a French mile around it, Peter Kalm, a Swedish professor on his way to Canada in 1749, was royally received by the Governor, who "heaped obligations" upon him and treated him with as much civility as if he had been one of his relations. He ate at his table, and his servant was allowed to eat with the Governor's; he had his own room, and when he left, the Governor stocked him with provisions for his voyage to St. Jean. Kalm's journal, rich with detail, provides us with one of the few glimpses of mid-eighteenth century life on Lake Champlain:

The English call this fortress Crown Point, but its French name is derived from the French secretary of state, Frederic Maurepas. . . . As most places in Canada bear the names of saints, custom has made it necessary to prefix the word Saint to the name of the fortress. The fort is built on a rock, consisting of black-lime slates . . . it is nearly quadrangular, has high and thick walls, made of the same lime-stone of which there is a quarry about half a mile from the fort. On the eastern part of the fort is a high tower, which is proof against bombshells, provided with very thick and substantial walls, and well stored with cannon from the bottom almost to the very top; and the governor lives in the tower. In the terre-plein of the fort is a well built little church, and houses of stone for the officers and soldiers. . . .

The soil about Fort St. Frederic is said to be very fertile on both sides of the (lake); and before the last war a great many French families, especially old soldiers, have settled there; but the king obliged them to go to Canada, or to settle close to the fort, and to lie in it at night. A great number of them returned at this time, and it was thought that about forty or fifty families would go to settle here this autumn. Within one or two musket-shots to the east of the fort is a wind-mill built of stone, with very thick walls, and most of the flour which is wanted to supply the fort is ground here. This wind-mill is so contrived as to serve the purpose of the redoubt, and at the top of it are five or six small pieces of cannon. During the last war there was a number of soldiers quartered in this mill, because they could from thence look a great way . . . and observe whether the English boats approached; which could not be done from the fort itself, and which was a matter of great consequences, as the English might (if this guard had not been placed here) have gone in their little boats close under the western shore of the river, and then the hills would have prevented their being seen from the fort. Therefore, the fort ought to have been built on the spot where the mill stands, and all those who come to see it are immediately struck with the absurdity of its situation. If it had been erected in the place of the mill, it would have commanded the (lake) and prevented the approach of the enemy. . . .

The soldiers had built houses round the fort on grounds allotted to them, but most of these habitations were no more than wretched cottages, no better than those in the most wretched places of Sweden, with (the) difference, however, that their inhabitants here were rarely oppressed by hunger, and could eat good and pure wheat bread. The huts which they had erected consisted of boards, standing perpendicularly close to each other. The roofs were of wood, too. The crevices were stopped up with clay to keep the room warm. The floor was commonly clay, or a black lime-stone, except the place where the fire was to lie, which was made of grey sand-stones, which for the greatest part consist of particles of quartz. . . .

The soldiers enjoy such advantages here as they are not allowed in every part of the world. Those who formed the garrison of this place had a very plentiful allowance from their government. They get every day a pound and a half of wheat bread. They likewise get pease, bacon, and salt meat in plenty. Sometimes they kill oxen and other cattle, and flesh of which is distributed among the soldiers. All the officers kept cows at the expense of the king, and the milk they gave was more than sufficient to supply them. The soldiers had each a small garden without the fort, which they were allowed to attend and plant in it whatever they liked, and some of them had built summer-houses in them, and planted all kinds of pot-herbs. The governor told me that it was a general custom to allow the soldiers a spot of ground for kitchen-gardens at such of the French forts hereabouts as were not situated near great towns, from whence they could be supplied with greens. In time of peace the soldiers have very little trouble with being upon guard at the fort; and as the lake close by is full of fish, and the woods abound with birds and animals, those amongst them who choose to be diligent may live extremely well and very grand in regard to food. Each soldier got a new coat every two years; but annually, a waistcoat, cap, hat, breeches, cravat, two pair of stockings, two pair of shoes, and as much wood as he had occasion for in winter. They likewise got five sols (cents) apiece every day, which is augmented to thirty sols when they have any particular labour for the king. When this is considered, it is not surprising to find the men are very fresh, well fed, strong, and lively here. When a soldier falls sick he is brought to the hospital, where the king provides him with a bed, food, medicines, and people to take care of and serve him. When some of them asked leave to be absent for a day or two . . . it was generally granted them if circumstances would permit, and they enjoyed as usual

21. Scale model of Fort St. Frederic (1734) at Crown Point was constructed by A.S. Hopkins of Albany from the original plans. A French community grew up around the fort.

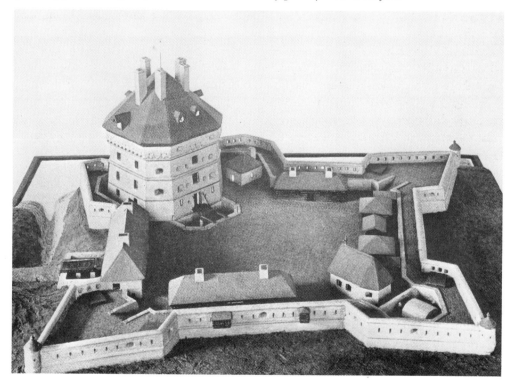

their share of provisions and money, but were obliged to get some of their comrades to mount the guard for them as often as it came to their turns, for which they gave them an equivalent. The governor and officers were duly honoured by the soldiers; however, the soldiers and officers often spoke together as comrades, without any ceremonies, and with a very becoming freedom. The soldiers who are sent hither from France commonly serve till they are forty or fifty years old, after which they are dismissed and allowed to settle upon, and cultivate a piece of ground. . . . Those who are born here commonly agree to serve the crown during six, eight, or ten years, after which they are dismissed, and set up for farmers in the country. The king presents each dismissed soldier with a piece of land. . . . As soon as a soldier settles . . . he is at first assisted by the king, who supplies himself, his wife, and children with provisions during the three and four first years. The king likewise gives him a cow and the most necessary instruments for agriculture. Some soldiers are sent to assist him in building a house, for which the king pays them. These are great helps to a poor man who begins to keep house, and it seems that in a country where the troops are so highly distinguished by the royal favour, the king cannot be at a loss for soldiers. . . .

Fort St. Frederic served the French both as a military base and as an outpost of settlement in a howling wilderness a hundred miles removed from any other in any direction. Ancient foundations of houses discovered in the vicinity would at least support Robert Rogers's description of it as a "small village." From 1731 to 1759 198 deaths, 31 marriages, and 243 baptisms were recorded.

The community of Fort St. Frederic thus served notice on the British that the French were now not only in a position to protect the lake but to settle its shores on both sides. They had parceled out the whole valley to landholders in sections called seigneuries, the largest of which had a frontage on the lake of twelve miles. It included the Lamoille River and extended back fifteen miles, encompassing what are now the towns of Milton and Westford, and parts of Georgia, Colchester, Fairfax, Fletcher, and Underhill.

There are a number of references to another early center of French activity along the Missisquoi. Guy Coolidge (in his study of the French occupation of the Champlain Valley) reports 180 Abnakis as having returned following the plague that struck them there, and French missionaries as building a stone chapel in an upper village near the falls. Finding mast pines on the Saranac and Au Sable rivers, Rene Levasseur, a naval contractor appointed by the King as chief of construction in Canada, built a sawmill at the falls of the Missisquoi about 1749. Traces of his canal or channel furnishing water along the right bank above the falls could be seen a century later. Vessels could navigate the river as far as the falls and easily transport the products of his mill to Canada. A wooden stockade above the mill was built to protect the upper

22. *Primitive view by T. Davies of Crown Point (after the French had blown up the tower) shows the magnitude of France's strongest bastion other than Louisbourg and Quebec.*

French village of 50 houses clustered around the missionaries' stone church. The mission was flourishing in 1759; 20 years later a Jesuit priest still ministered to the needs of the Christian Abnakis who, having survived the wars, remained in the lower village.

At least two smaller French missions appear to have been established in the valley. A stone chapel with a bell was built near Ferrisburg convenient to the Otter Creek, the Indians' pathway to the hinterlands and to the Connecticut Valley. An Indian village is reported to have stood at the mouth of this river about 1690. There is also mention of another early chapel at the mouth of the Winooski, the Indians' other important avenue from the lake to the east. Indeed, the French may have occupied Colchester Point, near the river's outlet, as early as they did Isle La Motte. "At least three houses," writes Guy Coolidge:

... were built on the Point during the French occupation. The first English settler, Benjamin Boardman, on his arrival in 1789, found the remains of stone fortifications and other defensive works, three chimney bottoms ... and remains of walls near them. On these sites have been found leaden bullets, Indian arrowheads, rusted iron utensils, and pieces of silver and copper coin; two skeletons were washed out of the earth nearby in 1867....

The first English map of the lake, published after the close of the war, indicated both the point in West Alburgh and Colchester point as "Windmill Point." It is difficult to see any reason for the name unless from the fact that a mill stood there either then or formerly. Dr. E. Tudor . . . told his grandchildren (Hon. John W. Strong and Mrs. Emeline Hard of Ferrisburg) that there was a French blockhouse fort on Colchester Point at the time of the English invasion of Canada (1759). . . .

A short distance north of Colchester Point, another vestige of French settlement is found at the head of Malletts Bay. Here was the home of Captain Mallet, of whom little is known; a Frenchman, he had probably settled there under a French grant many years before the Revolution; he was known to be there from 1774 until his death in 1790. Captain Mallet (whose name probably should be written "Maillet" or "Malet") was apparently a man of considerable independence of spirit; he feared no one and acknowledged allegiance neither to the English King nor to the American colonies. It seems that he never accepted the Treaty of Peace which gave control over his lands to the English; his sympathies were on the side of rebellion, for he welcomed spies and smugglers into his home all through the Revolutionary period.

As for settlements other than Fort Sainte Anne in the North, Peter Kalm reported seeing a stone windmill in the western part of Alburgh "on a projecting piece of ground. Some Frenchmen have lived near it, but left when the war broke out, and are not yet come back to it. . . . The English have burnt the houses here several times, but the mill remained unhurt." This settlement was begun about 1740 by Sieur Francis Foucault, a member of the Supreme Council of Quebec, according to terms of the grant that he locate settlers there. His stone windmill was no doubt an enticement. Other French houses opposite these stood on the west side of the lake and north for ten miles toward St. Jean.

By the time France and England again locked horns in what in Europe was called the War of the Austrian Succession (1744-48) but was known in North America as King George's War, the French claim to the Champlain Valley was somewhat stronger. While their efforts to colonize it had not amounted to much, Fort St. Frederic at least served them as a staging area over half way from Montreal to the enemy stronghold at Albany. The northernmost British outpost at Saratoga, manned by twelve soldiers, was so weak as hardly to deserve mention except perhaps as a symbol of British vacillation, caused in part by secret trading carried on among a good many British subjects with the French in Canada. The Iroquois were disgruntled with the failure of their allies to deal with incessant attacks upon their villages of the French from their new fort on Lake Champlain. In the eyes of the Iroquois the British were losers, and their capture of Louisbourg on far-away Cape Breton did little to change their minds.

To rehearse the lesser events leading up to the clash of great armies on the northern gateway is to jumble rather than clarify the crowded military and naval calendar of the final fifteen years of French power, yet to ignore the prologue would do the climax a disservice:

1745.   Only a few months after the fall of their Nova Scotia bastion, a French force of from five to six hundred out of Fort St. Frederic crossed Wood Creek to the Hudson, totally burned Saratoga, killed and scalped about a third of the inhabitants and carried the rest, as many as a hundred, back over the lake to Canada.

1746.   A larger Canadian expedition (500 French and 200 Indians) arrived in a flotilla of canoes at St. Frederic in August and there decided to attack Fort Massachusetts on the northwest border of that colony. The commander of this hapless garrison, Captain Ephraim Williams, for whom Williams College was named, fought bravely but since some of his soldiers had gone for ammunition and many of the rest were sick with dysentery, he was forced to surrender. The French commander, Rigaud de Vaudreuil, tried to prevent his Indians from taking scalps but did not succeed. The war party burned and plundered their way through a wide swath of North Massachusetts countryside, finally returning to Canada.

1746-48.   French attacks south through the lake by way of Lake George, or east by way of the Winooski and south on the Connecticut rivers continued to terrify English settlements. In 1746 alone, the northernmost English stronghold, called Number 4, at Charlestown, New Hampshire was assaulted five times, and might have been captured in 1747 had the dogs the English resourcefully recruited not smelled Indians and alerted the defenders with their barking.

In the treaty of Aix-la-Chapelle, signed by France and England in 1748, the latter returned Louisbourg to the French, but nothing to clarify the ownership of Lake Champlain was decided, with the result that the French continued to occupy Fort St. Frederic and even to station troops at the southern end of navigation and on Lake George. The Iroquois were so disgusted with the British that they would have broken their alliance were it not for the fur trade.

1754.   Just after daybreak on the 29th of August Algonquins from the Canadian village of St. Francis attacked the log house of James Johnson, about 100 yards distant from Fort Number 4 on the Connecticut, and "fixed horribly for war, rushed furiously in," wrote his wife Miriam, in one of the most remarkable journals of captivity in the French and Indian War. During the frightful march of the prisoners westward over the height of land and down the Otter Creek Mrs. Johnson gave birth to a daughter, called Captive. The food supply ran out and the horse she was riding had to be eaten. Nearly perishing on foot she managed to struggle forward to the lake. "The hour I sat on the shore of Lake Champlain was one of the happiest I ever experienced," she wrote. Arriving by canoe at St. Frederic Mrs. Johnson was put to bed with a nurse in attendance, and her baby and other children were decently clothed. Several days later they set forth by canoe down the lake and the Richelieu, eventually arriving at St. Francis. After suffering three years of captivity she was released in an exchange of prisoners and sent to England, at last returning to America and to her home near Fort Number 4 in January, 1758. Then her husband joined the war and was killed. Mrs. Johnson married again and had seven more children (four of whom died in infancy) and as an old lady could count 38 grandchildren and 28 great-grandchildren, to whom her daughter Captive often showed the dress she appeared in when brought to her mother's bedside by the French nurse at St. Frederic.

1755.   At the end of a breathing spell the exertions of France and England for empire in the New World became more violent. To restore their tarnished prestige the British took the offensive and reoccupied Nova Scotia, but because of their custom of appointing incompetent generals failed in two other thrusts against French power in the Ohio Valley and at Fort Niagara. In a fourth offensive to capture Fort St. Frederic they sent another military incompetent, Sir William Johnson, lord of the Iroquois manor and spouse of a Mohawk squaw. A talented and engaging but vain and calculating entrepreneur who was born to succeed, Johnson did not capture St. Frederic but won a notable victory at Lake George entirely on the strength of Phineas Lyman, a subordinate officer from Connecticut. Johnson conveniently forgot

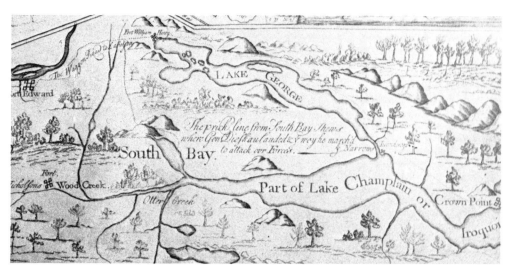

23. *Section of early map shows route taken in 1755 by Baron de Dieskau from South Bay through the forests to his defeat by the English between Fort Edward and the head of Lake George.*

Lyman's services and by advertising his own at Court received the title of baronet, 5,000 pounds, and 110,000 acres on the north bank of the Mohawk.

His ego would not even permit the name of a small outpost built by his deputy at the southern doorstep to the lakes to remain Fort Lyman: Johnson changed it to Fort Edward. Starting from there toward Champlain down swampy Wood Creek with 2,800 untrained militia and volunteers, he changed his mind and decided to take the other route by way of Lake George. Changing the lake's name from St. Sacrement to that of his King, he curried further favor by naming the fort he built there for the King's grandson, William Henry. There he established his headquarters, more as if he were in rest camp than on a military campaign.

Meanwhile from Canada an army of some 3,500 French regulars, Canadians, and Indians was sailing south on Champlain to protect their endangered fortress at Crown Point and if possible to forge further south and destroy the invaders. An able veteran of the European wars, Baron de Dieskau struggled with a long supply line from Canada and with the problem of 600 unmanageable Indians. "They drive us crazy from morning till night," he wrote. "There is no end to their demands. They have already eaten five oxen and as many hogs, without counting the kegs of brandy they have drunk. In short, one needs the patience of an angel to get on with these devils, and yet one must always force himself to seem pleased with them."

The fate of an army often hangs on the smallest judgment. An English

24. *Prominent casualty of the Battle of Lake George
was aged Mohawk chief and English ally, King Hendrick.*

prisoner lied to Dieskau that Johnson had only 500 men at Fort Edward, and
that the rest had gone back to Albany. Purely on the strength of this information Dieskau decided to leave half of his army at Ticonderoga, and with a
force of only 1100 men, not counting the 600 Indians, he embarked by canoe
for South Bay, where he took to the forests. Within three miles of Fort
Edward, upon learning he had been deceived by the English prisoner and that
the number of Johnson's troops was a great deal larger, he decided to withdraw to South Bay. But Johnson had learned of his presence and sent Ephraim
Williams and 1,200 troops to intercept him. Although the British marched
straight into a French ambush they managed to fight their way out of it and,
despite the death of Colonel Williams, all but rout the French force in a
sanguinary battle fought at close quarters.

The thrice-wounded Dieskau would surely have fallen to the tomahawk
had he not been protected by Johnson's white troops from Johnson's Indians,

whose aged commander, King Hendrick, had been killed. The so-called Battle of Lake George actually comprised several engagements fought to the very breastworks at the rear of Johnson's lakeside fort, during which he himself was wounded. Despite his heedless oversight of the services of General Lyman, who had saved the day, Johnson at least had the civility to attend to Dieskau's wounds before his own, and to remove him to Albany. Dieskau died in France a few years later from the effects of his wounds. The remainder of his regiment returned to Ticonderoga.

If Johnson had followed his subordinates' advice instead of basking in his victory at Fort William Henry, he might have driven the French back to Canada. Although the Battle of Lake George gave the British and Iroquois a badly needed victory, all they really won was a stalemate that allowed the French to rally their forces and fight another day.

❧❦❧

Spread out as they were in the Champlain Valley the French could hardly have attributed their possession of it for nearly a century and a half to superior armies or a vigorous program of colonization. They owed their good luck to the British, who in the beginning were even less competent and purposeful in extending their domain to the north. True, the French had built St. Frederic, but their generals had never thought much of it and by 1755 it was deteriorating. What they needed was a stronger fort that would protect the entrance to the broad lake either from the Narrows or from Lake George. The place they chose, a rocky height north of the waterfall draining Lake George into Champlain, afforded a sweeping command of the lower reaches of the larger lake (the very spot, or close to it, that Champlain fought the Iroquois in 1609.) The logistics of such an enterprise a hundred miles removed from the base of supply are not easy to appreciate from the vantage point of two centuries.

Work began in September of 1755 under the aegis of Michael Chartier (later the Marquis de Lotboniere) who had been sent from Crown Point by the Governor-General of Canada to pick the site and superintend construction. His first task was to fell trees, level the top of the promontory, and to build some kind of shelter for 650 soldiers and, presumably, the civilian carpenters, masons, and other artisans. The next summer an enlarged force of 2,000 soldiers laid the foundations for the walls. The colonial ranger, Robert Rogers, reported in September to the British that he had been "within a mile of Ticonderoga fort where I endeavored to reconnoitre the enemy's works and strength. They were engaged in raising the corner of the fort with ports in it for cannon. East of the blockhouse was a battery which I imagine commanded the lake." Returning in October Rogers wrote that he scalped a prisoner in full view of the fort, but added little to his previous observations.

By December four barracks and twenty-one huts had been constructed inside the rising walls; two months later twelve cannon were mounted. The original walls were formed of oak timbers fourteen or fifteen inches square laid one on top of the other in rows ten feet apart. Dovetailed together with cross pieces and filled with earth they offered as good protection against cannon fire as masonry, but since the wood eventually rotted, some or most of it had to be replaced with stone. By July of 1756 the army of workmen at Carillon, as the French called the fort, apparently after the music of the nearby rushing stream, numbered 5,000.

Planning and progress seemed to be proceeding with a will, but as Colonel Edward Hamilton has observed in his intriguing chronicle of the fort, those seamy bedfellows, politics and graft, were diligently at work. The administration of Canadian Governor Vaudreuil (whose vanity easily matched that of the enemy's Sir William Johnson but who does not appear to have engaged in graft) contained an all-powerful *intendant* or financial overlord so notorious that his name, Bigot, for the hypocrites in Normandy, became part of the language. Presented in a new country with every kind of opportunity to enrich himself and the cronies gathered around him with speculations in land, currency, trade with the Indians, army payrolls and supplies, he undertook his machinations with a relish that put later practitioners to shame. Such behavior in the highest quarter was greedily adopted down the line. While the majority of army officers appear to have resisted temptation, some of them succumbed to the overtures of their superiors or of civilian procurers. Most military field units were understrength, and it was a simple matter for the commissary to draw rations for a full complement and sell the excess.

New forts provided the best sources of graft and therefore cost about twice what they did in France. Carillon was far from an exception. No account of what went on there serves better than Colonel Hamilton's:

One plum considered the rightful perquisite of the officer building a fort was the canteen concession. It was particularly true in a place like Ticonderoga that a soldier had nothing upon which to spend his pay, both his regular pittance and those extra francs received for work on the fortifications, except on wine and brandy at the canteen. At Ticonderoga, Le Roux, keeper of the canteen, sold wine for just twice what it cost at Montreal and brandy three times. In the same way the farther one went away from Montreal the greater the cost of the soldier's ration. In 1756 the value of the soldier's daily portion of food was ten and one-half sous at Montreal, while at La Chine, only twelve miles upstream, it was twenty-seven sous. A small bit of this fearful increase of course was chargeable to transport costs, but most of it was due to graft. The King gave daily to each soldier about a pound each of bread and salt pork, perhaps half as much of dried peas, and an allowance of wine. Save for salt and other condiments, that was all. At times fresh beef was issued, but salt pork was usual. Sometimes when a barrel of salt pork was broached, it was found to contain only the heads and feet of pigs. . . . Montcalm at one time, in order to set an example, even tried eating bread made partly from *"grouillee"* (squirming) flour — flour constantly in motion from the activity of the vermin within it.

The profit of the canteen was great and continuing. The longer it took to build the fort, the greater the engineer's profit. Thus de Lotbiniere had no real incentive to expedite the construction at Ticonderoga, but instead had every reason to make the work drag out. A French regular engineer officer who served at the fort estimated that the annual profits of the canteen at Carillon amounted to 100,000 livres, certainly equivalent to $150,000 today. Another moneymaking opportunity was open to anyone who had a little capital. De Lotbiniere paid his workers in paper chits, rather than the usual Canadian "card" money which was bad enough in itself. If one had hard money at Carillon he could buy "card" money at a material discount, and then with this latter currency he could acquire de Lotbiniere notes at anywhere from one-half to three-quarters of their face value. Then, if he sent these chits to the treasurer at Montreal, they would be exchanged for their face value in "card" money less a small discount. The process could then be repeated. It was even said that de Lotbiniere kept a clerk at the fort who would expedite these various exchanges.

A third operation, illicit and open only to the engineer himself, was quite out of the ordinary. The sand used in the mortar — much of the later work at Carillon was in masonry — had to be hauled a hundred or two hundred yards from the sandpit, so horses were provided by the engineer, although presumed to be hired from various fictitious owners. De Lotbiniere had to pay for the oats the horses ate, but hay and shoeing were provided by the King, as well as the supply and repair of the wagons used. Twenty-five livres, say thirty-five dollars or so in today's values, was paid for each trip, but it was considered too much trouble to bother to count the number of trips actually made, so it was assumed that each horse made sixteen or seventeen trips in a day. There were at least fifteen horses in 1756 and each horse must have grossed about ten thousand livres a month. This seems almost astronomical and would be hard to believe were the figures not reported by an honest professional officer recently arrived from France. Another officer has left a record confirming this operation, but he put the proceeds at a considerably smaller figure, believing that the seven horses working in 1758 earned de Lotbiniere 120,000 livres in all, a sum certainly not to be despised.

De Lotbiniere, as constructing engineer, certified for all work done, and no one appears to have audited his figures. It is most probable that a material part of the engineers' immense receipts were distributed to associates and subordinates — he

25. *Construction of the French Fort Carillon (later Ticonderoga) began in 1755 as a defense against English invasions northward from the Narrows or by way of Lake George.*

offered a third share in the canteen and horse concessions to a regular French officer who worked with him at Carillon, and who refused the offer in scorn — but he must have made a very sizable fortune through his operations. Today we would consider this an illegal and ill-gotten gain, but it appears that de Lotbiniere stayed within the letter of the law of that day, just as did Governor Vaudreuil. The former was not arraigned nor the latter found guilty in the wholesale trial of Bigot's crew after the fall of New France.

Whatever de Lotbiniere's shortcomings, the fort and various facilities around it — a lime kiln and brick works, a sawmill at the falls from Lake

George, a small separate redoubt further out on the point to better defend the Narrows — were being built. With the exceptions of a storehouse with a wine cellar hewed out of rock just outside the arched entrance to the inner fort, and a retaining wall of stone later built outside the oaken curtain wall of the fort proper, with a concourse between, Carillon had acquired its present contours by the fall of 1756.

Shortly thereafter thirty-six cannon were in place on the walls. There had been a scarcity of candles and wine (the latter happily arrived by bateaux) and thousands of feet of cord wood remained to be cut and brought in for the winter. Otherwise the fort was reasonably well prepared for whatever onslaught the British might be planning at William Henry, a mere 30 miles south at the head of Lake George.

⚜

The French built their fort at Ticonderoga not so much as a bastion of defense as a staging area on their southern frontier. Early in 1757 Rigaud de Vaudreuil, brother of the Canadian governor (and son of a veteran of previous forays against the British in the valley) led still another campaign of some 1600 regulars, Indians, and Canadians over the snow-driven highway of ice, this time to try to topple the Redcoats from their perch on the southern rim of Lake George. They brought with them 300 ladders to scale the walls of Fort William Henry, but never had a chance to use them, though the British had less than a quarter as many troops.

Among the defenders, who were suffering from a prolonged celebration of St. Patrick's Day, was the hardy New Hampshire scout, John Stark, who made sure that at least his sentries were sober. Before daybreak on March 19 they saw the distant fires Rigaud's men had lighted to keep warm, and alerted the fort. Rigaud's stealthy advance was thus greeted with a tumultuous volley of cannon and musket fire. With it all hope of capturing William Henry went glimmering. But the French had come too far merely to turn back and for several days tried such means of forcing a surrender as setting fire to icebound British bateaux, a hospital, sawmill, storehouses, and piles of lumber, which very nearly ignited the wooden fort itself. Then it began to snow and on the twenty-third Rigaud's dejected troops turned their backs on William Henry and on snowshoes started for Ticonderoga and Canada, dragging their heavily laden sleds behind them.

Thus far the story of the conquest of the Champlain Valley had dealt with few supermen, other than the discoverer himself and perhaps the Jesuit priest,

Father Joques. Now, however, there appeared one of the giants of any war or age, Louis Joseph, Marquis de Montcalm, a soldier all his life, a survivor of five wounds in the Battle of Piacenza in Italy, a gentle family man, a sensitive and spirited leader to whom the baser instincts of politicians and entrepreneurs were anathema. Given command of all Canadian troops in 1756, Montcalm captured Fort Oswego on Lake Ontario and by so-doing diverted the British from attacking Ticonderoga, which was then under construction and in no position to be defended.

Montcalm's winning personality failed, however, to disarm the Canadian governor, who had expected to be appointed commander himself and was jealous of his prerogatives as a seasoned colonial who had recently governed Louisiana and now all French America. French colonists tended to be just as disdainful of royal officers as were Americans of their titled commanders who knew nothing about fighting in the wilderness. Montcalm, however, proved to be a master at it and the Indians responded to his adaptability as if he were some kind of god. Among the qualities he lacked, however, was patience. Wrought up by the lagging construction of Fort Carillon under the corrupt Lotbiniere and by the machinations of Quebec, he gave vent to loud recriminations which further eroded his relationship with the governor and his options as commander-in-chief.

Montcalm's plans to move quickly against the enemy were helped by some very able subordinates, not to mention the customary assortment of stolid British generals, who, instead of striking at the heart of French power in central New York and on the northern thoroughfare of the lakes, mounted a fruitless attack on the Nova Scotia fortress at Cape Breton. This gave Montcalm a shining opportunity to assault Lake George's weakened garrison at Fort William Henry, commanded (from Fort Edward) by General Daniel Webb, who was unusually inept even by British standards.

Thus in the summer of 1757 the blue inland sea bore southward another motley flotilla: battalions of French regulars, militiamen, volunteers, and in 200 canoes a mob of howling Indians — a thousand wild ones from the area of the Great Lakes and 800 who had been converted to Christianity, chanting a cacophony of war songs and missionary hymns. To his utter dismay Montcalm found himself powerless to prevent them from boiling captured Englishmen in their pots, stealing the officers' poultry, and slaughtering oxen needed to haul the expedition from the lower lake to the upper at Ticonderoga. Bougainville, one of Montcalm's principal officers, described them as "naked, black-red, howling, bellowing, dancing, singing the war song, getting drunk, yelling for 'broth,' that is to say, blood drawn from 500 leagues away by the

26. *French commander Montcalm nearly turned the tide of empire.*

smell of fresh human blood, and the chance to teach their young men how one carved up a human being for the pot. Behold our comrades who night and day are our shadows. I shiver at the frightful spectacles they are preparing for us."

Their heads shaved except for a tuft of hair on top of which they affixed wampum or bird feathers, with collars also of wampum, with pendants dangling from their noses and from ear lobes stretched from childhood to their shoulders, and knives hanging from their chests, they daubed their faces with vermilion, white, green, yellow, and oily black scraped from their cooking pots. As the expedition started for William Henry, part of it by water and part by way of the old Mohawk trail along the steep western shore, they scrambled over the ledges catching rattlesnakes and tying their tails together to watch them struggle. Tiring of this they chopped off their heads and tails and committed them to their cooking pots and to their insatiable stomachs.

Compared to the swamps, forests, and rocky defiles confronting the division on shore, the water-borne contingent had a relatively easy time of it despite a raging storm that delayed it for several hours. By August 3 the army of 8,000, swollen by the troops at Ticonderoga, had surrounded the British fort and was hard at work digging trenches and placing siege guns and mortars. Three days later Montcalm opened fire on the 500 defenders of the hapless stockade and upon 1700 reinforcements trying to protect it with insufficient artillery from a barricade on a rocky knoll some distance away. With Montcalm's Indians cutting off the road to Fort Edward the outlook for Lt. Colonel Monro, the ranking British officer, was grim from the start. It became hopeless with the discovery of a letter from General Webb, found in the waistcoat of a dead British soldier, informing Monro that no further help from Fort Edward was forthcoming and that he had better make the best terms he could. Webb's backbone had previously been suspect but now proved scandalously soft when Sir William Johnson arrived at Fort Edward with reinforcements which Webb declined to forward to Lake George.

The French battered the walls of William Henry to splinters. One by one the British guns exploded. Beset by as deadly an enemy within the fort as without — smallpox — the doomed garrison put up as good a fight as the courageous Monro could muster and three days later raised the flag of surrender. Montcalm's terms were generous but not those of his Indians. Despite their promise to abide by the terms they went berserk in an orgy of carnage. No sooner had the prisoners left the fort than the Redskins rushed in and tomahawked all of the wounded but seventeen who had been placed under a French guard in the care of a surgeon. But these too fell to the tomahawk in the darkness when the guard was inexplicably removed before the British marched away the next morning.

Although the French warned their captives to throw away their liquor some did not, with ghastly consequences. Preying like buzzards upon the retreating English, the Indians plundered at will and killed any who tried to resist. A war whoop from an Abnaki Christian roused the red horde to a frenzy and to wholesale butchery. A hundred were slaughtered and hundreds more carried away before Montcalm was able to turn the bloody tide. Accounts differ of the number killed but that the massacre of Lake George was the most dreadful of the French and Indian War, none deny. Disgruntled Indians who felt they had been cheated of their share of scalps dug smallpox victims out of their graves near the fort. Thus they obtained their fair share of scalps and also of the wicked disease which raced in retribution from one Indian to the next, so that the conquerors sickened and died with the conquered.

With fear that approached panic — for he expected Montcalm any minute — General Webb at Fort Edward sent his personal belongings to the rear. But his thin skin was safe because Montcalm needed artillery to destroy Fort Edward but had no way of transporting it overland. Furthermore he knew that the militia that General Webb had summoned to Fort Edward were collecting there. (He could not guess that Webb did not know what to do with them when they arrived; offensive action was not in his lexicon.) The most important reason Montcalm could not march south was that Governor Vaudreuil had made him promise to have all his troops home by September so that they could gather their crops. Now the jealous governor had Montcalm where he wanted him; if he marched to Fort Edward he could censure him for not getting the troops home on time, and if he got them home on time he could flay him for not attacking Fort Edward.

While seriously misjudging his ability to manage his ferocious allies, Montcalm did all a victor could for the vanquished — he even begged the Indians to kill him instead of the prisoners. After the battle his army spent several days tearing down and setting fire to Fort William Henry, and the bodies in it, and the smallpox in the bodies. Reembarking on August 16 with a huge cargo of supplies and plunder, his army set sail for Ticonderoga and Canada.

Those of his Indians who did not die of smallpox eventually arrived in Montreal with their prisoners, some of whom Governor Vaudreuil bought for two kegs of brandy per prisoner. Then the Indians got drunk and started to abuse the captives not yet ransomed, one of whom they killed. Cooking his body in a kettle they forced the other prisoners to eat it. Most of the remaining captives were now mercifully ransomed.

Thus ended the massacre of Lake George, whose sound and fury signified little other than horror and depravity. While they had lost William Henry the British still held Fort Edward, however feebly. With their new fort at Ticonderoga the French remained the overlords of the Champlain Valley. A fall stillness stole over the lakes, broken only by the lofty honking of Canadian geese toward the southward sun. But they would be back in the spring, and so would the contenders for their flyway.

✿❦

Events now move so swiftly it is hard to understand why it took a century and a half for one side or the other to control the Champlain Valley. The answer has to be that England and France were so busy fighting in their own backyards that neither could summon the will to pour enough strength into the huge vacuum of North America.

Under the zealous William Pitt, Britain resolved to efface its smudgy record with a three-pronged assault on Louisbourg, the Cape Breton gate to the sea (which they had once conquered, given back, and failed to retake), Fort Duquesne (Pittsburgh) at the threshold to the midwest, and Ticonderoga. Louisbourg fell to Jeffrey Amherst, James Wolfe and Admiral Boscawen in July 1758. The expedition against Fort Duquesne also succeeded, but barely.

The thrust against Ticonderoga, the most strategic portal to New France, was entrusted to Gen. James Abercromby, successor in America to the Earl of Loudon, who had been cashiered for his failure to take Louisbourg and for General Webb's fiasco at Lake George. Abercromby was old, sick and nervous, and his military pedigree was average to uninspired. Perhaps the Prime Minister chose him as someone who would carry out the strategy he himself had prescribed. Pitt at least took the precaution of backing up Abercromby with "the noblest Englishman in my time," according to Gen. Wolfe, "and the best soldier in the British army" — the grandson of the King (unlikely as that may seem), George-Augustus, Viscount Howe. Only thirty-four, his was a rare spirit, equally at home with princes and peasants. Provincial soldiers revered him almost to the point of awe, for he went on scouting missions with Robert Rogers and had become an eager convert to the Rangers' strategy of fighting in the wilderness. The spectacle of the King's grandson, second in command of the largest army ever sent to America, washing his own clothes in a brook was as invigorating a boost to morale as Pitt's edict giving provincial officers the same authority as His Majesty's.

Early in July, after ascending the Hudson Valley, the great army embarked on Lake George in 900 bateaux and 135 whaleboats to the accompaniment of trumpets, bagpipes, and drums. Covering the lake for six miles the 15,000 troops presented an awesome sight under the cloudless sky: the British regulars in crimson, the Black Watch regiment in kilts, the provincials from the northern seaboard colonies in blue, the Rangers in green, and the Indians in every hue.

Outside the fort at Ticonderoga Montcalm directed a feverish last-minute defense of an earthen breastwork protected by limbs and branches with pointed ends, an early version of barbed wire. He needed far more than 3600 troops but his relationship with Governor Vaudreuil had so deteriorated that he must have counted himself lucky to have that many. A detachment he had stationed at the end of Lake George had destroyed the bridges over its outlet to Lake Champlain. Thus the British, who landed at the end of the upper lake on July 6, were forced to march through the woods, with Robert Rogers leading the way.

Now a devastating shock struck His Majesty's army. An exhausted band of 350 Frenchmen who had been scouting Lake George and had become lost in the forest trying to return to the fort, happened to stumble upon the British regulars, and a confused battle began. Hearing rifle fire, Rogers doubled back, catching the French in a trap in which 200 were killed and most of the rest taken prisoner. But the most fateful bullet struck Abercromby's young brigadier, Lord Howe, piercing his lungs, heart, and backbone, killing him

27. *Champlain Theater was vital to the outcome of the French and Indian War, culminating with Roger's raid on the St. Francis and Amherst's conquest of the lake.*

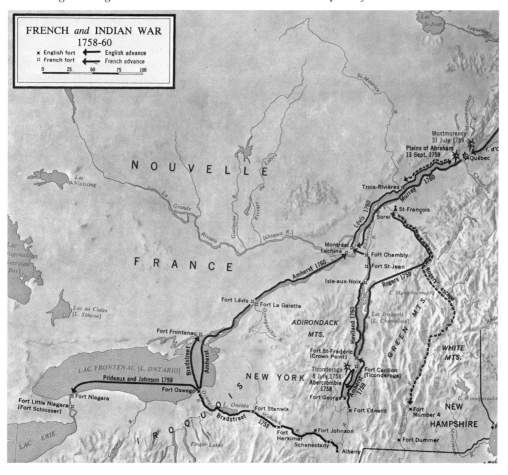

instantly. Thus departed the hope of England, who but a few hours before
had been seated on a bearskin rug with Robert Rogers discussing the
strategy that would put an end to French power in the Champlain Valley.
"When his body was brought into camp," wrote his aide de camp, "scarce
an eye was free from tears."

The dreadful tidings spread, and what shortly before had been a confident
and invincible army became a giant organism with no nervous system. For
now "Aunt Nabbycromby," as the troops called the bewildered old general
was now not nominally, but actually, in command. He ordered a retreat.
Then it was decided that General Bradstreet would rebuild the bridges, and
the army lumbered back toward the fort. So vastly superior were their numbers, the fort could have quickly or eventually been taken if Abercromby
had adopted any of several strategies other than the one he chose on July 8
— a frontal assault through the morass of trees and pointed branches. From
a safe vantage point two miles away he ordered wave after wave of infantry
against this breastwork. As quickly as they advanced, a murderous French
fire cut them down so that each crimson wave fell upon the one that preceded it. Such disaster befell the obedient and courageous British regulars
that over half of the eleven hundred soldiers in the Black Watch regiment
alone were killed or wounded. And all the while, Abercromby's Indians sat
in a spectators' gallery on the lower slopes of nearby Mount Defiance.

Although abundant reserves remained to be brought forward, every heart
was filled with the fear and desperation that strikes soldiers, no matter how
many, without a leader. Upon the failure of the heralded Highlanders to
penetrate the breastwork, the entire army panicked. Throwing down its
weapons it turned and fled in a mad scramble for the boats at the foot of
Lake George, the sickly Abercromby in its forefront. Even then the cannon
left at the water's edge could have been brought forward to pound the
wooden walls of the fort. Instead, Abercromby sailed away, while at the fort
the incredulous Montcalm stood victorious with his small but brilliantly
directed complement of regulars. He had not been able to count on his
militia, some of whom failed to carry out his commands in a flanking
maneuver against the Black Watch. Indeed, some had fled toward the boats
earlier in the day and he had been compelled to fire on his own troops. Yet
he had held the fort. In a defeat unprecedented in any battle yet fought in
America, the British lost 1,610 killed, wounded, and missing, most of them
regular troops; while Montcalm, still the master of Lake Champlain, lost
377.

A ghost story of Shakespearian dimensions arose out of the slaughter of

28. *Black Watch Regiment assaults Ticonderoga in Abercromby's bloody defeat of 1758.*

the Black Watch, a footnote to the Abercromby debacle of as much interest and significance as the campaign itself. On an expedition to the Scottish Highlands sixteen years before Ticonderoga, Duncan Campbell, the Lord of Inverawe, an officer of the illustrious Black Watch, had lost his way while serving in the Western Highlands. In the darkness he chanced to meet none other than his cousin, Donald Campbell, who gave him food and shelter, and the next morning directed him on his proper way. Duncan vowed someday to repay this favor.

Years passed, and he had almost forgotten the incident until one night, after the departure of the last guest from a party at his castle, he heard a frantic knocking at the gate. Supposing it to be one of his guests who had returned, he opened the gate to a stranger with a bloody face and torn clothing who begged to be admitted. He said he had killed a man, that his enemies were close behind, and implored Duncan to hide him.

"Swear by your dirk," the stranger pleaded, "that you will not betray me!" This Duncan did and led him to a secret place. Shortly thereafter, two armed men appeared with the shocking news that his own cousin, Donald, had been the victim of the murderer, and that they were hunting for him. Greatly disturbed because of the oath he had just given the stranger — and also his promise to Donald to repay his favor when he had been lost — he did nothing, and sent the two armed men on their way.

Falling asleep with a troubled conscience, the Lord of Inverawe suddenly awoke and to his consternation beheld, standing by his bedside, the bloody ghost of his cousin. "Inverawe! Inverawe!" warned a sepulchral voice. "Blood has been shed. Shield not the murderer!" Then the ghost faded into the darkness.

The horrified Duncan tossed and turned the rest of the night and in the morning went to the hiding place to tell the murderer he could shield him no longer. When reminded that he had given his oath to protect him, Duncan decided upon a compromise and led him to a nearby cave. That night the ghost of Donald again appeared and repeated his solemn warning not to protect the murderer. Deciding that he must choose between his promises, he returned to the cave only to find that the murderer had fled.

While he brooded over his plight before the fireplace on the third night, his dog began to growl and tremble and then to howl, and within a moment Donald stood before him with outstretched hands. "Farewell, Inverawe. Farewell, till we meet at Ticonderoga!" Then he vanished.

As agitated as before, Duncan pondered over the strange name, Ticonderoga, which he had never heard, but as the days passed and Donald's ghost did not reappear, he managed to put it in the back of his mind. Not long thereafter he was summoned to America with his Black Watch regiment and then it was that he learned, with consternation, that the army of which it was a part was setting forth on a campaign to take a fort named — Ticonderoga! So distraught did he become with each mention of the name that his fellow officers tried to convince him that the fort they were to attack was called George, not Ticonderoga.

The worst of Duncan's fears were realized when, the night before the battle, Donald's ghost appeared once more, though it said nothing. With trembling voice the next morning Duncan told his fellow officers that they had tried to deceive him about the army's objective. 'This" he said, "is Ticonderoga! I shall die today!" When the Black Watch tried to storm the barricade Duncan, in its midst, received a shot which shattered his arm. It had to be amputated. He died from the loss of blood and was buried between Hudson Falls and Fort Edward.

⁂

With the defeat of an army three times larger than his own, Montcalm ought to have become the hero of French Canada. But he knew his victory was an illusion. Sooner or later, if the law of averages meant anything, he would confront an able British general. Although reinforcements permitted him to conduct a number of raids at the heels of Abercromby's retreating army, he still lacked the troops to pursue it — even enough to retain the fort.

Quebec remained his chief frustration. Maligned and discredited by the spiteful Vaudreuil and a provincial government pock-marked with graft and corruption, he lamented that "all the knaves grow rich, and the honest men are ruined." Powerless to forestall the loss of Canada and its dependencies to England, he petitioned the King to return to France, but His Majesty would not hear of it. "There are situations," Montcalm confessed to a friend, "when nothing remains but for a general to die with honor."

In contrast to the hopeless scenario that the French were writing for themselves, Prime Minister Pitt had finally implanted in the British a sense of purpose and had weeded out the bad generals. Fresh from his victory at Louisbourg and now commander-in-chief of North America, Sir Jeffrey Amherst prepared a new plan to cut New France in half by seizing Ticonderoga and Crown Point and advancing to Montreal. The strategy for 1759 also called for General Wolfe to ascend the St. Lawrence with fresh troops from England. In the West another expedition would cross Lake Ontario and capture Fort Niagara.

Advancing down Lake George on July 21, 1759, with an army nearly as large as Abercromby's, the able but cautious Amherst found Fort Carillon to be a sitting duck. Starved everywhere for troops, Montcalm had departed for Canada leaving General Bourlamaque with a garrison of only 2300 men. Bourlamaque thought he might be able to attack the forward British lines with some 300 Indians, regulars, and volunteers, but as usual the Indians refused to expose themselves to open fire. Deciding that he had better

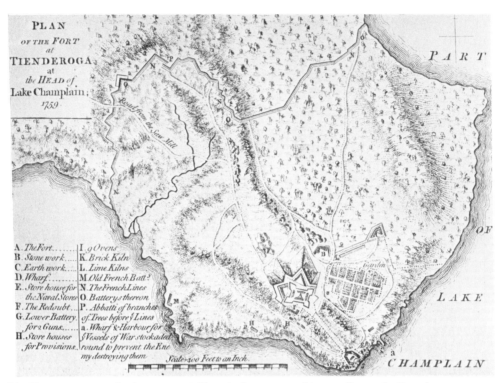

PLAN
OF THE FORT
at
TIENDEROGA,
at
the HEAD of
Lake Champlain;
1759

A. The Fort.......... I. 9 Ovens
B. Stone work..... K. Brick Kiln
C. Earth work..... L. Lime Kilns
D. Wharf.......... M. Old French Batt.²
E. Store house for N. The French Lines
   the Naval Stores O. Batterys thereon.
F. The Redoubt... P. Abbatti of branches
G. Lower Battery   of Trees before y Lines
   for 2 Guns...... a. Wharf & Harbour for
H. Store houses   y Vessels of War stockaded
   for Provisions. round to prevent the Ene-
                   my destroying them. Scale 400 Feet to an Inch.

29. *Upon conquering the fort in 1759 Jeffrey Amherst restored it according to the French plan and renamed it Ticonderoga. French "Jardin du Roi" is shown at right.*

retreat while he could, Bourlamaque embarked for Crown Point, with instructions to Captain Hebecourt to hold Carillon as long as possible with his 400 men, and then to blow it up.

The situation became desperate as the British brought up their heavy cannon. On July 26, three French deserters reported to Amherst that Hebecourt was leaving to join Bourlamaque and that he had lighted a slow fuse that soon would blow up the powder magazine. Wanting a whole fort, not just pieces, Amherst offered 100 guineas to the deserter who would lead his men to the fuse so they could extinguish it. None volunteered. About 10:30 that night a tremendous explosion rent the sky. Raging flames then discharged cannon that the French purposely had primed. Despite a bucket brigade of camp kettles passed up from the lake, the fire consumed the floors of the barracks, the roof timbers, and parts of the walls.

The next day a number of drunken French troops who had tapped kegs of brandy before the explosion were rounded up as they staggered about the area. When the flames died down the British found that the blast in the

30. *An extremely careful commander, Amherst also built a new fort at Crown Point and a road to the Connecticut River.*

powder magazine had carried away fifty horses stabled above it. But the damage was not beyond repair. Determining that the fort could be rebuilt Amherst chose to do it according to the French plan which, he said, would "save great expense and give no room for the engineers to exercise their genius."

Bourlamaque also had blown up Fort St. Frederic but that was too far gone to be restored. Moving to Crown Point early in August, Amherst engaged his army in the building of a new fort that cost what was then the enormous sum of 10 million dollars. Constructed not on the original site at the northeast edge of the point, but a few rods inland, Fort Amherst never saw any action other than a fire that gutted the fieldstone walls of the barracks. Amherst has been criticized for spending too much time on defensive projects instead of pursuing Bourlamaque into Canada and perhaps ending the war a year earlier. However, his policy of being safe rather than sorry had its advantages, among them the rebuilding of the old French road between Crown Point and Ticonderoga and the blazing of a new one on the

opposite shore from Chimney Point through the Green Mountains to Fort
Number 4. The Crown Point Road was intended to bind the Connecticut
Valley to Lake Champlain and facilitate the passage of troops and supplies
from southern New England.

In the absence of any roads on either side of the broadening lake's rugged
shores north of Crown Point, Amherst hurriedly built the nucleus of a fleet
— an armed brigantine carrying sixteen 18-pound cannon, three square-
rigged scows and 160 flat-bottomed bateaux. Rather than encounter these
vessels, the French scuttled their schooner and some barge-like xebecs near
Valcour Island, whereupon Champlain became a British lake.

Other than his conquest of the forts, action in the Champlain Valley in
1759 belonged, not to Amherst, but to the durable Rangers of Robert

*31. Without Robert Rogers's "academy" of fighting in the wilderness, and his band of
durable Rangers, the French and Indian War might have ended differently.*

Rogers, without whose "academy" of fighting in the wilderness the French and Indian War might have ended differently. The sooner His Majesty's officers and men learned Rogers's methods the safer, they found, were their scalps. It is an interesting coincidence that Rogers came from Dunbarton, New Hampshire, then called Starksville, the home of John Stark, whose services were to become so important in the American Revolution. He was appointed commander of the Rangers by the Royal Governor of New Hampshire, Benning Wentworth, in the same year, 1755, that John Stark was commissioned a second lieutenant.

Steeped as they were in traditional warfare, British generals soon found it essential that Rangers lead their armies and protect their flanks and rear from surprise attacks by Indians, or by Frenchmen who had adopted Indian tactics. None had learned them better than the Rangers. Superb scouts and masters of stealthy raids, they subsisted in all weather — in the water, in snow, and on the ice. In the woods they were likely to march single file, the ranger in the lead keeping some distance ahead of the others. To avoid ambush they were careful never to return the same way they went. While under fire, they hugged the ground. When those in front discharged their muskets, those behind moved forward while the leaders were reloading. Often they waited until their enemies were very close and then fell upon them with knives and hatchets. If overwhelmed, they dispersed and met later at a selected place. If trapped, they fought as a body until darkness permitted their escape. They always posted sentries and were always awake at dawn when Indians attacked. When outnumbered, they bluffed their adversaries by fighting at night.

In their many sorties on skates, snowshoes and in whaleboats near Ticonderoga, the Rangers generally inflicted more punishment than they received, although their losses were occasionally very heavy. During the Abercromby campaign one of the more illustrious Rangers, Israel Putnam, was sent to Fiddler's Elbow in the Champlain Narrows to intercept any French scouts or detachments trying to approach the British from that direction. Putnam had only a few men and chose as the point of ambush a high ledge known today as Put's Rock. When 500 French and Indians passed below in the moonlight Putnam opened fire, killing half of the enemy while losing only one Ranger.

Captured by the French, however, Putnam very nearly lost his own life when, after being forced to march through the woods with a heavy pack and with swollen hands and bloody feet, the Indians stripped him, bound him to a tree, and lighted a fire under him. With his death only moments away,

Marin, the French leader, rushed forward and scattered the burning branches. Putnam was sent to Ticonderoga and later to Montreal by Montcalm. He survived his imprisonment to fight again — in the American Revolution.

Because it embodies all the elements of adventure, the expedition of the Rangers against the St. Francis Indians has become more famous than it was critical to the outcome of the war. During their countless raids on New England settlements from their village south of the St. Lawrence about half way between Montreal and Quebec, the St. Francis had taken hundreds of scalps. In early autumn, 1759 General Amherst ordered Rogers to put an end to these menacing Abnakis.

Sailing north from Crown Point on September 12 with 200 men, Rogers used every precaution to avoid discovery by the French. On the fifth day 40 sick and injured Rangers had to leave the expedition when a keg of gunpowder exploded at their encampment on the eastern shore. After ten days on the lake the Rangers landed at the northern end of Missisquoi Bay, hid their boats, and started overland. They had not gone far when the two Indians they had left in charge of the boats caught up with them to report that 400 Indians and French from the Missisquoi village had discovered their boats, and half of them were in pursuit. Rogers had no option but to move faster and to return to Crown Point, not by way of the lake, but south to the English forts on the Connecticut River, and then west to Crown Point. To make certain his men would have enough to eat, assuming they even reached Coos (now Newbury), Rogers sent messengers to inform Amherst of what had happened and to request that he send food to Coos.

So gruelling was their journey — nine days through a spruce bog covered with a foot of water — that their number had shrunk by another 18 men as they neared their destination. Much weakened by dreadful demands on their strength, the remainder finally reached a point three miles from St. Francis. There Rogers and two of his men dressed themselves as Indians. Stealing in the darkness to the edge of the village they found the Indians "in a high frolic" celebrating a wedding. A half hour before dawn the Rangers struck — furiously enough to atone for the 600 English scalps on display in the village. By seven o'clock they had killed 200 of the 300 Indians, taken 20 prisoners, and set all but three of their dwellings on fire. Rogers lost only one man. Thus expired the feared and hated St. Francis in a massacre as brutal as their own at Fort William Henry.

But the scalps of the Rangers were anything but secure. Two war parties of 550 French and Indians were in close pursuit above and below them on the St. Francis River. Managing to keep ahead of them by striking through the forests to the shores of Lake Memphremagog, Rogers now faced an acute shortage of provisions. Shooting animals was out of the question since their remains would mark the route of his escape. If he kept his men together starvation would overtake them before the enemy, but if he divided them so they could forage for food they could not withstand an attack. At length he separated them into

32. Rogers Rangers' surprise attack on the St. Francis Indians resulted in a massacre.

small groups with instructions to meet at the mouth of the Ammonoosuc, a tributary of the Connecticut.

Already exhausted in body and spirit, some of the Rangers became lost in the mountains, some were overtaken and killed by the enemy, and some, reaching the rendezvous, pressed forward to Coos, where Amherst was to have sent fresh supplies. Rogers wrote that "after so many days tedious march over steep rocky mountains or thro' wet dirty swamps" it was "hardly possible to describe the grief and consternation of those of us who came to the Cohase Intervales." For the lieutenant sent by Amherst with supplies "being an indolent fellow, tarried at the place but two days, when he returned, taking all the provisions back with him, about two hours before our arrival." Finding the remains of a fire burning in his camp, Rogers fired guns to alert him. Although he heard the shots he would not return since he thought Rogers to be an enemy.

Our distress . . . was truly inexpressible; our spirits, greatly depressed by the hunger and fatigues we had already suffered, now almost entirely sunk within us, seeing no resource left, nor any reasonable ground to hope that we should escape a most miserable death by famine. At length I came to a resolution to push as fast as possible toward No. 4 leaving the remains of my party, now unable to march further, to get such wretched subsistence as the barren wilderness could afford (this was ground nuts and lilly roots) till I could get relief to them, which I engaged to do within ten days.

I, with Capt. Ogden, one Ranger, and a captive Indian boy, embarked upon a raft we had made of dry pine trees. The current carried us down the stream in the middle of the river, where we endeavoured to keep our wretched vessel by such paddles as we had made out of small trees, or spires split and hewed. The second day we reached White River Falls, and very narrowly escaped being carried over them by the current. Our little remains of strength however enabled us to land, and to march by them.

At the bottom of these falls, while Capt. Ogden and the Ranger hunted for red squirrels for refreshment . . . I attempted the forming a new raft for our further conveyance. Being not able to cut down trees, I burnt them down, and then burnt them off at proper lengths. This was our third day's work after leaving our companions. The next day we got our materials together, and completed our raft, and floated with the stream again till we came to Wattockquithey Falls, which are about fifty yards in length. Here we landed, and by a withe made of hazel bushes, Capt. Ogden held the raft, till I went to the bottom, prepared to swim in and board it when it came down, and if possible paddle it ashore, this being our only resource for life, as we were not able to make a third raft in case we had lost this. I had the good fortune to succeed, and the next morning we embarked, and floated down the stream to within a small distance of No. 4 where we found some men cutting of timber, who gave us the first relief, and assisted us to the fort, from whence I dispatched a canoe with provisions, which reached the men at Cohase four days after, which (agreeable to my engagement) was the tenth after I left them.

Finally returning to Crown Point on December 1, 79 days after the expedition had begun, Rogers found that he had lost to the wilderness and to the enemy three officers and 46 sergeants and privates.

The lowering of the fleur-de-lis above Quebec's rocky promontory was just a matter of time. The French had stressed exploration, conquest, and trade in the new world — not settlement. England, to the contrary, had planted there nearly fourteen times as many settlers by the beginning of the French and Indian War.

If France had not been exhausted by war at home, if dissension had not rent the Quebec government, if corruption had not reduced the average Canadian to penury, if an able governor had assisted Montcalm instead of trying to destroy him; if the Iroquois had gone over to the French which they constantly threatened to do because of British inaction, and if Pitt had not ended the succession of incompetent generals and fortified his countrymen with a sense of purpose, the French might have prevailed much longer. As it was, Montcalm's remark that there are situations when all that remains for a general is to die with honor was all too prophetic.

The British succeeded in their western campaign against Fort Niagara. And General Wolfe, sailing up the St. Lawrence, managed to scale the frowning bluff of Quebec. There remained one of the most tragic and decisive moments in the history of warfare — the death of Montcalm on the Plains of Abraham and, just as the British were winning an empire, the death of General Wolfe.

His posthumous victory was consummated in 1760 with the departure of Col. William Haviland's army of 3400 from Crown Point for the Richelieu, the capture of the rest of France's tiny Champlain navy, and the cutting off of Bouganville (at Isle Aux Noix) from his source of supplies at St. John.

On September 8 Vaudreuil capitulated to the combined British forces which advanced upon Montreal from the upper and lower St. Lawrence. Three years later at the Treaty of Paris, France formally relinquished to England a major part of North America.

IV

Daybreak of the Revolution.

❧❧❧❧❧

The Key to Liberty.

T HE American frontier always summons visions of the boundless West.
Yet after the treaty of 1763 the frontier was North. For over fifteen
decades the dense curtain of northern New England had been parted only
by scouts, raiding parties, and armies. Dark forests covered all but the
highest peaks from the English seaboard villages west for 200 miles to Lake
Champlain.

Of the settlers who streamed north after the cannon fire faded away, none
marked the future more indelibly than the brothers Allen of Litchfield, Connecticut. Ethan, the eldest, born in 1738, became the archetype of an American pioneer, with talents dwarfing those of later entries like Daniel Boone
and Davy Crockett. His strength and size were such that he could "seize by
his teeth, and throw over his head, bags containing each a bushel of salt, as
fast as two men could bring them round to him." It was said that he had
"grasped two enemies, one in each hand, and, lifting them off the ground,
held them out at arms' length and beat them together till they cried for
mercy." And that he alone had tackled a New York sheriff and a posse of six
men and left them sprawling on the ground.

In his biography of Ethan, John Pell describes the brothers, even in their
youth, as obstinate, domineering, bold, and clever, and Ethan as precocious
and mercurial, with a strange thirst for knowledge. At 19 he joined the French
and Indian War in a march to Lake George, but such was the turn of events

that he served only 14 days. At 23 he was working an iron mine in Salisbury, Connecticut. A religious skeptic under the influence of an itinerant doctor, he was also exploring the prospects of the hereafter. Following his marriage to a woman six years his senior he acquired a taste for real estate, specifically the Green Mountains and the valley of Lake Champlain. The evergreen wilderness between the lake and New Hampshire, then being parceled out by the Royal Governor, Benning Wentworth, provided a cheap and alluring haven for restless Connecticut malcontents who couldn't settle down. Covering vast areas of it on foot, Ethan and his brother, Ira, first obtained New Hampshire titles to 12,000 acres in Hubbardton and Castleton for a mere 60 pounds (a penny an acre). Since New York was granting the same land (and had gained legal right to it from the Crown in 1764) they had to form a posse, the Green Mountain Boys, to protect their New Hampshire titles. As Colonel Commandant, Ethan conducted their mission of chasing away New York agents and settlers with style and gusto.

The miner, theologian, scout, woodsman, and father of a growing family now acquired the talents of the military adventurer, lobbyist, orator, and pamphleteer. "This wicked, inhuman, most barbarous, infamous, cruel, villainous, and thievish act," he called one of the Yorkers' boldest aggressions. And "the gods of the hills are not the gods of the valleys," meaning, presumably, that the humble and honest settlers under New Hampshire would never submit to the imperious designs of the New York gentry, or the venal plots of their sheriffs and magistrates! Those not privileged to hear Ethan's wildly refreshing pronouncements could read them in the *Connecticut Courant,* or in pamphlets he wrote and distributed, chastising New York and extolling his own cause. He was a literary event, and his writings were widely enjoyed.

After Ira had gone down the lake in 1772 and mapped the land from the mouth of the Onion all the way up to the mountains, the brothers (including also Heman and Zimri and their uncle, Remember Baker) banded together as the Onion River Land Company, advertising that there "is no tract of land of so great quantity between New York and Canada that can be denominated equally good." Desiring to purchase adjacent lands granted by New Hampshire to several men living in enemy territory, they dressed as British officers and bought them secretly in White Plains, New York. Now in possession of an enormous tract of 60,000 acres of lakeshore and river lands, the Green Mountain Boys became ever more active against New York claimants, whose titles, if ever validated, would mean they would have to pay twice for the same lands. The complex dispute had arisen over the question of whether the

33. Traditional portrait of Ethan Allen. No true likeness exists.

Connecticut River was the eastern boundary of New York, or whether Lake Champlain was the western boundary of the New Hampshire Grants. The controversy was long argued in provincial capitals and at Court, and a final decision was just as long deferred.

The Green Mountain Boys ranged over much of what is now Vermont doing what they could to terrify New York settlers and surveyors. Stopping short of death, but not of whipping with what Ethan called "Twigs of the Wilderness," their violence sometimes consisted of such humiliating jokes as hoisting a Yorker to the top of the 20-foot signpost at the Catamount Tavern in Bennington, the early headquarters of the Green Mountain Boys, and letting him swing to the jeers of the inhabitants.

Among the Allens' most persistent adversaries in the Champlain Valley were some Scotch settlers who had settled at New Haven Falls under a New York title. The land had originally been granted by New Hampshire to settlers whom the Scotchmen had driven away. Ethan in turn deposed the Scots, only to find they had returned. This time the Green Mountain Boys rode in 100 strong, set fire to the Scots' cabins, pulled down their gristmill, broke the millstone and threw it in the river, and trampled their corn with their horses. When the Scotchmen demanded by what authority they had done this, the Colonel Commandant replied that he was Ethan Allen, Captain of the Mob, and his authority was his gun.

To forestall any further opposition Ethan built a fort at New Haven Falls and garrisoned it with Green Mountain Boys. Troubled in the north with a New York surveyor whom they first threatened to burn but then let go, they also built a blockhouse at the lower falls of the Onion. Its eight-inch timbers contained 32 portholes for small arms fire, and there were double doors and blocks for the windows. The second story jutted out over the first so that water could be poured over the walls in the event they were set on fire. Should the detachable roof be ignited by flaming arrows it could be thrown off.

By 1774 the Allens were exploring the possibility of forming a separate royal colony in the Champlain Valley with Colonel Philip Skene, who owned 30,000 acres around the head of the lake at Skenesborough (Whitehall). The province was to have embraced all the land east to the Connecticut, west to Lake Ontario, and north from the Massachusetts boundary to the 45th parallel. An officer in the armies of Abercromby and Amherst, Skene acquired his titles neither from New Hampshire or New York but directly from London, so that he held a more or less neutral position in the land controversy. Also proclaimed Governor of Ticonderoga and Crown Point, Skene had built at his fledgling principality a sawmill, military garrison, a sloop in which to transport supplies from Canada, and a fine two-and-a-half story stone house where he diplomatically received both the partisans of New York and New Hampshire. However, since he had been appointed a New York justice of the peace, and Ethan was the chief disturber of it, Skene had advised him as early as 1771 to "repair to Connecticut" until things quieted down, or he would be forced to arrest him.

Ethan replied that he could not flee to Connecticut, that a spirit above had directed that he should remain in the neighborhood until removed from it to the kingdom of Heaven. Recalling the Major's generous hospitality, Ethan flatteringly advised him that although his honorable station in life commanded submission from those of an inferior rank, that it was his character that merited admiration.

Ever Since my Small Acquaintance with You I have Retained the Most honourable Sentiments Toward You Not onely as the Most Consummate politician whose Eye pierces through Humane Nature but also as one that acts from Generous and brave

principles from hence I have infer'd you would not be an Adversary to the Setlers . . .
Undoubtedly You would pass Sentence on my Past and future Conduct. If by this
Rule I can be Denominated Disorderly and Riotous I Desire You would be my
adversary but if Otherways my friend . . . the law of Self preservation Urges me to
Defend my Property.

As for the reward Yorkers had posted for his capture, Ethan told Skene that
"they are not Allowed to hang any man before they have ketched him."

The separate Champlain Valley province never materialized because the
Revolution was near at hand and Skene was an ardent Tory. The Allens
intended to be independent both from Britain and New York even if they had
to erect their own government to legalize the claims to their land. Since the
swelling resentment against England presented a greater danger than New
York, Ethan determined early in 1775 that another kind of action was necessary. If war were declared Champlain would again become the main artery of
invasion from Canada, and the rich intervales of the Onion River Land
Company the stamping ground of the Redcoats. And the forts would become
strongholds of British repression.

During the 16 years since Ticonderoga had been blown up by the French
and rebuilt by the British it had decayed into "an Amazing Useless Mass of
Earth," according to a captain of the Royal Engineers. Although Amherst had
replaced the wooden walls with stone, the freezing and thawing of the earth
had toppled some of them. The wooden parapets covering the cannon had
rotted and the interior of the barracks had sadly deteriorated. Even so
Ticonderoga remained for Britain as it had for France the most important
stronghold in the American heartland. Although war with the colonies
seemed unthinkable, George the Third continued to maintain there a small
garrison of a captain, a lieutenant, and 42 soldiers.

Lying in the sphere of Philip Skene's grant and caught in the crossfire of
competing land claims between New Hampshire and New York, the forts and
the lake existed in a kind of vacuum. Sometime early in 1775 the overlord of
the Green Mountains appointed himself to fill it. While visiting with John
Brown, a Massachusetts lawyer who had been commissioned by the Boston
Committee of Correspondents to probe the sympathies of the Canadians,
Ethan volunteered two of his Green Mountain Boys to guide Brown to
Montreal. He also suggested a surprise attack on Ticonderoga.

The lake and its tributaries were swollen by a February thaw and Brown's
boat was driven against an island and frozen in for two days. Arriving at last in
Montreal, Brown wrote the Boston Committee that Canada was well disposed
toward New England. He also advised that Fort Ticonderoga be seized as soon

as possible, that the Green Mountain Boys had "engaged to do this Business, and in my opinion they are the most proper Persons for this Jobb."

Not long thereafter Heman Allen, fellow owner of the Onion River Land Company, arrived in the Grants with news of Lexington and Concord. At that moment, Ethan later recalled, the die was cast:

Ever since I arrived at the state of manhood and acquainted myself with the general history of mankind, I have felt a sincere passion for liberty. The history of nations, doomed to perpetual slavery, in consequence of yielding up to tyrants their natural-born liberties, I read with a sort of philosophical horror; so that the first systematical and bloody attempt, at Lexington, to enslave America, thoroughly electrified my mind, and fully determined me to take part with my country.

The capture of Ticonderoga would have to be swift, silent, and well planned. Galloping to Bennington, Ethan received the sanction of a committee of the Council of Connecticut to attack the fort, and 300 pounds to purchase ammunition and defray expenses. Guards were posted on all roads leading to Ticonderoga. A council of war convening in Castleton on May 8 directed that Ethan lead the expedition, that thirty men be sent to the head of the lake the following day to capture Skene's family and settlement, and that his boats be rounded up and brought that night to Hand's Cove, Shoreham, diagonally across from the fort on the east shore, the point of rendezvous.

Meanwhile Noah Phelps, commissary of the expedition, gathered some useful intelligence by posing as a British traveler seeking a shave from the Ticonderoga barber. According to the more plausible of several accounts, his spying was so credible that the officers discussed with him the unrest in the colonies, the poor condition of the fort, and even the fact that all the powder was wet and had to be dried out. Phelps boldly employed a boatman from the fort to row him across the lake. Although anxious and in a great hurry he declined to help row when the boatman asked him to, protesting that he was no boatman. But when safely out of range he willingly took an oar and rowed so vigorously that the boatman became suspicious, saying: "You have seen a boat before now, Sir." It appeared for a while that he might try to return Phelps to the fort but he feared his size. Landing safely, Phelps hurried to Castleton to report to the war party what he had seen and heard.

Another valuable service was performed by a blacksmith, Gersham Beach, when he set out to inform the scattered farmers of Rutland, Pittsford, Brandon, and Middlebury that they were needed at Castleton. While it seems hardly possible, as some sources claim, that he covered sixty miles in 24 hours entirely on foot, his must have been a marathon performance, since much of his route, unlike that of Paul Revere, lay through heavy forests.

Answering the call to arms, 170 men appeared at the tavern in Castleton, all except one eagerly awaiting Ethan's instructions — Captain Benedict Arnold, who had come with his own orders from the Massachusetts Provincial Congress to capture the fort. He was supposed to have raised 400 men but was in such a hurry to arrive before Ethan's expedition embarked that he was accompanied only by his servant. A hot dispute followed in Shoreham, where it was explained that the Green Mountain Boys had their own authority from Connecticut and would follow no leader but Ethan. When Arnold persisted in his demands the angry militia told him that rather than obey his orders they would return to their farms. When Arnold argued that Ethan, lacking authority from the Massachusetts Provincial Congress, would swing from a tree if something went wrong with the expedition, Ethan seems to have agreed that Arnold might share his command at least to the extent of marching by his side. However, since the troops would not otherwise have started out, Ethan did in fact command them.

With 200 Green Mountain Boys and two score more from Massachusetts and Connecticut milling around in the darkness at Hand's Cove early the next morning, his leadership was vital. The boats to ferry them across had not arrived and it would soon be too late to start if the fort was to be reached at dawn. A large rowboat belonging to Colonel Skene fortunately arrived in the nick of time. It had not come from Skenesborough, but from Bridport where it had been secured from one of Skene's servants with a taste for "strong water." Procuring a jug of rum, six young men told the boatman they were on their way to a Shoreham hunting party and, waving the jug of rum, volunteered to help him row the boat that way. By the time they arrived at Hand's Cove the boatman was too far gone to recognize the hunting party for what it was.

The ferrying operation had to begin with the rowboat and a scow. Although only 80 men had reached the west shore by dawn, Ethan decided he could wait no longer. On a beach north of the fort he addressed his men (according to his *Narrative)* as follows:

Friends and fellow soldiers, you have for a number of years past been a scourge and terror to arbitrary power. Your valor has been famed abroad, and acknowledged, as appears by the advice and orders to me from the General Assembly of Connecticut to surprise and take the garrison before us. I now propose to advance before you, and, in person, conduct you through the wicket-gate; for we must this morning either quit our pretensions to valor, or possess ourselves of this fortress in a few minutes; and, inasmuch as it is a desperate attempt, which none but the bravest of men dare undertake, I do not urge it on any contrary to his will. You that will undertake voluntarily, poise your fire-locks.

*Montcalm's troops celebrate their 1758 victory over superior British forces at Fort Carillon.
It was conquered and renamed Ticonderoga by Jeffrey Amherst in 1759. Courtesy Fort Ticonderoga.*

Air view shows Ticonderoga's strategic location at the outlet of Champlain's high tributary, Lake George. Courtesy Fort Ticonderoga. Below: Fort Crown Point ruins. By R.N. Hill.

Scene of Commodore Macdonough's triumph appeared on blue commemorative china, manufactured for export at Staffordshire, England. By Rik Jesse.

One of many versions of the crucial American victory at Plattsburgh harbor, September 11, 1814.

Sunk by the British at Valcour Island on October 11, 1776, Benedict Arnold's gondola Philadelphia, was salvaged 159 years later, her mast and cannon still in place. She is now displayed in a special wing of the Smithsonian Institution—the only such survivor of the American Revolution. Courtesy Vermont Historical Society.

Lithograph of Whitehall, from a drawing by Milbert, around the turn of the 18th century.
Below: Endicott lithograph of Burlington harbor in 1858 at the height of the steamboat era.

Every gun was raised.

Thus, in the Green Mountain daybreak, began the first offensive action of the American Revolution — Ethan leading the way in his green officer's coat with large gold epaulettes, Arnold beside him (still protesting his leadership) dressed as a captain in the Connecticut governor's footguard, and the motley company of provincials clad in deerskin and linsey-woolsey, wearing bearskin and beaver hats, and armed with rifles, blunderbusses, knives, and clubs with which they hoped to subdue the "Gibraltar of America."

Rounding the eastern ramparts they poured through a break in the south wall toward the wicket gate in the center of the south curtain. The sentry, in John Pell's words,

. . . saw in the pale grey light an enormous apparition rushing at him with a sword waving above his head. He had presence of mind enough to cock his musket and pull the trigger, but the flint flashed in the pan and the gun misfired. Taking to his heels, he ran through the long archway under the south barracks into the *place d'armes* and

34. Capture of Ticonderoga by Allen and Arnold is recreated in Fort's authentic diorama.

across it to a bombproof on the other side, shouting all the while to rouse the garrison. Ethan rushed after him, and the men, with Indian war-whoops, crowded through the wicket gate and climbed the walls of the bastions. Ethan ordered them to form a hollow square in the *place d'armes,* but after they had given three cheers their enthusiasm overcame their discipline and, shouting "No quarter!" they rushed at the doors and stairways of the barracks.

The first soldier to emerge from the guard-room in the south barracks made a pass at one of the invaders with a charged bayonet, but Ethan, coming up just then, hit him over the head with the flat of his sword. The man's life was probably saved by a comb he was wearing in his hair. He begged for quarter, which Ethan granted on condition that he point out the Commandant's room. The soldier led the way to a stairway leading up the facade of the west barracks. With Arnold beside him and a crowd of his men at his back, Ethan started up.

35. What Ethan Allen said at the moment the British commander surrendered Ticonderoga has been the subject of much folklore but was probably just what he reported that he said.

At this much-debated point, Ethan seems to have shouted: "Come out of there, you damned old rat!" The door opened to reveal a bewildered lieutenant, holding his breeches in his hand. Staring incredulously at the rabble in arms, he demanded to know by what authority they entered His Majesty's fort. "In the name of the Great Jehovah and the Continental Congress!" thundered Ethan. Waving his sword over the lieutenant's head he demanded immediate possession of the fort "and all the effects of George the Third!" or else he would not leave a man, woman, or child alive.

Now apparently realizing that the lieutenant was not the commander, Ethan began forcing his way through the door, when Captain William de la Place stepped out and, after a brief parley, handed Ethan his sword. The lieutenant was locked up in de la Place's quarters, while the Commandant was taken below so he could order his men to surrender. They already had. Breaking into their barracks the Green Mountain Boys ousted them from their beds and bundled them down to the parade ground, where their weapons were stacked in a pile. The Revolution's first prisoners were paraded in the dawn, and as Seth Warner arrived with a second contingent from Hand's Cove, the barracks were ransacked for the inevitable "souvenirs." In Captain de la Place's private cellar the Green Mountain Boys discovered 90 gallons of rum, which Ethan commandeered "for the refreshment of the fatigued soldiery."

"The sun seemed to rise that morning with a superior lustre," he wrote, "and Ticonderoga and its dependencies smiled on its conquerors, who tossed about the flowing bowl, and wished success to Congress and the liberty and freedom of America."

Word of the fall of a far-famed fortress to a band of farmers emboldened every patriot heart throughout the Colonies and even the cautious deliberations of the Continental Congress, which in the spring of 1775 had not yet declared independence, much less war. But the raid was a *fait accompli* and they had no option but to rationalize it as a measure of protective security. It was easier for Ethan to report to the governor of Connecticut that he was making him a present of "a Major, a Captain, and two Lieutenants in the regular Establishment of George the Third," than for the governor or other authorities to know what to do with them. It was a long time before they did.

To secure the lake the day after the capture of the fort, Ethan sent Seth Warner, his right bower in the Green Mountain Boys (who was disgruntled at having to arrive after the action was over) to capture Crown Point, where the British maintained a skeleton garrison. Since Ethan and Benedict Arnold could not dispose of one another they formed an uneasy alliance in the pursuit of the British sloop cruising the lake — Arnold to command Skene's captured sloop, the *Liberty*, and Allen, Skene's bateaux. Since the *Liberty* did not arrive fast enough to suit Arnold, he set sail in a smaller boat to clear the British from the northern part of the lake. On the way the mail boat fell into his hands, and with it a list of all the King's troops in the northern department. Meanwhile he transferred operations to the *Liberty*, which had caught up, and proceeding north, managed to seize without bloodshed the small garrison of a sergeant and 12 men at St. Jean; also a schooner which he renamed the *Enterprise*, and several bateaux. Loading aboard two cannon and other useful supplies and destroying everything else, he started south before the British garrison at Chambly caught wind of his raid. Midway in the lake he met Ethan, who was on his way north with his flotilla of bateaux and about 100 men.

Boarding the *Enterprise*, Ethan went below with Arnold and after excessive toasts to their success Ethan could not be dissuaded from going north to occupy the garrison Arnold had just left at St. Jean. Shortly after his arrival a British expedition (from Montreal), twice as large as his, forced his rather shamefaced withdrawal to Crown Point. He explained this away by writing the Continental Congress: "Provided I had but 500 men with me at St. Johns when we took the King's sloop I would have advanced to Montreal." Probably he would have, for the roster captured by Arnold on the mail boat listed a total of 550 British troops in all Canada.

The Green Mountain Boys returned to their farms, leaving Ethan without a command, whereas Arnold, with 150 enlistees, emerged as the undisputed authority on the lake. Moving to Crown Point he made plans to capture Canada, which might well have been possible at that time with a small well-trained army. But even if he could have recruited and trained it, the Continental Congress would not hear of such a rash gamble. Psychologically unprepared to fight, it directed that the forts be abandoned (until such a time as they could be returned to the King), and that the cannon be removed to the head of Lake George. An outcry from the northern provinces dependent upon the forts for protection forced the Congress in June to place them under the aegis of New York.

Now followed an interval of backing and filling — Ethan going to Philadelphia to get Congress and New York to authorize a regiment of 500 Green Mountain Boys, which was done, and Arnold, who had become involved in further disputes about his authority, to Cambridge and Connecticut to attend to his own affairs until plans for his march to Quebec could be formulated. Ethan's success in raising a regiment turned into a sour disappointment when his men chose Seth Warner as their commander. No doubt they considered him too impetuous. Capturing the fort in their backyards was one thing, invading Canada quite another. And there was not a shred of doubt that that was what he planned, with or without the sanction of Philadelphia. There was logic in his strategy; within a few months the opportunity for a relatively bloodless grafting of Canada to the American colonies was forever lost. By the time an invasion was undertaken it was too late, both in terms of the weather and of British resistance.

Finally getting down to the business of organizing the rebellion, the Continental Congress appointed an Albany patrician, General Philip Schuyler, as commander of the northern department. Since some 400 British regulars were then strengthening the defenses at St. Jean, Congress timidly suggested that if Schuyler found it practicable, and it was all right with the Canadians, he might try to capture St. Jean, Montreal, or any other parts of Canada. A veteran of the late campaigns under Johnson, Abercromby, and Bradstreet, Schuyler was no stranger to the lake or the northcountry. More competent as a planner and supply officer than as a field commander, he was nevertheless a valuable choice, since the acquisition and transport of provisions and materiel remained a most stubborn problem.

Arriving on the lake in July he found conditions deplorable and set diligently to work building a sawmill and hospital and getting supplies for Ticonderoga's starving and ragged defenders, many of whom were sick and most of them without shirts, shoes, underclothes, blankets, even firearms. With the arrival of fresh troops from Connecticut and New York conditions improved. By the end of August Schuyler had somehow managed to build two boats and to procure food, rum, and clothing for the 2400 men now at Ticonderoga and Crown Point — enough, he considered, to attack the British at St. Jean.

Schuyler's tactical strength reposed in his gallant brigadier, Richard Montgomery, an Irish officer who had served with Wolfe and Amherst; a former baronet, member of Parliament and subsequently of the Provincial Congress, and son-in-law of the eminent Robert Livingston of New York. With Schuyler ailing, it was Montgomery who commanded the new expedition of 1200 troops to the north. Sailing from Crown Point on the 30th of August, they bivouacked that night at what was to become Westport, and reached Isle La Motte the next day. They then sailed to Isle Aux Noix, where Montgomery placed a boom, protected by artillery, across the Richelieu to prevent the two 52-foot, 18-gun boats the British had built from sailing south. Despite driving rains, sickness in his ranks, short supplies, arguments among

Schuyler helped improve things conditions

the officers, and the prodigious task of dragging artillery through the dank swamps of the bordering river, he pushed north to St. Jean, which fell after a siege of nearly two months.

In the meantime another would-be conqueror of Canada without any troops, none other than the zealous hero of Ticonderoga, was at work as an official missionary trying to convert Canadians to the American cause. Well suited to this role, Ethan discharged it until he and John Brown (with whom he had connived to take Ticonderoga) hatched a plan to make themselves masters of Montreal. Meeting in a house in Longueil, they agreed that Ethan would cross the St. Lawrence a little north of Montreal, and Brown a little to the south. With 110 recruits, Ethan successfully launched his half of the invasion by crossing the river at night. Unfortunately Brown did not appear from the North and Ethan found himself in a trap with no possibility of recrossing the river by canoe in the daylight. In his inimitable account of this misadventure Ethan reported that when word of his presence reached the British "the town of Montreal was in great tumult."

Gen. Carlton and the royal party made every preparation to go on board their vessels . . . but the spy escaping from my guard to the town occasioned an alteration in their policy, and emboldened Gen. Carlton to send the force, which he had there collected, out against me. I had previously chosen my ground, but when I saw the number of the enemy as they sallied out of town, I perceived it would be a day of trouble, if not of rebuke; but I had no chance to fly, as Montreal was situated on an island, and the river St. Lawrence cut off my communication to Gen. Montgomery's camp. I encouraged my soldiery to bravely defend themselves, that we should soon have help, and that we should be able to keep the ground, if no more.

The enemy consisted of not more than forty regular troops, together with a mixed multitude, chiefly Canadians, with a number of English, who lived in the town, and some Indians; in all to the number of 500. The reader will notice that most of my party were Canadians; indeed it was a motley parcel of soldiery which composed both parties. However the enemy began the attack from wood-piles, ditches, buildings, and such places, at a considerable distance, and I returned the fire from a situation more than equally advantageous.

The attack began between two and three of the clock in the afternoon, just before which I ordered a volunteer by the name of Richard Young, with a detachment of nine men as a flank guard which, under the cover of the bank of the river, could not only annoy the enemy, but at the same time serve as a flank guard to the left of the main body.

The fire continued for some time on both sides; and I was confident that such a remote method of attack could not carry the ground (provided it should be continued till night), but near half the body of the enemy began to flank round to my right, upon

which I ordered a volunteer by the name of John Dugan, who had lived many years in
Canada and understood the French language, to detach about fifty of the Canadians,
and post himself at an advantageous ditch, which was at my right, to prevent my
being surrounded. He advanced with the detachment, but instead of occupying the
post, made his escape, as did likewise Mr. Young upon the left, with their
detachments.

I soon perceived that the enemy was in possession of the ground which Dugan
would have occupied. At this time I had but forty-five men with me, some of whom
were wounded. The enemy kept closing round me, nor was it in my power to prevent
it . . . and being almost entirely surrounded with such vast unequal numbers, I
ordered a retreat, but found that those of the enemy who were of the country, and
their Indians, could run as fast as my men, though the regulars could not. Thus I
retreated near a mile, and some of the enemy, with the savages, kept flanking me,
and others crowded hard in the rear. In fine I expected in a very short time to try the
world of spirits, for I was apprehensive that no quarter would be given to me, and
therefore had determined to sell my life as dear as I could.

One of the enemy's officers boldly pressing in the rear discharged his fusee at me;
the ball whistled near me, as did many others that day. I returned the salute and
missed him, as running had put us both out of breath. . . . I then saluted him with my
tongue in a harsh manner, and told him that inasmuch as his numbers were so far
superior to mine I would surrender, provided I could be treated with honor, and be
assured of good quarter for myself and the men who were with me, and he answered
I should. Another officer coming up directly after, confirmed the treaty, upon which
I agreed to surrender with my party, which then consisted of thirty-one effective
men, and seven wounded . . .

The officer I capitulated with then directed me and my party to advance towards
him, which was done. I handed him my sword, and in a half minute after, a savage,

part of whose head was shaved, being almost naked and painted, with feathers intermixed with the hair of the other side of his head, came running to me with an incredible swiftness; he seemed to advance with more than mortal speed. (As he approached near me his hellish visage was beyond all description: snakes' eyes appear innocent in comparison to his, his features extorted; malice, death, murder, and the wrath of devils and damned spirits are the emblems of his countenance).

In less than twelve feet of me he presented his firelock; at the instant of his present, I twitched the officer to whom I gave my sword between me and the savage, but he flew round with great fury, trying to single me out to shoot me without killing the officer. But by this time I was near as nimble as he, keeping the officer in such a position that his danger was my defence, but in less than half a minute I was attacked by just such another imp of hell. Then I made the officer fly around with incredible velocity, for a few seconds of time, when I perceived a Canadian (who had lost one eye as appeared afterwards) taking my part against the savages; and in an instant an Irishman came to my assistance with a fixed bayonet and drove away the fiends, swearing by Jasus he would kill them. This tragic scene composed my mind.

The escaping from so awful a death made even imprisonment happy, the more so as my conquerors on the field treated me with great civility and politeness. The regular officers said they were happy to see Col. Allen. I answered that I should rather choose to have seen them at Gen. Montgomery's camp. The gentlemen replied that they gave full credit to what I said ... a British officer walking at my right hand and one of the French noblesse at my left, the latter of which in the action had his eyebrow carried away by a glancing shot, but was nevertheless very merry and facetious.

No abuse was offered me till I came to the barrack-yard at Montreal, where I met Gen. Prescott, who asked me my name, which I told him. He then asked me whether I was that Col. Allen who took Ticonderoga. I told him I was the very man; then he shook his cane over my head calling many hard names, among which he frequently used the word rebel, and put himself in a great rage. I told him he would do well not to cane me, for I was not accustomed to it, and shook my fist at him, telling him that was the beetle of mortality for him if he offered to strike. Upon which Capt. M'Cloud of the British pulled him by the skirt, and whispered to him (as he afterwards told me) ... that it was inconsistent with his honor to strike a prisoner. He then ordered a sergeant's command with fixed bayonets to come forward and kill 13 Canadians, which were included in the treaty aforesaid.

It cut me to the heart to see the Canadians in so hard a case, in consequence of their having been true to me. They were wringing their hands, saying their prayers ... and expected immediate death. I therefore stepped between the executioners and the Canadians, opened my clothes, and told Gen. Prescott to thrust his bayonet into my breast, for I was the sole cause of the Canadians taking up arms. The guard, in the meantime rolling their eyeballs from the General to me as though impatient, waited his dread commands to sheath their bayonets in my heart. I could however

36. American campaigns against the British forts and Montreal in 1775, the ill-fated siege of Quebec, and the Battle of Valcour Island in 1776 demonstrate the lake's central role.

plainly discern that he was in a suspence and quandry about the matter: this gave me additional hopes of succeeding, for my design was not to die, but save the Canadians by a finesse. The General stood a minute, when he made the following reply: "I will not execute you now, but you shall grace a halter at Tyburn, God damn ye!"

Thus was the kindler of one of the rebellion's first sparks, the master spirit of Lake Champlain and of the defense of the New Hampshire Grants against New York, temporarily lost to the cause of liberty. George Washington, who thought there was "an original something" in Ethan that commanded admiration, wrote Schuyler: "Colonel Allen's misfortune will, I hope, teach a lesson of prudence and subordination to others who may be too ambitious to outshine their general officers, and regardless of order and duty rush into enterprises which have unfavorable effects to the public and are destructive to themselves."

Defiantly setting sail in irons for England, and haranguing anyone who would listen about liberty from his cell during his long confinement in Pendennis Castle, Ethan did not return until the worst of the Revolutionary hurricane had blown over the northcountry.

After the fall of St. Jean to General Montgomery early in November of 1775, British resistance evaporated. With winter dogging his footsteps, Montgomery filled his arsenal and the stomachs of his men with captured supplies and pushed on to Montreal, which surrendered with no resistance.

Governor Carleton, who only a short time previously had caught the captor of Ticonderoga in a trap, now found himself in one. He had sent to Boston the few remaining troops that might have defended the island town; the rebels had seized his ships, and his protection amounted to scarcely more than a bodyguard. Unfortunately for the Americans he managed to slip past their encampment at night in a whaleboat with muffled oars, and down the St. Lawrence to the safety of Quebec's high-walled fortress.

Otherwise, things were going well for Montgomery, and promised to go better, for Benedict Arnold was on his way up the Kennebec River in Maine (and down Canada's Chaudiere) in a diversionary move which, joining with Montgomery's advance from the West, was calculated to make short work of Carleton's small enclave. Arnold's mortal struggle with hunger and the elements is not central to this chronicle, nor the sufferings of the two commanders on the shores of the ice-caked St. Lawrence, nor their disastrous attempt to scale Quebec's frigid cliff in a year-end blizzard in which Montgomery perished in a hail of grapeshot; nor the agonizing siege Arnold's bedraggled troops hopelessly continued.

To bolster their frail and failing campaign in the later winter and spring, Schuyler sent reinforcements, among them Seth Warner with his Green Mountain Regiment, and Colonel John Stark. And Congress sent a three-man commission headed by Benjamin Franklin, Samuel Chase and Charles Carroll to try to rally the French Catholics to the American cause. They were accompanied by the latter's cousin, John Carroll, a Catholic priest. The bateau which in April carried them over the snow-fed waters of Lake George, was hauled down the portage to Champlain by oxen. A second 36-foot bateau with a single blanket sail here joined the first, the 70-year-old Franklin embarking with only an awning to protect him from the wind and icy spray.

Crown Point was their first stop, then Panton at the home of Peter Ferris, and the following day (April 25) Essex, where they were driven by a gale. Arriving in Montreal four days later, they found that Canadians were spurning Colonial paper and demanding hard cash (of which there was little) for what they sold Americans. Indifferent to the reforms Carleton had guided through Parliament, they also showed little interest in joining the lost cause of a faltering American expeditionary force. Empty-handed, Franklin and Father Carroll reembarked for the cold journey back over the lakes and down the Hudson, while Chase and Charles Carroll continued their efforts, to no avail.

The jig was up for the Canadian campaign. Schuyler's supply lines were too far extended. To feed the northern army 120 barrels of pork and flour had to leave Albany in a dozen bateaux every day. Unloaded on to wagons and reloaded on boats several times before reaching Lake Champlain, the pork barrels were subject to drilling and the loss of their brine to lighten the wagoner's load. The spasmodic arrival of spoiled meat was not the least of Arnold's problems. Critically short of heavy cannon and ammunition, his sick and threadbare army would soon confront fresh troops on their way up the St. Lawrence from Britain. Still suffering a wound acquired in the attack on the fortress when Montgomery was killed, Arnold finally relinquished his command in the spring. Although the army of his successor, General John Thomas, was increased to 3,000, he was fated to lose the St. Lawrence valley to Carleton, and his life to smallpox at Chambly. He was replaced there by General John Sullivan.

1776 brought grievous tidings to the lake. As the Americans, pressed by Carleton, retreated up the Richelieu they were besieged by a more sinister foe, a respecter of neither season, nor place, nor tactic — smallpox. As early as

1756 it had struck the French forts like a thunderclap. When it lay quiescent it was supplanted by dysentery, measles, or more lethal infections to which the wounded were particularly vulnerable. Bullets given soldiers to chew during the amputation of gangrenous limbs survive at Ticonderoga as tokens of their suffering.

Conditions at Valley Forge in the winter of 1776-77 could hardly have been deadlier than those a year previously at sub-zero Quebec and Lake Champlain. In the absence of blankets at Ticonderoga, tents had to be cut into sacks for the beds. Infectious organisms abounded in the well water, the food was rotten, and disease so rampant that Colonel Joseph Ward wrote Philadelphia that, "we have from ten to fifteen every week that Bids farewell to this world." The vice-president of the Philadelphia Council of Safety wrote Congress that "a few naked, sickly, and ill-attended troops must fall prey to their own distress if not to the enemy. The blessings of Heaven can scarcely be expected to attend a cause however good, which the men who expose their lives in support of it are so ill rewarded."

The only hopeful development, if the departure of Ticonderoga's artillery could be called that, had been its epic arrival at Dorchester Heights in Boston just in time for George Washington to dislodge the British from the city. The migration of the artillery under the direction of Henry Knox, a hulking 25-year-old Boston bookseller, became one of the Revolution's truly legendary exploits. Transported to the landing beneath the fort, and from there by barges and bateaux to the foot of the portage, 59 pieces of artillery weighing 60 tons were then somehow drawn up the hill and refloated on Lake George. Then loaded on 42 sledges harnessed to 81 yoke of oxen, they were dragged south through Saratoga and Albany and east the whole breadth of Massachusetts over snow-bound mountains, Knox said, "from which we might almost have seen all the Kingdoms of the Earth."

The remnants of the Canadian campaign — those who had not died, deserted, or previously been evacuated to the hospitals at the head of Lake George and at Crown Point — reached the latter fort on July 1. Colonel John Trumbull, son of the Connecticut governor, described the scene:

> At this place I found not an army but a mob, the shattered remains of twelve or fifteen very fine battalions, ruined by sickness fatigue, and desertion, and void of every idea of discipline or subordination. . . . Last spring there were ten battalions, amounting to about six thousand four hundred men, sent from New York to join this army; there were then here two battalions of Pennsylvanians, three from New England, and one or two from New Jersey, all of them strong and amounting to at least four thousand men more, which, joined with the others, make the army

37. *Artist's conception of the remarkable journey of Fort Ticonderoga's cannon across Massachusetts to enable General Washington to drive the British out of Boston.*

upwards of ten thousand strong. We now have three thousand sick, and about the same number well; this leaves near five thousand men to be accounted for. Of these, the enemy has cost us perhaps one, sickness another thousand, and the others, God alone knows what manner they are disposed of. Among the few we have remaining, there is neither order, subordination, nor harmony; the officers as well as men of one colony, insulting and quarreling with those of another.

Dr. Lewis Beebe, Yale graduate and brother-in-law of Ethan Allen, revealed that there had been "not the least preparation for fortifying the garrison, which has tumbled to ruin and decay. The generals have their hands full in riding about the camp, prancing their gay horses; the field officers set much of their time upon court martials; the captains and subs may generally be found at the grog shops; the soldiers either sleeping, swimming, fishing, or cursing and swearing, most generally the latter."

Conditions were as bad or worse at Ticonderoga, which Colonel Anthony Wayne called "the last part of the world that God made & I have some ground to believe it was finished in the dark. . . . I believe it to be the ancient Golgotha or place of skulls — they are so plenty here that our people for want of other vessels drink out of them, whilst the soldiers make tent pins of the shin and thigh bones of Abercromby's men. . . ." As for the whole demoralized northern army, Colonel Joseph Wait described it as having "generals without men, and a small artillery without supplies, and commissaries without provisions, paymasters without money, and quartermasters without stores, and physicians without medicine."

It would be convenient to blame this calamity on General Schuyler, had he not foreseen the obstacles and originally doubted the feasibility of the campaign. Allen and Arnold might have been right that Canada could be taken if its population had been won over before the British had time to mobilize. Assuming that that had happened, it would nevertheless have been another matter to retain that vast country, since just the defense of New England and the seaboard required the utmost exertions. In any case, orders for the campaign came, not from the slow and methodical Schuyler, but from the Continental Congress.

The dismal outlook on Champlain was not, however, considered hopeless even when Lord Howe occupied New York City and threatened to cut off New England by moving north, for preparations were afoot to prevent or delay Carleton from advancing south to meet him. These plans took quite a while to gel, and in the meantime newly-arrived settlers, especially those north of the forts, were clamoring for protection. Many picked up and left, while others, like those at Shelburne with large crops of wheat in the ground and stocks of cattle, took steps to defend themselves. They joined with the military in building a stockade fort at Shelburne Harbor (identified in a petition as "a very good harbor" where boats were often obliged to put in to avoid "sudden gusts during the summer").

In the absence of Ethan Allen, his brother Ira was doing everything in his power to persuade the military to defend the northern settlers (not to mention the rich intervales of the Onion River Land Company). He so far succeeded that General Sullivan ordered 200 men to Onion River for the safety of the inhabitants. Even Schuyler and Arnold appear to have gone there to inspect their defenses (which ultimately became the responsibility of Seth Warner's Green Mountain Regiment). Meanwhile Point au Fer in the extreme north, Colchester Point, and Jericho joined Shelburne Harbor as outposts.

A surprising decision by the generals on July 7 to abandon Crown Point and withdraw to Ticonderoga drew stiff rejoinders from John Stark and some twenty other field officers — and even their commander-in-chief. "I confess the determination of the council of general officers on the 7th to retreat from Crown Point surprised me much," Washington wrote John Hancock, "and the more I consider it the more striking does the impropriety appear." In another letter written the same day to Schuyler, Washington called Crown Point "a key to all these colonies," declaring that "Nothing but a belief that you have actually removed the army from Crown Point to Ticonderoga and demolished the works of the former" prevented him from directing that Crown Point be held until Congress decided otherwise.

Schuyler replied that Crown Point could not be defended as well from the north (as it formerly had been from the south by the French) because boats could avoid its guns by passing near the shore of the bay behind it. Troops might then be landed who could sever its lifeline across the peninsula leading to the mainland. Ticonderoga, he thought, was similarly vulnerable.

When General Horatio Gates arrived to share the northern command, its axis was already shifting south. Preparations were going forward to make Mount Independence (on the east shore opposite Ticonderoga) the lake's main bastion. General Schuyler, Colonel Trumbull, and Benjamin Franklin, who had so recently passed by, were impressed with its superior location. Schuyler wrote Washington that he had found it "so remarkably strong as to require little labor to make it tenable against a vast superiority of force, and fully to answer the purpose of preventing the enemy from penetrating into the country south of it." Surrounded as it is on three sides by walls of natural rock, and on the fourth by a creek, Schuyler was convinced that 20,000 men could not drive away a quarter that many defending it.

Accordingly, the forest was cleared from its summit 200 feet above the lake, batteries were built, and three brigades were transferred from Ticonderoga. Later a hospital was erected, and a star-shaped fort of pickets surrounding a square of barracks.

A 13-gun salute on July 18 inaugurated the christening ceremonies, according to a letter quoted by the *Boston Gazette*. "Immediately after divine worship the Declaration of Independence was read by Colonel St. Clair, and having said 'God save the free independent States of America!' the army manifested their joy with three cheers. It was remarkably pleasing to see the spirits of the soldiers so raised after all their calamities; the language of every man's countenance was, 'Now we are a people! We have name among the states of the world!' "

❧❦❧

The short swarthy man with the hooked nose and the light blue eyes had survived more danger in six months than most soldiers in a lifetime. A man driven to excel and to succeed, he did not merely react to dangerous circumstances, he created them. The key to his personality was very likely his admission that he had been a coward until he was fifteen years old. Thereafter his boundless determination and energy seems to have prevented his insecurity from catching up with him.

His great-great-grandfather was one of the founders of Rhode Island; his great-grandfather, grandfather, and father, Benedict Arnold I, II, and III, had run the gamut from wealth to near poverty, to wealth and back to poverty. Born in Norwich, Connecticut in 1741, Benedict V (his brother, Benedict IV died in infancy) started out as an heir-apparent to wealth and position, but his father's reverses forced him to pursue on his own such trappings of wealth as the fine clothes to which he was accustomed.

For a while he ran an apothecary shop. Later he went to sea on his own sloops and brigantines, trading from St. Croix to New Haven, to Albany, to Quebec and Montreal. That was when he learned to sail and to become something of a philanderer. Marriage did not cure his wanderlust, his craving for action, or his gnawing and jealous ego. Acquiring many enemies after the capture of Ticonderoga with Ethan Allen, he ended his pursuit of authority on the lake by resigning in disgust and withdrawing to his home in Connecticut. (There was nothing unique about that; the Revolution was a hothouse of disgruntled commanders. When General Sullivan was replaced by General Gates after the retreat from Quebec, Sullivan bitterly resigned from the army. And General Gates, as tactical commander of the northern army, constantly sparred with General Schuyler, nominally his superior in Albany.)

Bounding back at Washington's behest to lead the gruelling trek through Maine to Quebec, Arnold had no option but to yield to adversity in the Canadian campaign. Summer of 1776 found him back on Lake Champlain, bristling from real or imagined slights but brimming with energy for his new mission: to build America's first fleet from scratch and sail it north against the

British — an assignment he had received from Gates. But Schuyler had appointed another commander of the lake, Captain Jacobus Wyncoop. Gates and Arnold responded to this affront by arresting Wyncoop when he countermanded Arnold's orders for a training cruise. (He was apparently no great loss. Having seen British sails in the distance, he had summoned his fellow captains to a council of war, only to be informed that the sails were a flock of seagulls.)

Now a brigadier general, Arnold had everything his own way in the building of his fleet, probably because no other general coveted such a formidable task. Many of his shipwrights were house carpenters, and the rigging and other fittings had to come 200 miles by wagon from the Atlantic coast. Since there was very little seasoned wood at Skenesborough, most of the timber that sailed north late in the summer had been growing in the local forests in the spring. With 200 carpenters laboring on the heavy gondolas and row-galleys, Skenesborough was busy as a hive — and as hot as one. Only liberal allowances of rum enabled the workers to endure the swarms of giant mosquitoes drifting in from the surrounding swamps. (When George Washington later visited the port it acquired the reputation of having the largest and most voracious mosquitoes that had ever bitten the father of his country.)

[handwritten margin note: Mosquitos! So True!]

Fortunately the iron forge built by the Tory, Philip Skene, remained in good condition, as did his two sawmills, one of them a few miles to the south near Fort Ann (a companion outpost to Fort Edward during the late wars with the French). As soon as the flat-bottomed hulls of the 53-foot open gondolas were finished (four were completed in July) they were rowed to Ticonderoga to receive their masts and rigging. From there they sailed to a rendezvous near Crown Point to join the schooner *Royal Savage* and the sloop *Enterprise*, which Arnold had captured from the British the previous year. Since the guns had been stripped from the 70-ton *Royal Savage* and carted to Washington in Cambridge during the siege of Boston, she had had to be refitted.

Arnold pinned his principal hope on his 72-foot, round-hulled row-galleys. Designed with two masts carrying lateen sails, they could also be propelled by seven pairs of two-man sweeps on each side. They had 20-foot quarter decks and contained considerable covered space for 80 crewmen and supplies. Their triangular lateen sails were unusual on Lake Champlain, although they had previously appeared on the French xebecs. Armed with 8 or 10 quite heavy guns and several swivels, the row-galleys took longer to build than the gondolas, but as the main source of fire power were worth the time.

The scene 125 miles to the north much resembled that at Skenesborough, except that the British were nearer the source of supplies and labor at

38. *Silhouettes of Arnold's vessels appear in little-known contemporary drawing—all built at Whitehall except the schooner* Royal Savage *and the sloop* Enterprise, *captured*

Montreal. They also had the advantage, if it could be called that, of disassembling ships already constructed on the St. Lawrence, hauling them up or around the rapids at Chambly, and reassembling them in the basin at St. Jean. The largest of them, a ship of war called the *Inflexible,* had been commandeered on the stocks at Quebec, taken apart in some 30 6-ton sections and loaded on as many long boats, which were drawn up the Richelieu rapids. A 32-ton gondola, 400 bateaux, and several other flat-bottomed boats ascended the rapids intact, while two schooners, *Maria* and *Carleton,* and ten small gunboats journeyed over the portage in pieces aboard wagons. Upon reaching the shipyard at St. Jean the *Inflexible's* thirty sections were feverishly joined together in 28 days.

Also under construction there was a nondescript 400-ton scow called a "radeau." Designed for a crew of 300, its length was 92 feet, its width 33, and depth about 7, with a cabin and small quarterdeck, and bulwarks with ports for 24-pound guns. Too cumbersome to be propelled and maneuvered solely

*from the British. All but four of the makeshift American flotilla were lost in a defeat
that nevertheless proved to be the turning point of the American Revolution.*

Scow

Newer
Designs!

by two huge sails, the *Thunderer* was also designed to be winched along by
having its anchor carried forward in a long boat and dropped. The advantage
of this ungainly dreadnaught, assuming it could be properly maneuvered, was
its concentrated fire power.

On August 24 Arnold sailed from Crown Point with 9 vessels carrying 55
guns, 78 swivels, and 395 men. A savage northeaster arose the next night while
the fleet was anchored at Willsboro, and the following afternoon it was forced
to retreat to Button Mould Bay on the east shore at Ferrisburg. On September
6 it reached the northern part of the lake, where it was joined by another
gondola and row-galley. While the fleet lay at anchor off Isle La Motte
guarding the channel at St. Jean, 18 crewmen were sent ashore to gather
fascines, or branches, to be bound together and affixed to the bows and sides of
the gondolas (in order to ward off sniper fire and keep the enemy from
boarding). Their work had barely begun when they were ambushed by a war
party of Canadian Algonquins. Before the fleet could cover their return, three

were killed and six wounded. When the British started erecting batteries on the shores the next day, Arnold withdrew to a point north of Cumberland Head, where 300 Canadians and Indians on the shore greeted him with another volley.

On September 23 he sailed his fleet into the deep channel between the western shore and Valcour Island, there to be joined by Captain Warner with the Galley *Trumbull,* and Brigadier General Waterbury with the 125-ton galleys *Washington* and *Congress.* Except for another 8-gun galley being armed at Ticonderoga, and the supply schooner *Liberty* loading at Crown Point, the flotilla was complete: 15 vessels with a total of 86 guns and 152 swivels, manned by a crew of 500.

Although spies had scouted the rival shipyards during the summer, Arnold had no accurate estimate of the size of the British fleet until September 15. Nor, until a day later, any inkling of the three-masted *Inflexible* with its superior fire power of 18 12-pounders — enough (with the dozen 24-and-12-pounders and two howitzers on the great radeau) to pulverize the American fleet. With this dismaying intelligence Arnold changed his tactics from offense to defense. Hence his presence in the mile-wide trough between Valcour Island and the mainland, protected on both shores by a heavy screen of pines and cedars. Since an enemy approach through the narrow pass at the northern end of the three-mile channel was unlikely or impossible, Arnold could ignore his flanks and rear and concentrate on the deep south entrance. A favorable north wind carrying the British ships past the outside of the island would, he

39. Variety of craft appear in this primitive view of the Richelieu River at St. Jean during the Revolution. British redouts are in background.

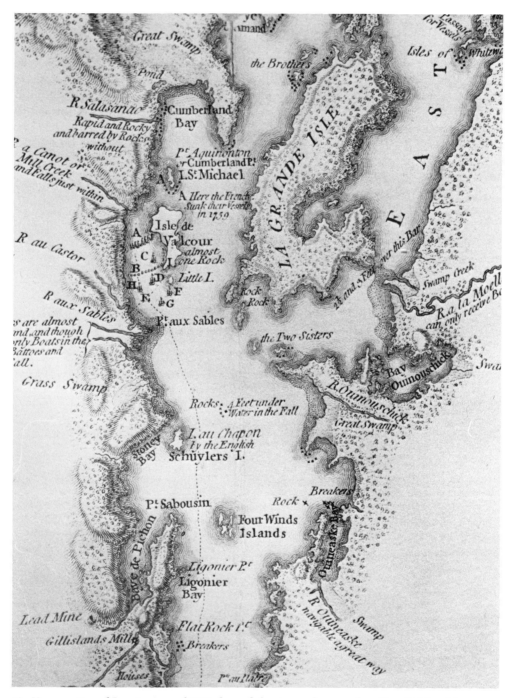

40. *Upper section of Brassier map of 1776 shows defensive anchorage where Benedict Arnold
awaited the British fleet. Winston Churchill wrote that "The Battle of Valcour
may have been the most important naval battle in the history of the United States."*

calculated, severely handicap them as they turned and tacked toward his anchorage. Since they could not do this in unison, he planned to pick them off one by one by virtue of a network of anchor cables which gave his cannon a wide range over the bay to the south.

From his flagship, *Royal Savage,* Arnold wrote Gates that his plan would permit the row-galleys to attack the enemy in the open lake, and to withdraw to the channel if the battle proved too hot. He begged that "one hundred good seamen may be sent to me as soon as possible. We have a wretched motley crew in the fleet; the marines the refuse of every regiment and the seamen few of them ever wet with salt water." He hoped that not too much was expected of him "if with 500 men half-naked, I should not be able to beat the enemy with seven thousand men, well-clothed, and a naval force, by the best accounts, near equal to ours." (By seven thousand men he meant, of course, the army in Quebec awaiting developments on the lake.)

News that the British had driven Washington out of New York City served to emphasize how vulnerable the entire northern gateway had become. Now all that stood in the jaws of a British vise was Arnold's little flotilla. Upon it, acknowledged George Washington, rested the hope of America.

A fresh north wind, whistling over the white-crested Adirondacks, carried the British fleet out of the Richelieu on the morning of October 11. It was just as well that the Americans, huddling with their homemade squadron in the lee of Valcour, could not see the *Inflexible* and her consorts as they cleared Cumberland Head — every strake and spar the handiwork of professionals. Compared to the Admiralty's nearly 700 well-drilled seamen, the rebel sailors must have presented an even sharper contrast.

But there was at least one advantage Arnold could count as His Majesty's square-riggers scudded past Valcour: the British knew nothing of his hiding place. Their ships were strung out as if they were holding a regatta, the *Inflexible* and the schooners *Carleton* and *Maria* in the lead, the gondola *Loyal Convert* in their wake, and the trundling radeau miles behind. Still out of sight were the bateaux carrying Carleton's supporting ground troops, some of whom had landed at Pointe au Fer to await the destiny of the fleet, commanded by Carleton's deputy, Captain Thomas Pringle.

When the *Inflexible* and the two schooners appeared in full view southeast of the American anchorage, the *Royal Savage* and four row-galleys (at the urging of General Waterbury, despite Arnold's reservations about a running encounter with the faster *Inflexible)* started out into the bay. What happened then — whether the American schooner engaged the British close up or at a distance, or whether Arnold thought better of this sortie and decided to return

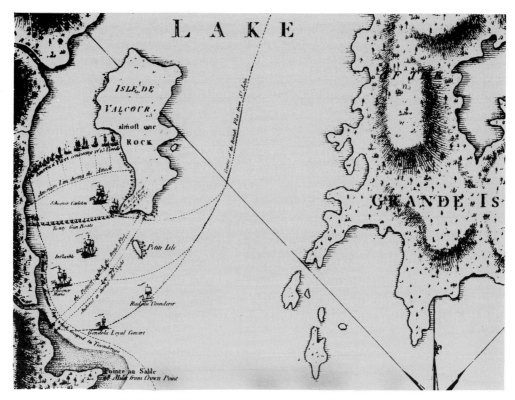

41. Section of map of the Battle of Valcour, from a sketch by an officer on the scene, shows deployment of the British fleet and grounded American flagship on southern point.

to the Channel — is not clear. Having in any event received several shots from some 12-pounders, the *Royal Savage* fetched hard up in the shallows on the tip of the island. Attempts to free her from this costly miscalculation failed and she had to be abandoned.

The British flagship *Maria*, carrying both General Carleton and Captain Pringle, and the *Inflexible* were meanwhile having trouble beating up-wind — so much so that they could not get near enough to fire. But the *Carleton* managed to approach the anchorage, and 17 of the 20 British gunboats advanced to within point-blank range. Arriving by longboat with part of his crew, the captain of the gondola *Loyal Convert* boarded the grounded *Royal Savage* and turned her guns on her own fleet. The Americans, however, returned such a heavy fire that he lost a number of men before he too was forced to abandon her. Later the British returned and set her ablaze, whereupon she blew up with a roar.

According to Baron von Reidesel, later a central figure in the Battle of

42. *The fury of a battle fought at close quarters by what Arnold called his "wretched motley crew" is recaptured in this retrospective painting.*

Bennington, a "tremendous cannonade was opened on both sides," the *Carleton* pouring a merciless barrage into the line of galleys and gondolas ranged across the channel. If the rebels were going to show their mettle now was the time. Bringing every jury-rigged firing piece they could lay their hands on to bear on the *Carleton,* they let loose a thunderous volley of cannon fire and grapeshot, scoring one splintering shot after another. The *Carleton's* commander was knocked senseless, the arm of a second officer was severed, and half her crew lay killed or wounded in the wreckage on her deck. A fortunate American shot then severed her aft cable, and she swung stern-first to the American artillery. When it seemed likely that she would have to strike her flag, Midshipman Edward Pellew, later to become an admiral and a lord, crawled out on her bowsprit amidst a tattoo of musket fire, and managed to bear her jib to the wind. Too crippled to sail, and with two feet of water in her hold, she was presently towed out of range by two British artillery boats, to which Pellew had thrown a tow line from his perch on the bowsprit.

The removal of the *Carleton* and the sinking of a British artillery boat by no means meant that the Americans were gaining the upper hand. The gunboats were raising havoc from fairly close quarters, while several hundred Indians whom the British had landed on the island were firing from the trees. Although the Indians' poor markmanship and the fascines protecting the gunwales nullified their efforts, the galleys and gondolas were receiving the most grievous artillery fire. Amidst tattered sails and rigging under a pall of smoke, Arnold was everywhere present on the *Congress*, shouting orders and pointing the guns himself.

"The *Congress* and *Washington* suffered greatly," he reported; "the latter lost her First Lieutenant killed, Captain and Master wounded. The *New York* lost all her officers except the captain. The *Philadelphia* was hulled in so many places, that she sunk about one hour after the engagement was over. . . . The *Congress* received seven shot between wind and water; she was hulled a dozen times; had her main mast wounded in two places and her yard in one. The *Washington* was hulled a number of times, her mainmast shot through. . . ."

Late in the afternoon the *Inflexible* finally managed to approach, and with five broadsides silenced the whole American line. But twilight was at hand. Although hundreds of British seamen in bateaux were prepared to board the American vessels, the *Inflexible* and all her consorts withdrew to form a floating barricade across the entrance to the channel. With the Indians remaining on the island and a contingent of British regulars guarding the mainland, Carleton and Pringle apparently did not bother to post lookouts. They thought that nothing remained for the Americans, bottled up in the channel, but to surrender the next morning.

After conferring in the darkness with his captains, Arnold set in motion a daring plan to weigh anchor. So silently was this done that one of his boats after another, the galley *Trumbull* leading, gondolas and schooners following — each with a tiny light that could only be seen astern — were able to steal undetected along the mainland shore past the left wing of the British anchorage.

That night Providence laid a fog on the channel, and when it lifted in the morning Carleton and Pringle were confounded to find that the entire American fleet had eluded their grasp. Carleton was so infuriated that he started out in immediate pursuit, forgetting to leave orders for his troops encamped at Cumberland Head. Finding no trace of the enemy, and with an adverse wind, he apparently returned briefly to Valcour, where he received word that the rebels had reached Schuyler Island, eight miles to the south. After making provision for the ground troops to follow in bateaux, Carleton got under way

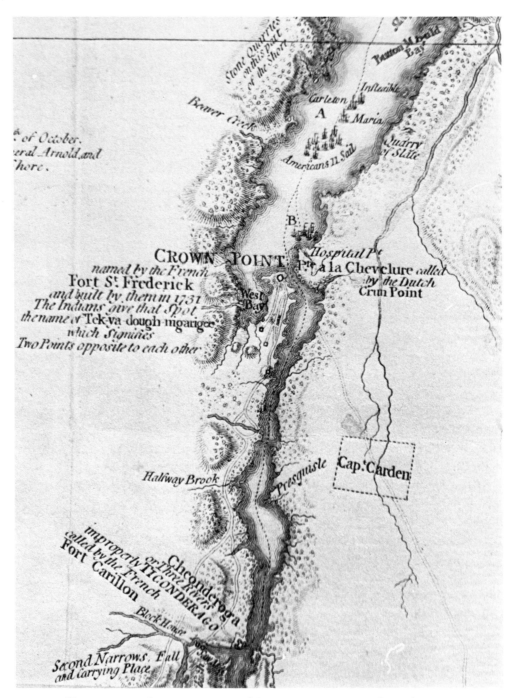

43. *Dotted line continuing from upper section of Brassier map on page 99 shows the
Americans' southward retreat from Valcour Island. After the second engagement (A) Arnold
beached and burned four vessels on the Vermont side (B) and escaped overland to Crown Point.*

again, this time encountering trouble with the wallowing radeau. Having lost its lee boards it developed such a severe list that water poured through its lower gun ports. Confusion about the British position on the day and night of the 12th makes the time sequence difficult to determine, but by noon of the 13th they were moving briskly south.

Having sailed and rowed his battered and leaking vessels all night after the battle, Arnold was forced to sink two of his gondolas near Schuyler Island. Further time was sacrificed plugging leaks, mending sails, and, on the second sleepless night, bucking fickle winds. With his sails scarcely filled off Willsboro on the morning of the 13th, and with the British catching up because of still-conflicting winds, Arnold gradually lost hope of beating them to Crown Point — although the schooner *Revenge,* the sloop *Enterprise,* the galley *Trumbull,* and one gondola managed to do so. Almost overtaken north of Split Rock, the galley *Lee* was run into a bay on the east shore. The shattered *Washington* had suffered so many killed and wounded that General Waterbury struck her colors after receiving another battering. The gondola *Jersey* also surrendered.

"Then," Arnold wrote Schuyler, "we were attacked in the *Congress* galley by a ship mounting twelve eighteen-pounders, a schooner of fourteen sixes, and one of twelve sixes, two under our stern, and one on our broadside, within musket-shot. They kept up an incessant fire on us for about five glasses, with round and grape-shot, which we returned as briskly. The sails, rigging, and hull of the *Congress* were shattered and torn in pieces . . . when, to prevent her falling into the enemy's hands, who had seven sail around me, I ran her ashore in a small creek ten miles from Crown Point, on the east side. . . . After saving our small-arms, I set her on fire with four gondolas, with whose crews I reached Crown Point through the woods that evening, and very luckily escaped the savages, who waylaid the road in two hours after we passed."

With the destruction or capture of two-thirds of the enemy fleet, Carleton had reason to advertise his victory at court, although the fierce resistance of the rebels must have restrained his pen:

"The Rebel fleet upon Lake Champlain has been entirely defeated in two actions, the first on the 11th instant between the Island of Valcour and the Main, and the second on the 13th, within a few leagues of Crown Point. We have taken Mr. Waterbury, the second in command, one of their Brigadier Generals, with two of their vessels, ten others having been burnt and destroyed."

Of course Carleton made no mention of the paralysis of the *Inflexible* and *Maria* at Valcour, or the thrashing the *Carleton* had received, or the sinking of two of his gunboats and the blowing up of another, or the failure of the ponderous radeau to fight at all, or of Commander Pringle's ineptitude (to which the master of the *Inflexible,* John Schank, later attested). But a victory was a victory, and Carleton personally emerged with an unsullied reputation; a grateful king dubbed him Knight of the Bath.

British pushed back!

Although he planned to attack Ticonderoga at once, a strong wind arose on October 15 and held his fleet windbound for four days. When some of his ships finally approached Ticonderoga they found the redouts and batteries there and on Mount Independence bristling with artillery and a splendid show of flags. Confronted by some 13,000 troops, most of them militia raised by General Gates, and with the days growing short and cold, Carleton turned his fleet around and sailed back to Canada for the winter.

On November 3rd his rear guard left beleaguered Crown Point, which was promptly reoccupied by the Americans. Since 1609 it had passed from the French to the British, back to the French, then to the British, to the Americans, to the British, and now to the Americans. Yet its destiny was still far from secure.

***

Three weeks after the withdrawal of the British to St. Jean, the Narrows were frozen solid. With the danger of an invasion now postponed to 1777, General Gates dismissed the forts' 13,000 shivering militia. For the 2500 who remained, survival was the watchword.

On December 4 Joseph Wood wrote from Ticonderoga that one-third of the garrison was barefoot. "If you was here your heart would melt. I paid a visit to the sick yesterday, in a small house called a hospital. The first object presented my eyes, one man lying dead at the door. The inside two more laying dead, two living lying between them; the living with the dead has laid so for four and twenty hours."

"Mad Anthony" Wayne, the new commander, may or may not have been responsible, but might have earned his nickname when General Schuyler instructed him to have the chimneys swept every fortnight, to prepare dumplings to thicken the soldiers' stew, and to burn tar in the tents to purify the air.

Christmas was the occasion of a near-riot when a drunken Pennsylvania colonel assaulted a Massachusetts colonel because the latter's son was repairing soldiers' shoes, which was apparently beneath the dignity of the Pennsylvanian. Several Yankee soldiers were wounded during the ensuing fray, which ended when the Massachusetts colonel forgave the Pennsylvanian, who in turn invited all the combatants to a feast of fresh bear or venison.

Such rivalry might be dismissed as of small consequence if it did not also afflict the general officers. Gates and Schuyler often seemed to give more attention to their personal vendetta than to the war. Schuyler had proved too much of a symbol of the silk-stocking aristocracy of the Hudson to suit the New England farmers. Playing upon this prejudice in Congress, Gates succeeded in having Schuyler removed and himself appointed commander of the northern department in March. Two months later Gates was removed and his predecessor reinstated. Schuyler now offered Gates command of Ticonderoga, which he indignantly refused.

The militia should all have returned in the spring, but Washington was so convinced that the British would send their Canadian army down the St. Lawrence and around the coast to bolster General William Howe in New York, that the garrisons remained desperately undermanned. In June General Arthur St. Clair, a veteran of the last French war, of the recent Canadian campaign, and the chief strategist of Washington's victory at Trenton, arrived at the forts to replace Anthony Wayne.

"Had every man I had, been disposed of in single file on the different works, and along the lines of defense," St. Clair despaired, "they would have been scarcely within the reach of each other's voices; but Congress had been persuaded that the enemy would make no attempt in that quarter, and such a number of men only as were judged to be sufficient for constructing the works that had been projected were assigned to me." With these he was expected to defend both forts and all their outlying entrenchments, batteries, and outposts such as Mount Hope, which protected the road from Lake George. Upon the arrival of General Schuyler it was decided that the available troops could not defend both sides of the lake. If they could not hold Ticonderoga they would make a stand at Mount Independence, and failing in that they were to retreat to the southeast.

When at last it became clear that the Redcoats were indeed coming, and in great numbers, Mount Independence became an anthill of activity as St. Clair strove to complete the defenses laid out by Lt. Col. Jeduthan Baldwin and the ardent Polish patriot, Thaddeus Kosciusko. During the winter and spring a bridge had been constructed between Ticonderoga and Mount Independence. Twenty-one stone-filled cribs built fifty feet apart on the ice were then sunk as anchors for the floating sections of a roadway twelve feet wide.

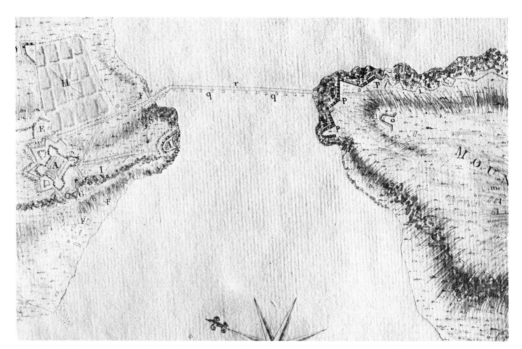

44. The bridge Americans built of piers, joined by floating sections, connected their fortifications at Ticonderoga and Mount Independence during winter of 1776-77.

To stop the enemy fleet north of the bridge a boom was installed of heavy timbers joined together, and alongside it a double iron chain with links an inch and a half square. New breastworks were raised on both sides of the lake, the star-shaped fort was completed on Mount Independence, also a small fort on Mount Hope, and a blockhouse at the northern end of Lake George — all of which defenses ranged in a crescent two and a half miles long.

Since Americans were well versed in counter-espionage, it is surprising that St. Clair knew no more about the size of His Majesty's expeditionary force than Arnold had learned about the superior British fleet the previous fall. At almost the last minute an Irish prisoner who had been tricked into talking (by an American officer disguised as another prisoner) disclosed the imminent arrival of one of the most professional armies ever sent to America.

The mission of George the Third's new army was to divide the rebels once and for all with the time-honored strategy of isolating New England by invading the Champlain-Hudson waterway. To command it the King had appointed John Burgoyne, a member of Parliament whose social graces overshadowed his considerable military talent. As the architect of the campaign, "Gentleman Johnny's" knowledge of warfare in America nevertheless compared unfavorably with that of General Carleton, and his ability as a planner was soon open to question. He gravely overestimated the willingness of Canadians to part with horses to pull his cannon over the portages and, at the insistence of his artillery officer, was still searching for them at the last moment.

His plans for an army of 11,000 were considerably abridged when only a few Canadians enlisted. He commanded, nonetheless, an imposing fighting machine composed of about half British regulars and half German mercenaries, with 600 Indians, and 250 Canadians and provincials. While fewer than Abercromby's army, his 7500 troops were more than enough to crush the scattered and disorganized rebels. After moving through the lake and seizing the forts he planned to meet Barry St. Leger's expedition from the Mohawk Valley at Albany, and to join Lord Howe's army somewhere on the Hudson — just where or when seems to have been left up in the air.

In addition to the fleet that swept the lake the previous fall, Burgoyne also commanded three vessels captured from Arnold and a new frigate, the flagship *Royal George*. With the raising of the royal standard the army sailed out of St. Jean late in June, pausing at Cumberland Head for several hundred carts and fifteen hundred horses to catch up. While some of these, according to the journal of a British officer, appear to have been transported the rest of the way on barges, the majority traversed the west shore. (Horses could travel through the woods but how the carts managed to do so remains an enigma.)

A young Britisher, Thomas Anburey, wrote that it was remarkably clear with not a breeze stirring on the broad lake "when the whole army appeared at one view in such perfect regularity as to form the most complete and splendid regatta ever beheld. In the front the Indians went in their birch canoes containing twenty or thirty each; then the advance corps in a regular line with the gunboats; then followed the *Royal George*, and the *Inflexible*, towing large booms which are to be thrown across two points of land, with the other brigs and sloops following. . ." After these came the first British brigade, followed by Lt. General Burgoyne and Major Generals von Reidesel and Phillips in their pinnaces, then another brigade, and finally a miscellany of women and camp followers.

The spectacle of the diverse flotilla was rivaled by the brilliant patchwork of its cargo: the Indians in war paint, the German and English regulars in white, the British infantry and artillery in scarlet and blue respectively, the

German chasseurs in green coats with red facings and cuffs, the Brunswick dragoons in buff — all with an assortment of headgear: bearskin, leather, three-cornered, cocked, and plumed. To designate their respective regiments many British soldiers had cut off the tails of Canadian cows and dyed them with bright colors.

On June 21 the fleet halted at the mouth of the Bouquet River. There Burgoyne presided over an elaborate feast and pow-wow, which served to galvanize the Indians, and at the same time, Burgoyne hoped, to restrain them. Railing against "the enemies of Great Britian and America, disturbers of public order, peace and happiness, destroyers of commerce, parricides of the state," he nevertheless beseeched the Indians "to regulate your passions when they overbear, to point out when it is nobler to spare than to revenge, to discriminate degrees of guilt, to suspend the uplifted stroke, to chastise and not to destroy." Forbidding bloodshed when not opposed in arms, he exhorted them to spare aged men, women, children, and prisoners from the hatchet. He promised compensation for prisoners, but declared they would be called to account for any scalps, except from those killed by their fire.

This speech was ridiculed in Parliament, and in the House of Commons, sarcastically derided by Edmund Burke: "Suppose there was a riot in Tower Hill. What would the keeper of His Majesty's lions do? Would he not fling open the dens of the wild beasts, and address them thus: 'My gentle lions, my humane bears, my tender-hearted hyenas, go forth! But I exhort you as you are Christians and members of civil society, to take care not to hurt any man, woman, or child.' "

On the 23rd the main army tried for four hours to round Ligonier (Willsboro) Point in a gale, but was driven back each time. Success the next day proved short-lived; the squadron was struck by a thunderstorm and then enveloped in a fog so thick that in order to keep it intact the drummers had to beat their drums all day. Then a fresh gale arose, forcing five vessels to land their occupants on the Islands of the Four Winds (Isles des Quatres Vents, later the Four Brothers).

On the 25th they encamped at Button Mould Bay on the east shore near Ferrisburg, and the following day rendezvoused (some units had gone ahead) at Crown and Chimney Points — two English brigades at the former and the German brigades at the latter. Teutonic voices thus joined the echoes of Iroquois, Algonquin, French, and English at this historic crossing.

From Chimney Point General Fraser sent a large party of Tories and Indians up Otter Creek. After they had captured some cattle and halted two miles above Middlebury Falls, St. Clair summoned Seth Warner to mobilize the Green Mountain militia. With the British in their cornfields, town delegates rallied in Windsor early in July to adopt a constitution — and to proclaim that the New Hampshire Grants had become the independent Republic of Vermont.

With good luck 2500 Americans might have been able to hold Ticonderoga and Mount Independence against three times that many British and Germans. The British planned to try to flank the forts by land, since an approach by water would have drawn artillery fire. While the New York shore offered relatively few obstacles, the Vermont side, where the Germans had landed, presented a minefield of heavy timber and brush, bordering the steaming and swampy muck of East Creek.

Why his fellow generals had not persuaded von Reidesel that to travel light was the only way in the northcountry, escapes the imagination. The high boots anchored to the thighs of his dismounted dragoons weighed 12 pounds a pair, and their heavy spurs caught every obstruction. Sweltering under their stiff leather breeches and gauntlets, they carried straight broadswords weighing three and a half pounds without the scabbard, and heavy muskets and haversacks.

While it is true that Burgoyne had abbreviated some of the uniforms and made certain other concessions to his strange new environment, his unwieldy and heterogeneous army was ill-adapted to it. His prospects were not improved by the indifference of the German mercenaries, and their ignorance of warfare in the woods. Torn from their hearths, fighting in a distant wilderness for a cause about which they knew little and cared less, the Hessians were homesick and disgruntled. There was animosity between their immediate commanders, Colonels Friedrick Baum and Heinrich Breymann, and their commanders, in turn, Baron von Reidesel and Simon Fraser.

Among Burgoyne's other encumbrances were the volatile and devious Indians, led by the notorious Frenchman, La Corne St. Luc, whose barbarity aroused Americans to fighting pitch; a supply line from Canada already stretched; the burden of no less than 138 pieces of artillery, and a miscellany of excess baggage calculated to improve the morale of the officers, if not the campaign's chances of success. The weaknesses in the crazy-quilt army that Burgoyne had patched together eventually became all too clear, but it at least had strength and momentum, which was more than could be said for the Americans.

Even so, the British might have been arrested or even repulsed had it not been for a glaring flaw in the American defenses: Sugar Loaf Hill. Not that the Americans were unaware that its 750-foot summit just to the south of

Colonists an
Complaint

Fort Ticonderoga commanded all of the defenses on both sides of the lake; it
was just that the commanders thought it too steep to fortify. In so deciding
they had ignored the advice of John Trumbull, Benedict Arnold, Thaddeus
Kosciusko, and even one of Amherst's lieutenants, who had advised him
eight years previously that the hill could and should be fortified. Trumbull
was actually ridiculed for this heretical opinion despite a demonstration
conducted for General Gates, in which a double charge fired from a cannon
on Mount Independence, landed half way up Sugar Hill across the water.
Obviously, a barrage from the higher summit could wipe out the defenses of
Mount Independence and easily destroy Ticonderoga, which was even
nearer.

When the demonstration failed to convince Gates, Trumbull and Arnold
climbed the hill and came down with definite assurance that cannon could
be drawn to its summit. Trumbull took the pains to draw up plans which he
presented to Gates, Schuyler and Congress — to no avail. Kosciusko fer-
vently advocated the plan, still to no avail; the generals decided instead to
strengthen the existing defenses of the forts.

With Burgoyne's Indians prowling in the nearby woods and the regulars
moving closer on both sides of the lake, St. Clair decided to put the torch to
the works at the foot of Lake George, the sawmills at the falls to Lake
Champlain, the fort on Mount Hope, and to withdraw to the old French
lines west of Ticonderoga. Whether or not his decision, based on lack of
troops, was sound, it resulted in the enemy's immediate occupation of
Mount Hope, the creek, and the gateway to what had been a possible route
of escape through Lake George. On the Vermont shore the Germans were
meanwhile plodding toward Mount Independence.

On July 4, the great British radeau or gun platform that had failed to
participate in the naval battle the previous fall approached and began
unloading cannon. By this time Lt. Twiss of the Royal Engineers and
General Phillips had observed the strategic importance of Sugar Hill, had
climbed it, and convinced Burgoyne that "where a goat can go a man can go
and where a man can go he can drag a gun." By dint of day and night labor
the road up Mount Defiance, as they renamed it, was built and oxen had
begun the onerous task of drawing up the cannon.

Upon discovering the activity at its summit, St. Clair, convinced at last of
the size and strength of the British army and the alarming threat of elevated
artillery, decided in council to retreat over the only available road, southeast
from Mount Independence to Hubbardton and Castleton. The remnants of
Arnold's fleet, loaded with the sick and the wounded and any supplies he had

45. *The British commander, General John Burgoyne, by Joshua Reynolds.*

time to gather, would depart simultaneously for Skenesborough.

The exodus began with the Ticonderoga garrison streaming across the floating bridge not long after sunset on the 5th. It became a mad scramble in the darkness as men, animals, and supplies competed for space on the 12-foot floats, and struggled up Mount Independence to the road leading to Castleton. Feverishly loaded along the shore were two schooners, a sloop, two row-galleys and, according to some accounts, nearly 200 bateaux.

After the last troops had crossed the bridge it was set on fire and guarded on the Vermont shore by several cannon and a crew who had tapped a keg of Madeira and were dead drunk at their posts. Although St. Clair had given orders that the highly visible summit of Independence be evacuated in the darkness, a French adventurer, General Roche de Fermoy, inexplicably a member of St. Clair's staff, put his quarters to the torch, which exposed the retreat in bold relief. It seems hard to believe that it could continue until 3:00 a.m. before being discovered by the British nearby, but General Fraser's first inkling of it appears to have been gained from two artillerymen who deserted the Americans in a small boat.

At first Fraser thought their story was a trick to decoy the British into the range of the rebels' artillery, but upon investigating he found it to be true. Immediately notifying General Burgoyne, who was asleep on the *Royal George,* he marshalled his troops, repaired the planks of the great bridge damaged by fire and by the American evacuation, and crossed to Mount Independence. Upon reaching the summit his soldiers discovered booty in the fort to be plundered, and he reported that "it was with very great difficulty I could prevent horrid irregularities." Not until five o'clock was he able to mobilize a detachment of grenadiers and light infantry and start off across the Vermont countryside in pursuit of St. Clair.

The burning sun was no hotter than the scene of retreat and pursuit on July 6. After a brutal trek of thirty miles the bulk of St. Clair's army reached Castleton at nightfall. The rear guard, led by the Green Mountain Boys' towering Seth Warner, bivouacked at Hubbardton. The pursuing Redcoats under Fraser caught up with them early in the morning and a wild, confused battle began. Rallying his troops Warner fought effectively for over an hour until von Reidesel arrived with his detachment of Brunswickers. When Colonel Francis of the Massachusetts militia was killed and Colonel Hale surrendered his beleaguered regiment, Warner, who had shocked the British with spirited defense, is said to have thrown himself on a log and "poured forth a torrent of curses and execrations." Recovering his composure he ordered his men to scatter through the woods and meet him at Manchester.

St. Clair, hearing gunfire at Castleton, had ordered two of his regiments, encamped only two miles from the battlefield, to Warner's aid, but instead they started for Castleton. Warner had, however, fought a successful rear-guard action. The exhausted British and Germans were in neither mood nor condition for pursuit. Thirty-five of Fraser's officers and men had been killed, 148 wounded, and with some 274 captives to manage in a strange land, he and von Reidesel ordered the whole lumbering contingent to Ticonderoga and Skenesborough.

Although St. Clair's army managed, on the whole, a successful retreat to Fort Edward, Congress did not allow him a single excuse. There had to be scapegoats and what better ones were available, regardless of the circumstances, than the commanders of an army that had so easily yielded a vital valley to the British, "I think we shall never be able to defend a post until we shoot a general," complained John Adams. Even George Washington considered the loss of Ticonderoga and Mount Independence "an event of chagrin and surprise not apprehended nor within the compass of my reasoning." Amidst villainous accusations that St. Clair and Schuyler had sold out to the enemy (who had embarrassed them by firing into their camps silver bullets which their men had scrambled to pick up) both were court-martialed. Their acquittal was inevitable, the facts being what they were: that the entire general staff from Washington on down were responsible for the failure to man the forts with sufficient troops. Some of them, moreover, shared the decision not to fortify Mount Defiance.

There was no relieving the Republic of the gloom that pervaded it in defeat. Nor any limits to the good cheer of the British. His Majesty's ministerial party thought the war was over. The betting odds on the recognition of American independence changed from even money to odds of five to one against it. Upon hearing the news, the King rushed into the Queen's apartment, announcing with delight that he had beaten all the Americans. There was an immediate cooling of the warm camaraderie the French had displayed toward America; they did not want to back a loser. And New England patriots discovered that there were many more Tories than they had thought.

The people in Vermont were despondent to the point of desperation: they considered St. Clair's retreat from the lake without a last-ditch fight nothing short of treacherous. Colonel Warner wrote the authorities in New Hampshire: "Many of the inhabitants have fled and left all in the hands of the enemy, and many more have taken protections of the British, and remain on their farms, and should the enemy march this way with any considerable force, many more will submit, and what will be the consequence cannot be foreseen." Everywhere in this frightened land, it seemed, the Eagle was taking wing.

⁂

With the British flag fluttering once again over Ticonderoga Burgoyne had every reason to expect 1777 would be his vintage year. The rebels had abandoned 15,000 stands of arms, a large store of ammunition, a great many tents, no less than 143,000 pounds of salted meat, a number of cattle, and 349,000 pounds of flour.

A few well-directed cannon shots on the morning of July 6 had parted the boom of timbers and the great iron chain that the Americans had supposed would protect the Narrows. With Fraser and von Reidesel pursuing St. Clair's army through Vermont, all that now stood between His Majesty's fleet and Skenesborough was the American flotilla of galleys and long boats that had started up the channel early in the morning with 600 troops, the sick, the women, and whatever supplies they had had time to load. Confident that pursuit would be difficult, or at least long-delayed, the Americans took their time at their oars. They had brought with them a plentiful supply of wine from the hospital stores, which transformed their retreat into a fife-and-drum diversion.

Upon reaching Skenesborough at 3 in the afternoon, great was their consternation to find three regiments at their heels aboard the *Inflexible,* the *Royal George,* and a number of gunboats. Near panic prevailed as two of their galleys surrendered and three others were blown up by their crews. Setting fire to the waterfront shops, storehouses and sawmills, whose flames touched off the whole hillside, they were forced to abandon their cannon, provisions, and some of the sick. As they evacuated the upper end of town for Fort Ann, the British landed in the basin below.

The new keeper of the gateway to the lake arrived with all the assurance of a permanent landlord. While consolidating his gains and awaiting supplies Burgoyne settled comfortably into Philip Skene's spacious fieldstone house to drink vintage wines with his comely mistress, the wife of one of his officers, generally referred to as "Mrs. Commissary." Here he pondered which way to pursue the Americans to Fort Ann, Fort Edward, and the Hudson Valley — whether by the route of their retreat along Wood Creek, or by Lake George. If it were to be the latter he would of course have to sail back to Ticonderoga and negotiate the portage to the upper lake.

It is generally thought that his decision to traverse swampy Wood Creek was at least partly engineered by Skene. Reclaiming his principality, captured by Allen's men two years previously, was obviously his dominant motive in accompanying the British army. If the Wood Creek route were chosen, Burgoyne would have to improve the wagon trail to Fort Ann, which would later enhance the value of Skene's lands. The canny Scot was apparently quite capable of such scheming. A story had recently circulated in town of the corpse of an old woman found in the basement of his house. It developed that he had been receiving an annuity which was to continue as long as his mother "remained above ground," and had conceived of a literal interpretation of the phrase which would allow him to receive it long after it was meant to cease.

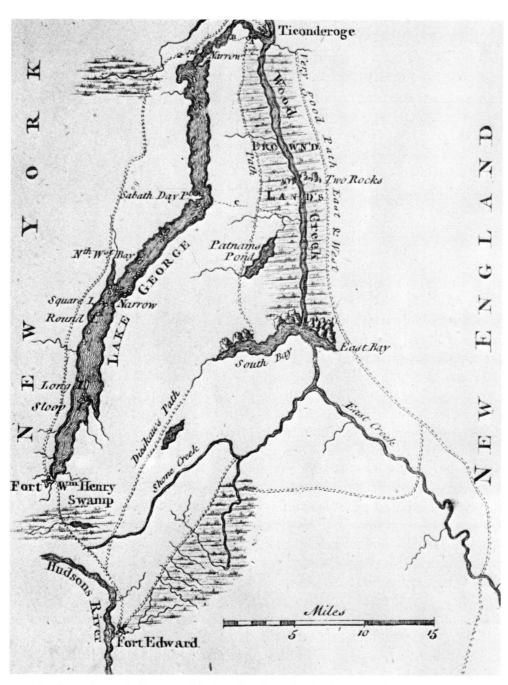

46. Map drawn during the French and Indian War shows Dieskau's route, and
also the locale of General Burgoyne's advance 22 years later to Fort
Edward. Delays encountered while slashing his way through the 26-mile
swamp of Wood Creek were critical in his march to Saratoga.

Much has been written about Burgoyne's logic, or lack of it, in deciding to hack his way through the swamps to the south. Hoffman Nickerson has devoted an entire book, *The Turning Point of the American Revolution,* to this critical juncture in Burgoyne's fortunes, and the events that immediately followed. Acknowledging that Skene must have played a principal role in Burgoyne's decision, he nevertheless points out that if the Lake George route had been chosen, Burgoyne would have had to drag all his boats, guns, and stores 220 feet up the hill at Ticonderoga.

Other scholars have emphasized Burgoyne's need of a continuing stream of supplies from Canada and for a direct and stable road over which to transport his boats to the Hudson. Since there were not enough of them to carry his whole army through Lake George, he presently decided to send the infantry over Wood Creek and, pending the building of his new road, the artillery and most of his supplies by way of Lake George. This took 11 days, which were also spent accumulating a month's provisions from the north in the event that he was forced to live off the land when he entered the Hudson Valley. One reason, generally overlooked, that his infantry took the Wood Creek route must have been that he was obliged to follow a retreating army, and would have been roundly criticized had he not done so.

In any case he had, in the meantime, sent von Reidesel to Castleton and vicinity to rally the inhabitants to the British standard, and to collect horses and cattle. To keep him from doing so Seth Warner rounded up large droves and herded them to Bennington, with the result that Reidesel's pickings were relatively thin. Burgoyne's efforts to return the people's sympathies to the Crown by proclamations and meetings also availed him little, since the patriots used such occasions to identify the Tories among them.

As he tried to penetrate the 26 miles of mosquito-and-gnat-infested miasma between Skenesborough and Fort Edward, Burgoyne had his work cut out, or down, for him. As the Americans retreated they laid waste to their crops, hid their stores, drove their cattle from the vicinity, dug channels to submerge drier lands, rolled large rocks into the creek, destroyed bridges, and felled great first-growth trees over the existing wagon trail. This labor was provided, among other troops, by Lt. Colonel Samuel Herrick's newly-formed company of Green Mountain Rangers.

The militia were paid from the proceeds of the confiscation of Tory properties in Vermont — a brilliant and timely scheme concocted by the 26-year-old Ira Allen, Secretary of the Vermont Council of Safety, architect of the new government, and lobbyist at large. Without the money he raised, the notable contribution of the infant republic to the outcome of the war could never have been made. Fifteen days after the Council had adopted Allen's policy of sequestration the regiment was at work trying to block Burgoyne's advance. To cut away the trees they had felled, to remove the obstacles from Wood Creek, and also to build 40 bridges, one of them across a swamp two miles long, Burgoyne's troops labored just as diligently. Their exertions had taken a considerable toll by the time they reached Fort Ann.

Near that small outpost now occurred an event that no tactician could have foreseen, but which made as much difference as a military factor in the outcome of the campaign — the scalping of Jane McCrea. Among the several versions of the tragedy is that of Isaac Weld, who traveled through the valley when people who remembered it were still alive:

The landlord of the tavern where we stopped . . . related all the circumstances attending Miss McCrea's death, and pointed out a hill, not far from the house, the very spot where she was murdered by the Indians, and the place of her interment.

47. Americans are destroying the sawmill as they evacuate Fort Ann in the path of Burgoyne's advance along Wood Creek. Garrison was built during the French and Indian War.

This beautiful young lady had been engaged to an officer in Burgoyne's army, who, anxious for her safety ... sent a party of trusty Indians to escort her to the camp. These Indians had partly executed their commission, and were approaching with their charge in sight of the British camp, when they were met by another set of Indians belonging to a different tribe, that was also attending the British army at this time. In a few minutes it became a matter of dispute between them, which should have the honour of conducting her to the camp; from words they came to blows, and blood was on the point of being drawn, when one of their chiefs, to settle the matter without farther mischief, went up to Miss McCrea, and killed her on the spot with a blow of his tomahawk.

When her bloodstained curls were brought into camp, Burgoyne, greatly shocked, wished to execute the murderer but the commander of the Indian troops, La Corne St. Luc, warned him that if he did all his Indians would desert. So the murderer was pardoned and "Remember Jane McCrea!" echoed through the hills, posts and stations, and what George Washington or the Congress could not do in heating the blood of patriots, the slaying of Jane McCrea and the pardon of her murderer did.

Upon reaching Fort Edward, Burgoyne's army, though exhausted, was still capable of meeting any contingency if its supply lines, which ran all the way to England, could be straightened out. Since horses for the dragoons and for hauling the artillery and baggage wagons remained the most critical need, Burgoyne contemplated an expedition east to Bennington. He had learned he could find there all he needed, in addition to oxen, wagons, cattle, corn, and flour. He had furthermore learned that the Friends of England in that town numbered five to one and "that they wanted only the appearance of a protecting force to show themselves." (His information proved faulty; he was to find nothing friendly about Bennington.) On August 11, upon reaching Fort Miller on the east bank of the Hudson opposite the Saratoga heights, Burgoyne ordered Lt. Colonel Baum to Bennington with a force of 800 German dragoons, chasseurs, British marksmen, Canadian volunteers, and Indians.

The scene there in sultry early August was quite as Burgoyne had been informed — abundant animals and provisions to be had for the taking. What he had not learned was that the Vermont and New Hampshire governments had resolved that they would not be taken without a fight, and had engaged John Stark of New Hampshire to join with Seth Warner in their defense. Stark and his militia were to be responsible to no one but the New Hampshire Assembly. Since that body did not know how to conduct a military campaign, Stark was responsible to no one but himself.

The veteran lieutenant and captain in Rogers Rangers had served bravely at

48. General John Stark, the victor (with Seth Warner) at Bennington.

Ticonderoga in the Abercromby fiasco, and subsequently with General Amherst, as the builder of half of the Crown Point Road connecting Lake
Champlain with the Connecticut River. As a colonel he had led a New
Hampshire regiment in the American left wing at Bunker Hill, and helped
arrange the defenses of New York City. In May, 1776, he arrived in Canada
just in time to meet, and retreat with, the ragged army from Quebec. That
summer he commanded a brigade which cleared and fortified the wilderness

of Mount Independence. Later he led the right wing in the advance guard of Washington's successful assault at Trenton.

In spite of his obvious attainments and the high opinion of him held by officers and men alike, his name (and Benedict Arnold's) were not included among lesser ones appearing on a new list of generals in 1777. Politics was the only reason conceivable unless a general's grammar was not supposed to slip, and Stark was no college man. In vain they tried to dissuade him from leaving the army but he declared that an officer who would not stand up for his own rights ought not to stand for the rights of his country. Feeling as he did he thought it improper to hold a commission and retired to his New Hampshire farm.

Within a week after he had received his commission from New Hampshire some 1500 volunteers had marched to Charlestown on the Connecticut, where they paused to cast bullets from the only pair of bullet moulds in town. They then marched to Manchester, where Seth Warner waited with the remainder of the regiment that had fought at Hubbardton. When Stark arrived he was flabbergasted to find Benjamin Lincoln, one of the generals promoted over his head, in charge. Producing his orders and commission from the New Hampshire Assembly, Colonel Stark in no uncertain terms told the General that his troops would remain with the Vermonters under Warner to guard the homeland from Burgoyne's left flank. Realizing that the local militia would not follow him, Lincoln diplomatically agreed to leave the troops under Stark and Warner, and departed to consult with headquarters.

On August 8 Stark marched his militia to Bennington (Warner remained in Manchester with the Vermont regiment, whose numbers had been increased by 200 recruits). It was pure accident that Stark was in Bennington when the British approached. By the time they reached Cambridge (New York), 18 miles from Bennington, Stark's scouts had reported a large force, and a courier was sent to summon Warner's regiment from Manchester. Baum, drawing closer, found not a hamlet full of Tories but a hornet's nest of provincials, and he sent to Burgoyne for help. Despite a flooding downpour that drowned their powder the next day, detachments went forth to harass the enemy from Stark's base about four miles northwest of Bennington.

His deserting Indians having reported that the woods were full of Yankees, Baum had been feverishly throwing up breastworks around the road over which his reinforcements would come. The strategic hill he had chosen might have been impregnable had he not deployed troops to hold what he considered a vital bridge half a mile down the slope. Stark's strategy was to attack from both sides, and he sent out groups of his men in shirtsleeves whom Baum mistook for Tory sympathizers seeking safety behind his lines. Stark meanwhile moved up gradually with his main force.

When he announced (in one of folklore's great moments), "There are the Redcoats, and they are ours, or this night Molly Stark sleeps a widow!" and Colonel Nichols started for Baum's right rear with 200 New Hampshire troops and Colonel Herrick for the left rear with 300 Vermonters, and the shooting, hot and heavy, began from all sides, Baum must have realized with a rush that this was a hellish place for a proud professional to die. As the Hessians under the hill tried desperately to climb to safety, the sharpshooting farmers picked them off. When the Yankees gained the crest of the hill it was war by bayonet, rifle butt, saber and pike. At length Baum received a mortal bullet in his abdomen and by three in the afternoon the routed Germans were retreating from an onslaught that Stark described as "one continued clap of thunder."

But the Battle of Bennington was not over. After a mud-soaked march more in the road from Cambridge than on it (with the Hessians nevertheless pausing every few minutes to re-dress their lines in military precision) the brave but bullying von Breymann arrived. Stark's forces were not prepared for a new enemy and now in turn it was they who were confused. Fortunately Colonel Warner's troops arrived from North Bennington just at this time and joined a battle so fierce that one soldier reported his musket too hot to hold.

49. Prisoners captured by New Hampshire and Vermont regiments at the Battle of Bennington. (Mural by Roy Williams)

With his empire at the head of the lake in the balance, Philip Skene was struggling mightily in the enemy lines. After his mount was shot from under him he found an artillery horse and rode off for an ammunition cart, which exploded as it was brought up. With a flesh wound in his leg and five holes in his clothing, Breymann at sunset had had enough and was retreating with the Americans in pursuit through the dim forest. Stark and Warner abandoned the chase, for they did not want to press too far their luck with the force of citizens-in-arms, who now could not see whom they were fighting.

It was a greater hour for the Americans than the people of Bennington, untying their rope beds to bind the prisoners, could conceive. Attesting to their fortitude and spirit, Burgoyne declared: "The Hampshire Grants, a country unpeopled and almost unknown in the last war, now abounds in the most active and rebellious race on the continent and hangs like a gathering storm at my left."

❦

The Battle of Bennington was the beginning of the end for Burgoyne. He later agreed with Lord George Germaine, Secretary of State for the Colonies, that it was "fatal" to his campaign. It was not just that some 250 of his best troops had been killed and 400 taken prisoner, but that the Americans' morale had been greatly restored by their first real victory. One of its immediate consequences was the defection of the hated La Corne St. Luc from Burgoyne's ranks and the departure of his Indians for Canada.

Although the leading figures in the drama on the lake became involved in the British downfall at Saratoga, it is not within the purview of this narrative to recount it. Burgoyne's only remaining option was then to retreat the way he had come, but he lost all hope of that when John Stark appeared on the east side of the Hudson to block his exit to the lake. Mopping up operations in the north had already begun before he finally capitulated on October 17.

Having returned to Bennington and Manchester to command all local forces (except Stark's), General Lincoln sent Colonel John Brown, the former "associate" of Ethan Allen, to retake the garrison at Ticonderoga if he could do it without too great a loss. He was accompanied by Colonel Herrick's Rangers, who had so recently labored as axemen to delay Burgoyne's southern passage through Wood Creek. Lincoln sent 500 other troops to harass the Redcoats on Mount Independence, and a third contingent to Skenesborough to protect the first two if they had to retreat that way.

The task of taking Mount Defiance was entrusted to Captain Ebenezer

Allen, who with his Rangers climbed it early in the morning of September 18. With a signal of three hoots of an owl to keep them together in the darkness, they swiftly reached the summit, although in one place the cliff was so steep that they had to climb over it on each others' shoulders. With a "hideous yell" they attacked the garrison, Allen reported, "like a stream of hornets to the charge." So startling was their assault that a British gunner trying to touch off his cannon fled with the match in his hand.

After a brief volley of musket fire and the flight of the Redcoats down the mountain to their capture, the hero of this mini-war proclaimed himself Commandant of Mount Defiance. Meanwhile Colonel Brown seized all the British shipping at the Lake George and Champlain landings (some 200 longboats, several gunboats, and a sloop), also the blockhouses at the falls and at Mount Hope. But Ticonderoga would not surrender, its commandant declaring: "The garrison committed to my charge I shall defend to the last." Since Mount Independence was also too strongly fortified the Americans decided to withdraw with their 293 British and Canadian prisoners, and also 100 jubilant veterans of the Battle of Hubbardton whom the Redcoats had imprisoned.

Later, after burning all the buildings and spiking the cannon, the British yielded Mount Independence, but Ticonderoga held on until after Burgoyne's surrender, when the local remnants of what a few months previously had been a seemingly invincible army withdrew to Canada. In the flush of victory Congress now hatched plans for another invasion of Quebec, first to be commanded by Stark and then by Lafayette, but this never materialized. In the absence of any large defensive force the lake remained vulnerable to British raids until the end of the war.

In November, 1778 they swept south as far as Ticonderoga, razing Vermont homesteads and taking prisoners. They set fire to every building in Middlebury except a barn made of lumber too green to burn. In November, 1779 they attacked Brandon and six months later passed through the lake to raid the Mohawk Valley. In October of 1780 one expedition ascended the Onion River to sack Royalton while another large one — 1,000 regulars, loyalists, and Indians aboard eight vessels — sailed south to capture Fort George and Fort Ann.

In 1781 British vessels were still cruising the lake and they still held outposts at Point au Fer, New York, and at Dutchman's Point, North Hero, Vermont. Little wonder that settlement, particularly along the northern shores, did not begin in earnest until after the Revolution. In 1783, while awaiting the formal end of hostilities, General Washington came down the

50. Green Mountain Ranger at left (Warner's Regiment, Fort Ticonderoga, September, 1775) is flanked by a fifer (First New York Regiment, Fort Ticonderoga, January, 1776).

lake as if to pronounce a benediction upon the crumbling ramparts of Ticonderoga and Crown Point.

The critical influence of the lake upon the outcome of the war has been stressed by a number of historians through the years, not the least of them Admiral Mahan, the naval historian, who wrote:

That the Americans were strong enough to impose the capitulation of Saratoga was due to the invaluable year of delay, secured to them in 1776, by their little navy on Lake Champlain, created by the indomitable energy and . . . courage of the traitor, Benedict Arnold. That the war spread from America to Europe, from the English Channel to the Baltic, from the Bay of Biscay to the Mediterranean, from the West Indies to the Mississippi, and ultimately involved the waters of the French peninsula of Hindustan, is traceable through Saratoga to the rude flotilla which, in 1776, anticipated the enemy in the possession of Lake Champlain.

The little American navy . . . was wiped out, but never had any force, big or small, lived to better purpose or died more gloriously; for it had saved the lake for that year. Whatever deductions may be made for the blunders and for circumstances of every character, which made the British campaign of 1777 abortive and disastrous, and so led directly to the American alliance with France in 1778, the delay, with all that involved, was obtained by the lake campaign of 1776. . . .

Further tracing the accession of Spain in 1779 to the intervention of France, Mahan demonstrates that the "war with these two powers led to the maritime occurrences, the interferences with neutral trade, that gave rise to the Armed Neutrality; the concurrence of Holland in which brought war between that country and Great Britain in 1780 . . ."

It is indisputable that events set in motion on the lake bore the heaviest of responsibilities for the outcome of the Revolution. The gateway to the country had become no less than the key to liberty. And if Valcour was one of its tines, another was Bennington which turned upon the raising of Stark's New Hampshire militia through the pledge of John Langdon's hard cash, silver, plate, and hogsheads of rum; and upon the confiscation and sale of Tory properties in Vermont by Ira Allen's Council of Safety. Such exercises in provincial exaltation can be carried too far, but not if destiny so obviously bears them out.

And what of the actors in this timeless drama? General St. Clair, whose misfortune was to be assigned the command of undermanned Ticonderoga and Mount Independence so soon before Burgoyne's arrival, suffered months of anguish. Despite his acquittal by his court-martial with honor and his election as president of the last Continental Congress, and subsequently as governor of what was then the Northwest Territory, he bore the stigma of a general who had failed, and died in penury at 84.

Gates continued, like a banty rooster, to peck away at Schuyler. Removed in August, 1777 from his command because of his court-martial with St. Clair, Schuyler was denied the opportunity he had largely created to defeat Burgoyne. That went to Gates, who covered himself with glory he should have shared with others. In 1779 Schuyler resigned from the army to foster his prerogatives as an illustrious Hudson River patroon, to work with his son-in-law, Alexander Hamilton, for the ratification by New York of the Federal Constitution, and to serve as an early member of the U.S. Senate.

The temporary success of Gates's intrigues to replace George Washington as commander-in-chief, together with his victory at Saratoga, won him the presidency of the Board of War, but not for long. Botching his final assignment as commander of the American army in the South, he withdrew to his Virginia estate.

Benedict Arnold's sensitive ego suffered another setback with the defeat of America's first naval squadron at Valcour. When Congress passed over his name for promotion to major-general in February, 1777 it was all George Washington could do to keep him in uniform. Belatedly promoted for outstanding service in Connecticut, he prevented St. Leger from joining Burgoyne on the Hudson, and with Daniel Morgan won for Gates both battles of Saratoga.

Thereafter his second marriage into a family of wealthy Philadelphia Tories, his implacable enemies, and his instability led him gradually but irrevocably to the dark moment when he plotted with John Andre to betray West Point to the British. Despised for his treachery even in England where he spent his final melancholic years, he asked on his deathbed to be clothed in his continental uniform, saying "Let me lie in my old American uniform in which I fought my battles. God forgive me for ever putting on any other."

Despite his defeat at Saratoga the attractive and well-meaning Burgoyne might yet have enjoyed a commanding reputation were it not for his sensuality. The holder of important political and military posts, he also enjoyed some small success as a playwright, but his 11-year liaison with a mistress who presented him with four bastards reduced him to the ranks of lesser men.

As for the local leaders, John Stark put away his sword and returned to his New Hampshire farm. Refusing every blandishment to be lured away from it, he lived to an old age, much respected and beloved by his neighbors as the archetypal laconic Yankee, every inch his own man.

In the face of every kind of privation Ethan Allen survived 32 months of British captivity with undiminished spirit. Numerous Englishmen came to see this lawless frontier libertarian and to hear the vigorous rebuttal with which he always put down his critics. At least he says he did in the ebullient narrative of his captivity. On one occasion while he was extolling the virtues of freedom in the parade ground outside his cell at Pendennis Castle he gained

> ... the resentment of a young beardless gentleman of the company, who gave himself very great airs, and replied that "he knew the Americans very well and was certain that they could not bear the smell of powder." I replied that I accepted it as a challenge, and was ready to convince him on the spot ... he answered that he should not put himself on a par with me. I then demanded of him to treat the character of Americans with due respect. He answered that I was an Irishman; but I assured him that I was a *full blooded Yankee,* and, in fine, bantered him so much that he left me in possession of the ground, and the laugh went against him. Two clergymen came to see me and, inasmuch as they behaved with civility, I returned the same! We discoursed on several parts of moral philosophy and Christianity; and they seemed to be surprized that I should be acquainted with such topics, or that I should understand a syllogism.

After numerous debates in high conference rooms as to what should be done with the indomitable and somewhat embarrassing Colonel Allen, the British sent him aboard a frigate which put in at the Cove of Cork on the way to America. Having heard that a rebel of their own stripe was incarcerated in their harbor, the Irishmen of the town assembled a large hamper of food, wine, and clothing, which Ethan said supplied him not only "with the necessaries and conveniences of life, but with the grandeurs and superfluities of it."

Following a series of brutal experiences, during which he was observed as a robust, large-framed man worn down by confinement and hard fare, yet with a strong mind and sense of generosity and honor, he was finally exchanged at Washington's behest for none other than General Prescott, who had thrown him in chains and had subsequently been captured himself.

Upon his release he went to Valley Forge to see Washington, who thought Ethan's "fortitude and firmness to have placed him out of the reach of misfortune" and recommended that Congress make him a full colonel. This was done, and he rode north with General Gates like a conquering hero. Upon reaching Bennington on May 30, 1778, he wrote that he appeared "as one rose from the dead . . . three cannon were fired that evening, and the next morning . . . 14 more were discharged welcoming me to Bennington, my usual place of abode; 13 for the United States, and 1 for young Vermont."

Thereupon he resumed his former role as protector of what in his absence had become the republic of Vermont, and of his lands on the lake and the Onion River. In some respects it was as if he had never been away. Throughout the Revolution the land wars with the neighboring states had been going on tumultously, at times quiescent under the numbing effects of the greater struggle, but again threatening to shake the little republic to its foundations. Although the war had migrated to the south, the British in Canada were ready at any moment to launch another invasion up the lake. That the Allens managed to keep His Majesty's Canadian army of several thousand from their borders with mere words was an accomplishment worthy of Talleyrand or Disraeli.

The so-called Haldimand Negotiations, named after the new governor of Canada, British General Sir Frederick Haldimand, with whom they were conducted, began in the fall of 1780 under the guise of an exchange of prisoners. Aware that the American Congress had shown little interest in admitting the Vermont republic as a state, the British were intrigued with the possibility that if Vermont's leaders were well enough rewarded, the republic might become a British colony and as such a wedge for invasion to the south.

By nourishing British hopes without actually promising anything, and by spinning out the negotiations, the Allens were able to keep the enemy from their borders for two years. In the meantime they applied pressure upon Congress for statehood by virtue of what they had done for the common cause. Unless Vermont was admitted to the Union, they assured Congress, its people could not be blamed for turning toward Great Britain. Why should their republic fight for the Union only to be swallowed up by New York after the shooting was over?

Ethan entered into the negotiations gingerly for, as he told Justice Sherwood, the British emissary, he did not wish to engage in any "dam'd Arnold plan to sell his country and his own honor by betraying the trust reposed in him." He realized, however, that to gain the diplomatic advantages of a string of conferences he would have to risk a whispering campaign that he was dealing, or at least conferring with, the enemy.

Haldimand's agent, after meeting with Ethan, reported to his commander that he was not able to tell whether things were going well or poorly from the British standpoint, for "he (Allen) is a most subtle and designing fellow." Ethan was not the least subtle in his memorials to Congress. He made no bones about declaring that since Vermont was an independent republic it had a right to agree to end hostilities with England if it so desired, and that he was "resolutely determined to defend the independence of Vermont as Congress are that of the United States, and rather than fail, will retire with hardy Green Mountain Boys into the desolate caverns of the mountains and wage war with human nature at large."

In 1781 rumors were flying so fast and thick that there was actually a movement by Ethan's enemies in the legislature for his impeachment. While it failed to pass, he resentfully turned in his uniform as brigadier general of the state militia, while his brother Ira took over the negotiations with the British. Impatient, and wary of the double-talk of the Vermont emissaries, Haldimand at length sent St. Leger up the lake to augment a force that he had sent a year earlier to seize Forts Ann and Edward; but before this large army could accomplish anything Lord Cornwallis surrendered at Yorktown and nothing remained for St. Leger but to return to Canada.

So Vermont fought this last campaign of the north with conversation. Despite obvious benefits to the Union, Congress still would not reward Vermont with statehood. Thus the Allens resumed conferences with Haldimand, Ethan declaring on one occasion that he would do everything in his power to make the republic a British province. Toward the end of the 1780's, with the adoption of the Constitution of the United States, it at last began to look as though the impossible might be achieved. The final stumbling block was removed when Vermont paid $30,000 to New York to end forever that state's claims to Green Mountain lands, and in 1791 the unwanted stepchild was received into the arms of the Union.

In 1787 Ethan moved north to Burlington with his second wife and their children (his first wife had died) and settled in a modest house on the Onion near the lake, there to farm his lands in the Intervale and to write his free-thinking book on religion, *Reason the Only Oracle of Man.*

Early in February, 1789 he and his servant drove his team of oxen north over the ice on the lake to Grand Isle to get a load of hay at Ebenezer Allen's. Convivially renewing old friendships there through the night, he started back early the next morning. About noon, as the sleigh approached the mouth of the Onion, he said: "It seems as if the trees are very thick here." He then struggled so violently that it was all his man could do to keep him from tumbling off. He then lay still. Carried into his house where he was bled and "physicked" by a physician, he lingered only a few hours longer.

V

Tales of the Frontier.

I. The Piersons

(Edited from a monograph by Lyman Thayer in
the *Vermont Historical Gazetteer*)

AMONG the settlers near the lake in Shelburne before the Revolution
was Moses Pierson. In 1776 he had raised a large crop of wheat. Soon
after it was harvested the British and Indians came up the lake. Deeming it
unsafe to remain, he and other settlers left this part of the state. The following March he returned with his family and a guard under the command of
Capt. Sawyer to thresh out the wheat and secure it.

While doing this they were attacked by a large company, apparently of
Indians, who with terrific yells made a furious attack in the latter part of the
night. The house was constructed of large logs laid close together, which
protected those inside from the balls of the enemy, except for shots fired
through the door or windows.

A desperate encounter was held for two hours, during which the house was
set on fire by the enemy, but was extinguished by some of those inside going
out and throwing on water and returning safe. But in a short time it was fired
a second time. All the water in the house had been used extinguishing the first
fire, and the question was, what could be done? Fortunately Mrs. Pierson had
made a barrel of beer the day before. Since it was outside the house, a reward

was offered by Pierson to the man that would get it and put out the fire. Barnabus Barnum made the attempt and succeeded, only to be shot down before reentering the house. Joshua Woodward was also killed by a ball entering through the door.

These two men had by chance come to the Piersons the previous day for the purpose of purchasing wheat, and the necessity of remaining through the night proved fatal to them. Others of the party were wounded, but they succeeded in repelling and driving off the raiders, killing and wounding many of them and taking a number of prisoners. The party in the house saw them after daylight carrying their dead to a crack in the ice and throwing them into the lake; and some who were probably considered mortally wounded were also thrown in.

Ziba and Uzal, the 17 and 15-year-old sons of Moses, were among the party and were active in this encounter. An infant daughter, who in after years became the wife of Nehemiah Pray, was lying in a bed at the time and fortunately escaped unharmed, although several balls were found in her bed and several went through the headboard.

The attacking party was apparently Indians, but it was strongly suspected at the time that many of them were in disguise. This suspicion was confirmed by a train of circumstances many years after this event. In the course of the War of 1812 a number of British officers that were captured at Missisco Bay were brought to Burlington, and by chance were visited by Ziba Pierson. While telling him his name and place of residence, one of the captives, a lieutenant, said: "Piersons — Shelburne. At Piersons in Shelburne my father fell. He was a Captain in the British service in the time of the Revolutionary war, and was shot down at Shelburne — his name was Larama."

This fully confirmed their former suspicions. His body was probably conveyed back to Canada, as it was known to the Piersons that some of the dead were carried on hand-sleds. The Piersons attributed their success and preservation from captivity or death to the fact that the raiders were under the influence of intoxicating liquor. The defeat of the enemy at this time and place evidently greatly exasperated the English leaders of the army. A large bounty was offered to the person that would capture and deliver to them the body of Moses Pierson, dead or alive, and a party was sent out the following April for the express purpose of capturing this notorious rebel.

After Pierson secured the wheat in Shelburne he retired with his family to Orwell. Since fodder for cattle was scarce, Ziba and Uzal, with an elderly man, were sent with a lot of cattle to Shoreham to browse these cattle in the forest. While thus employed they were surprised by this scouting party from

Canada. Ziba, Uzal, and the elderly man were taken prisoners and conveyed to Montreal, where they were confined until the next winter. The prison was situated directly on the river St. Lawrence, and when the ice formed on the river the three found means to escape. The aged man went first, and the two young men made their escape through the privy, which was directly over the river. They never learned the fate of the old man. Unfortunately for themselves a light snow fell that night, and they knew they would be pursued. When they reached the forest on the opposite side of the river they crossed and recrossed their tracks, reversed their shoes, retraced a portion of the distance they had traveled, and then hid themselves in the forest.

Soon after daylight a large party in hot pursuit passed directly by where they were concealed and obliterated their tracks with their own so that they were not discovered. Not daring to proceed, they remained in their hiding place the next night. The third night they moved cautiously forward and made their way as best they could, traveling for some time in the night only, and lying concealed in the wilderness through the day. They had no means of subsistence but what chance threw in their way, sometimes procuring milk from the cows they found in some of the French settlements through which they passed. They traveled most of the time in the forest, with no guide and often in the wrong direction, as they learned when the sun revealed itself.

When about 25 days from Montreal, and near the north line of New York, they discovered some lumbermen who camped in the forest in a log cabin. They concealed themselves nearby until the workmen left in the morning. Approaching the cabin cautiously, they ascertained that an old man was left to take care of the cabin and its contents, that he was fast asleep and, as they judged afterwards, intoxicated. They entered the cabin cautiously, with the understanding that one of them was to watch the old man, and if need be, to dispatch him at once to prevent their discovery. The other was to procure provisions for present and future use. They succeeded in getting as much as they could carry, which was a great relief to them in the remainder of their journey. The old man on guard made no move, and they did not harm him.

They proceeded on and reached Lake Champlain, and in crossing to the mainland found they were on Grand Isle, which was then occupied by Indians in considerable numbers, though they did not discover them. After 40 days in cold winter weather without the benefit of fire (for fear of its being a means of their being discovered and recaptured) they reached Shelburne, and found nought but desolation — no living person there. They found a few peas and some frozen potatoes at their former residence, and cooked and ate them with a relish, and proceeded on to Orwell. There they found their parents and were received with a joyful welcome, after almost a year's absence — appearing more like walking skeletons than living beings.

II. The Plot

(Edited from a monograph by Lyman Thayer in
the *Vermont Historical Gazetteer*)

T HE Plot River rises in the southeast part of Hinesburg and runs through the northeast corner of Charlotte, and through Shelburne Falls into Shelburne Bay. The circumstance which gave this river its name happened in the fall of 1775.

A band of Indians was discovered, probably from Grand Isle, making their way up Shelburne Bay in their bark canoes. From the head of the bay they proceeded about 100 rods up this stream. Landing on the west side and drawing their canoes up on shore, they concealed them among the bushes and moved cautiously forward for the purpose of plundering the settlers. Their motions having been watched, the alarm was spread among the settlers. Ten of them were mustered and a consultation was held as to what they should do.

Concluding that the Indians, if vigorously attacked, would retreat to their canoes, they decided that three of their number should proceed to the landing place and disable their canoes by cutting slits through the bark in various places. They would then conceal themselves nearby and await the result — while the other seven would make a furious and tumultuous assault upon the enemy, who had already commenced their work of plunder.

The plot succeeded beyond their most sanguine expectations. The onset of the seven in the darkness was made with so much show and spirit as to lead the

Indians to suppose they were assailed by a force far superior to their own, and that their only chance of escape consisted in a hasty retreat to their canoes. They accordingly betook themselves to flight and when they reached their landing place seized their canoes, hurried them into the stream, and leapt on board.

But what was their surprise when they found their canoes were disabled and were all filling with water. In this forlorn condition they were attacked by the three men who had lain concealed on the bank: The pursuing party soon came to their aid and the Indians were all shot while struggling to keep themselves afloat. None of them escaped to tell their tale of woe. This well contrived and successful strategem gave the name to this stream — Plot River. Relics of guns were found at this place not many years after.

III. Captain Thomas

(Edited from *Travels Through North America*, 1796, by Isaac Weld)

ON board our little vessel we had a poor Canadian, whom we took in at Skenesborough. Having asked this little fellow, as we sailed along, some questions about the Indians, he immediately gave us a long account of a Captain Thomas, a chief of the Cachenonaga nation, in the neighborhood of whose village he said he lived.

Thomas, he told us, was a very rich man, and had a most excellent house in which he lived as well as a signeur; and he was sure we should be well received if we went to see him. He told us also that he had built a church and was a Christian, and that he was very charitable. It was not long before we were gratified, for the party of Indians that arrived while we were at Chimney Point were from the Cachenonaga village, and at their head was Captain Thomas.

Thomas appeared to be about 45 years of age; he was nearly six feet high and very bulky in proportion. This is the sort of make uncommon among the Indians, who are generally slender. He was dressed like a white man, in boots; his hair untied but cut short. The people who attended him were all in Indian habit. Not one of his followers could speak a word of English or French, but Thomas could speak both languages. English he spoke with some little hesitation and not correctly, but French seemed as familiar to him as his native tongue.

His principal attention seemed to be directed towards trade, which he had pursued with great success, so much so that we afterwards heard he could get credit in any store in Montreal for five hundred pounds. He had along with him at Chimney Point thirty horses and a quantity of furs in the canoe, which he was taking for sale to Albany.

His people, he told us, had but very few wants; he took care to have these always supplied. In return they brought him furs taken in hunting, they attended his horses, and voluntarily accompanied him when he went on a trading expedition. During the course of conversation he told us that if we came to see him he would make us very happy; that there were some very

51. None of the names given landmarks in Burlington Bay by British surveyor have survived.

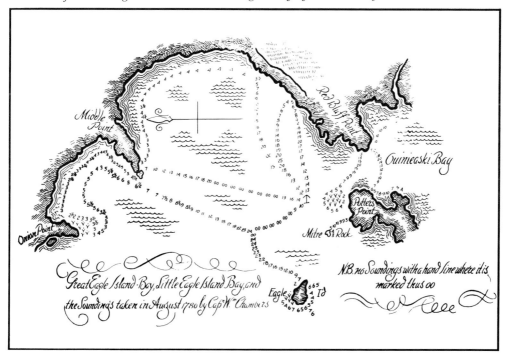

handsome squaws in his village and that each of us should have a wife. We promised to visit him if it was in our power, and parted very good friends.

Thomas, as we afterwards found, is not a man respected among the Indians in general, who think much more of a chief who is a good warrior and hunter, and retains the habits of his nation; than of one who becomes a trader and assimilates his manners to those of the whites.

IV. Benjamin Everest

(Edited from a monograph by John Strong in
the *Vermont Historical Gazetteer*)

WHEN 16 years of age Benjamin Everest, born in Seabury, Connecticut, moved with his father to Addison. This was in 1769. As a boy and young man he was noted for his prowess and activity in all athletic exercises. There was not one in all the settlement that could run, jump, or wrestle with him. He was by nature well fitted to take a part in those troubled times.

In August, 1773, when Allen, Warner, and Baker came up to help the settlers drive off Col. Reid and his Yorkers from their position at Vergennes, Everest with his brother Zadock and other neighbors joined them. After having torn down the mills, burnt the dwellings, and destroyed the settlement, Allen made such an impression on Benjamin — their spirits were so much in unison — that Everest wished to go with Allen, as more trouble with the Yorkers was expected. Allen was glad of his service and very soon gave him a sergeant's warrant in his band.

On receipt of intelligence of the battle of Lexington, Everest immediately repaired to Allen's headquarters, where he received a commission as lieutenant. He was very active and useful in procuring men and information to aid in the capture of Ticonderoga and Crown Point, and was with Allen when he entered the fort at Ticonderoga, and went up with Warner to take Crown Point. After Allen was taken prisoner at Montreal, Everest and his company were incorporated into Col. Seth Warner's regiment.

He was with Warner at the battles of Hubbardton and Bennington. Col. Baum having been mortally wounded, and his troops broken and flying, the militia, under the impression that the battle was over, had dispersed in every direction in search of plunder, when Col. Breymann, who had been sent to Baum's relief, arrived on the ground. When Warner arrived and at a glance saw the peril of our troops, he gave the word to "Close!" Like an eagle swooping to its prey, he and his Green Mountain Boys came down on the enemy and scattered them like dust before the wind.

After the capture of Burgoyne, Everest obtained a furlough with the intention of visiting Addison to look after his father's property (his father having gone back to Connecticut with his family). Not knowing how matters stood in that section, he approached warily, keeping on the highlands between Otter Creek and the lake. Arriving at the Falls at dark, he kindled a

fire and lay down. About midnight he was awakened by the war-whoop, and found himself a prisoner of a party of Indians on their way to Lake Memphremagog to attend a council of most of the tribes of Canada, New York, and New England.

He suffered much from the thongs with which he was bound, but understanding the nature of the Indians very well, so gained their confidence that they showed him more leniency afterwards. On the breaking up of the council he was brought back to the western shore of Lake Champlain near Whallons Bay, where they encamped for the winter. He had been pondering for a long time various plans for escape, but concluded to wait until the lake was frozen.

It was now December and the lake had been frozen some two or three days, the ice as smooth as glass. The sun shone quite pleasantly and the air was comfortable. The Indians prepared for a frolic on the ice; many of them had skates and were very good skaters. Everest asked permission to go down and see the sport, as he had never seen anyone skate. They gave him leave to go, two or three evidently keeping an eye on him. He expressed his wonder and delight at their performances so naturally that all suspicion was lulled.

After a time, when the Indians began to be tired and many were taking off their skates, he asked a young Indian who had just taken off a very fine pair, to let him try and skate. This the Indian readily consented to, expecting to have sport out of the white man's falls and awkwardness. Everest put on the skates, got up, and no sooner up than down he came, striking heavily on the ice. Again he tried to stand and down he fell, and so continued to play the novice until all the Indians had come in from outside on the lake. He had contrived to stumble and work his way some 15 or 20 rods from the nearest, when he turned and skated a rod or two towards them, and partly falling he got on his knees and began to fix and tighten his skates.

This being done he rose, and striking a few strokes towards the eastern shore, he bent to his work, giving, as he leaned forward, a few insulting slaps to denote that he was off. With a whoop and a yell of rage, the Indians that had on their skates started in pursuit. He soon saw that none could overtake him and felt quite confident of his escape. After getting more than half across the lake, and the ice behind him covered with Indians, he looked toward the east shore and saw two Indians coming round a point directly in front of him. This did not alarm him, for he turned his course directly up the lake. Again he looked and saw his pursuers (except two of their best skaters who followed directly in his track) had spread themselves in a line from shore to shore.

He did not at first understand it, but after having passed up the lake about three miles he came suddenly upon one of those immense cracks or fissures in the ice that so frequently occur when the ice is glare. It ran in the form of a semicircle from shore to shore, the arch in the center and up the lake. He saw he was in a trap. The Indians on his flanks had already reached the crack and were coming down towards the middle. He flew along the edge of the crack, but no place that seemed possible for human power to leap was there. But the enemy were close upon him; he took a short run backward, and then shooting forward like lightning, with every nerve strained, he took the leap and just reached the farther side. None of the Indians dared to follow.

Finding snow on the ice at Panton, he left it and made good his way to his regiment. He commanded the fort at Rutland during the summer of 1778. Having come up the lake during the fall of that year, Carleton undertook some repairs at Crown Point. The Americans wanted some information in regard to it and Everest was asked to go. Doffing his uniform, he procured a Tory dress (gray)and boldly entered the garrison and offered his services as a workman. He was set to tend masons and made himself very acceptable by his industry.

He had acquired about all the information he wanted and would have left in a day or two, when, as ill-fortune would have it, a man by the name of Benedict, also an early settler in Addison but who espoused the British cause, came into the fort, saw Everest and knew him, but Everest did not see Benedict. Benedict gave notice to the officer in command that one of his men was a spy, a lieutenant in the American army, and before Everest was aware that he was suspected, he was arrested, thrown into prison and kept there for nine days.

Having in the meantime collected 39 men and boys as prisoners (most of them neighbors and acquaintances of Everest) Major Carleton concluded to take Everest to Canada before he was tried, and ordered him on board the vessel just ready to sail for Canada. It was now the latter part of November; a severe storm from the northeast came on, sleet and snow, with the wind blowing furiously. The vessel had run up to Ticonderoga to take on board some freight. During the day Everest had bribed one of the sailors to bring on board a bottle of liquor, which was secreted by Everest. At sunset the vessel was taken into the middle of the lake and anchored there. The night was very wild and tempestuous. At the solicitation of the prisoners the captain had ordered a tent pitched on deck to shield them from the storm.

Everest now proposed to his fellow prisoners to try to escape. They were anchored about half a mile north of the bridge that crossed the lake at that place, and he proposed to invite the sentry to take a drink or two out of the bottle and shelter themselves from the storm, while they watched their opportunity to let themselves into the lake and to swim to the bridge. Only two dared to think of trying it. When everything was quiet Everest gave the sentry a drink out of the bottle, and in a little while asked him to come under the tent and have another glass. This was complied with and in a short time Everest, saying "What a storm it is!" went out as if to take a look. He took off his clothing and tied it about his head, let himself down into the water near the stern, and struck out for the bridge. It almost made him cry out aloud when he first went into the water, it was so piercing cold. Spaulding followed next, but the water was so cold when he touched it that he shrank back and crawled on board again. No other one attempted it.

Everest succeeded in reaching the bridge, on which he crawled, and where, before he could dress himself, he came near perishing, being much colder than in the water. Seeing and hearing nothing of his companions, he concluded they had not started, or perished in the attempt. There was a party of British on the east shore at the end of the bridge, and Indians at the west end. Everest thought he could pass the Indians the best. His dress was gray, the Tory uniform, and he resolved to make the Indians think he came from the British encampment and was on his way with special orders. A narrow path led through a pile of goods near the end of the bridge, a sentinel leaning against it. Everest looked about for a stick or some weapon, but could find nothing. He recollected he had a razor in his pocket, and opening it, approached very cautiously. He saw the man was asleep. With his razor ready and his face toward the sleeper, he passed within six inches of him, prepared, if the man stirred, to cut his throat.

He passed the Indian camp without suspicion on their part, but soon after fell into one of the ditches of the fort, getting thoroughly wet. He now took a northwest course for about four or five miles and came upon a fire where a party of Indians had camped the day before. After he had satisfied himself that no one was lurking in the neighborhood, he came to the fire, built a good one, and warmed himself and thoroughly dried his clothes. Just before daybreak the storm ceased, the moon came out, and he started north, keeping along the range of mountains.

About sunrise he came to Put's Creek; here he stopped and rested awhile. He then kept back on the hills, yet still in sight of the lake, until he came to Webster's, an old acquaintance, whom he found chopping in the woods. They started to go down to the house but on coming into the clearing they saw the British fleet coming down the lake with a very light breeze. Everest immediately went back and secreted himself in the woods. Since he had eaten nothing for 24 hours, Webster carried him some food, and agreed to keep a look out until after dark, and when the coast was clear to stand in his doorway and chop a few sticks of wood and whistle a tune agreed upon.

The fleet anchored right opposite Webster's, and when all was quiet Everest came out upon receiving the signal. Webster let him have his canoe. Giving the fleet a wide berth, he landed safely on the east shore and made his way to Castleton.

He was afterwards taken prisoner by seven Indians but escaped the next day. After the war he went to Connecticut and moved his mother and the younger children up to Pawlet, his father having died previously. There he resided some two or three years, and was married. Soon after, his family came back to the old farm in Addison, where some of his descendants now live. He died at a good old age, a member of the Baptist church, and much respected.

V. The Strongs

(Edited from a monograph by John Strong in
the *Vermont Historical Gazetteer*)

I N February, 1776 John Strong, with his wife Agnes and three children, started north from Salisbury, Connecticut with all their goods piled in a sleigh drawn by two mares. Their route lay through Albany and across the Hudson, then on the ice on Lake George to Ticonderoga, then on the ice on Lake Champlain to their house erected in Addison the fall before.

He at once commenced chopping a fallow, and as soon as the spring opened, planted corn and potatoes. About the first of June he was taken with chills and fever, but his wife and children were dependent on his constant exertions. Kind neighbors had come in but they were no better off than himself. So when the fit came on he would lie down by a log heap until it was partly over, and then up and at it again.

Wild animals were very troublesome, especially bears, with which he had many encounters. In September Mrs. Strong (while her husband had gone up the lake in a bateau to Albany to procure necessaries for the settlement) one evening was sitting by the fire with her children. The evenings had become somewhat chilly. The kettle of samp intended for supper had just been taken from the fire when, hearing a noise, she looked towards the door and saw the blanket that served the purpose of one, raised up, and an old bear protruding her head into the room. The sight of the fire caused her to dodge back. Mrs. Strong caught the baby, and sending the older children to the loft, she followed and drew the ladder after her. The floor of this loft was made by

NORTHERN PORTION OF THE LAKE

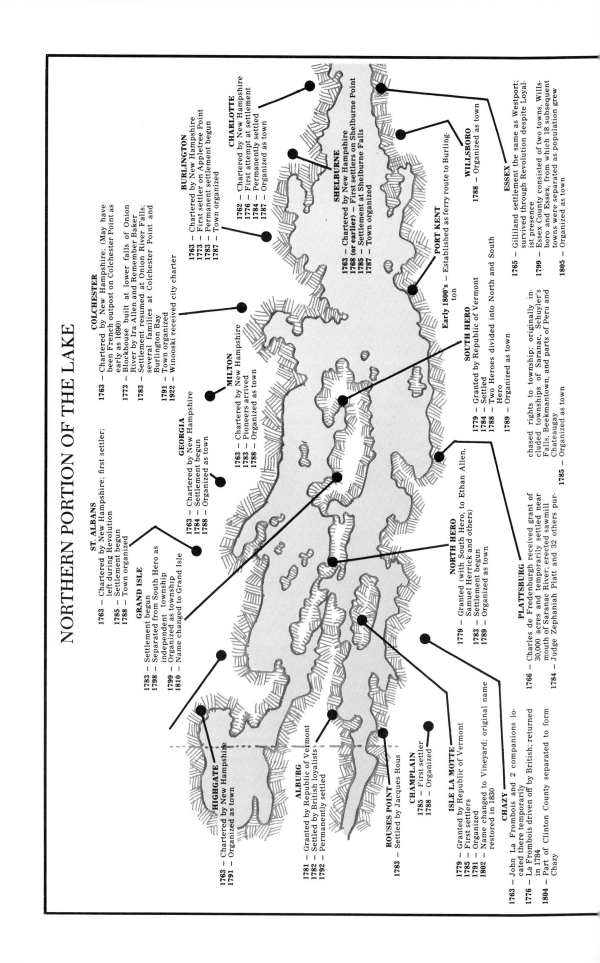

ST. ALBANS
1763 – Chartered by New Hampshire; first settler; left during Revolution
1785 – Settlement begun
1788 – Town organized

COLCHESTER
1763 – Chartered by New Hampshire; (May have been French outpost on Colchester Point as early as 1690)
1773 – Blockhouse built at lower falls of Onion River by Ira Allen and Remember Baker
1783 – Settlement resumed at Onion River Falls; several families at Colchester Point and Burlington Bay
1791 – Town organized
1922 – Winooski received city charter

BURLINGTON
1763 – Chartered by New Hampshire
1773 – First settler on Appletree Point
1783 – Permanent settlement begun
1787 – Town organized

CHARLOTTE
1762 – Chartered by New Hampshire
1776 – First attempt at settlement
1784 – Permanently settled
1787 – Organized as town

SHELBURNE
1763 – Chartered by New Hampshire
1768 (or earlier) – First settlers on Shelburne Point
1785 – Settlement at Shelburne Falls
1787 – Town organized

WILLSBORO
1788 – Organized as town

PORT KENT
Early 1800's – Established as ferry route to Burlington

GRAND ISLE
1783 – Settlement begun
1798 – Separated from South Hero as independent township
1799 – Organized as township
1810 – Name changed to Grand Isle

GEORGIA
1763 – Chartered by New Hampshire
1784 – Settlement begun
1788 – Organized as town

MILTON
1763 – Chartered by New Hampshire
1783 – Pioneers arrived
1788 – Organized as town

SOUTH HERO
1779 – Granted by Republic of Vermont
1784 – Settled
1788 – Two Heroes divided into North and South Hero
1789 – Organized as town

ESSEX
1765 – Gilliland settlement the same as Westport; survived through Revolution despite Loyalist presence
1799 – Essex County consisted of two towns, Willsboro and Essex, from which 18 subsequent towns were separated as population grew
1805 – Organized as town

HIGHGATE
1763 – Chartered by New Hampshire
1791 – Organized as town

ALBURG
1781 – Granted by Republic of Vermont
1782 – Settled by British loyalists
1792 – Permanently settled

CHAMPLAIN
1785 – First settler
1788 – Organized

ISLE LA MOTTE
1779 – Granted by Republic of Vermont
1785 – First settlers
1791 – Organized
1802 – Name changed to Vineyard; original name restored in 1830

CHAZY
1763 – John La Frombois and 2 companions located there temporarily
1776 – La Frombois driven off by British; returned in 1784
1804 – Part of Clinton County separated to form Chazy

ROUSES POINT
1783 – Settled by Jacques Rous

NORTH HERO
1779 – Granted (with South Hero, to Ethan Allen, Samuel Herrick and others)
1783 – Settlement begun
1789 – Organized as town

PLATTSBURG
1766 – Charles de Fredenburgh received grant of 30,000 acres and temporarily settled near mouth of Saranac River; erected sawmill
1784 – Judge Zephaniah Platt and 32 others purchased rights to township; originally included townships of Saranac, Schuyler's Falls, Beekmantown, and parts of Peru and Chateaugay
1785 – Organized as town

SETTLING
THE CHAMPLAIN VALLEY

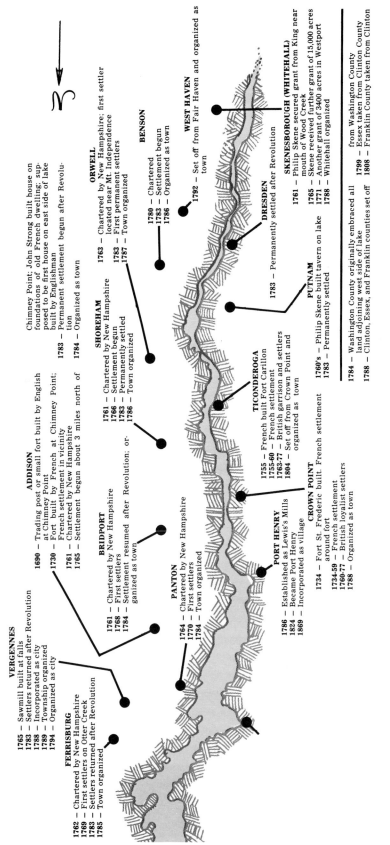

VERGENNES

1765 – Sawmill built at falls
1783 – Settlers returned after Revolution
1788 – Incorporated as city
1789 – Township organized
1794 – Organized as city

FERRISBURG

1762 – Chartered by New Hampshire
1769 – First settlers on Otter Creek
1783 – Settlers returned after Revolution
1785 – Town organized

PANTON

1764 – Chartered by New Hampshire
1770 – First settlers
1784 – Town organized

BRIDPORT

1761 – Chartered by New Hampshire
1768 – First settlers
1784 – Settlement resumed after Revolution; organized as town

ADDISON

1690 – Trading post or small fort built by English at Chimney Point
1730 – Fort built by French at Chimney Point; French settlement in vicinity
1761 – Chartered by New Hampshire
1765 – Settlement begun about 3 miles north of Chimney Point; John Strong built house on foundations of old French dwelling; supposed to be first house on east side of lake built by Englishman
1783 – Permanent settlement begun after Revolution
1784 – Organized as town

SHOREHAM

1761 – Chartered by New Hampshire
1766 – Settlement begun
1783 – Permanently settled
1786 – Town organized

ORWELL

1763 – Chartered by New Hampshire; first settler located near Mt. Independence
1783 – First permanent settlers
1787 – Town organized

BENSON

1780 – Chartered
1783 – Settlement begun
1786 – Organized as town

WEST HAVEN

1792 – Set off from Fair Haven and organized as town

DRESDEN

1783 – Permanently settled after Revolution

SKENESBOROUGH (WHITEHALL)

1761 – Philip Skene secured grant from King near mouth of Wood Creek
1765 – Skene received further grant of 15,000 acres
1771 – Another grant of 3400 acres in Westport
1788 – Whitehall organized

PORT HENRY

1786 – Established as Lewis's Mills
1824 – Became Port Henry
1869 – Incorporated as village

CROWN POINT

1734 – Fort St. Frederic built. French settlement around fort
1734-59 – French settlement
1760-77 – British loyalist settlers
1788 – Organized as town

TICONDEROGA

1755 – French built Fort Carillon
1755-60 – French settlement
1763-77 – British garrison and settlers
1804 – Set off from Crown Point and organized as town

PUTNAM

1760's – Philip Skene built tavern on lake
1783 – Permanently settled

1784 – Washington County originally embraced all land adjoining west side of lake
1788 – Clinton, Essex, and Franklin counties set off from Washington County
1799 – Essex taken from Clinton County
1808 – Franklin County taken from Clinton

Drawn by Howard Johnson

SOUTHERN PORTION OF THE LAKE

52. *John Strong survived all the vicissitudes of the frontier to build this fine second home.*

laying small poles close together, which gave ample opportunity to see all passing below.

The bear, after reconnoitering the place several times, came in with two cubs. They first upset the milk that had been placed on the table for supper. The old bear then made a dash at the pudding pot and, thrusting in her head, swallowed a large mouthful and filled her mouth with another before she found it was boiling hot. Giving a furious growl, she struck the pot with her paw, upsetting and breaking it. She then set herself up on end, endeavoring to poke the pudding from her mouth, whining and growling all the time.

This was so ludicrous, the cubs sitting up on end, one on each side and wondering what ailed their mother, that it drew a loud laugh from the children above. This seemed to excite the anger of the beast more than ever, and with a roar she rushed for the place where they had escaped, up aloft. This they had covered up when they drew up the ladder, and now commenced a struggle; the bear to get up, the mother and children to keep her down. After many fruitless attempts the bear gave up and towards morning moved off. After Strong's return, a door made from slabs split from basswood and hung on wooden hinges gave them some security from such inroads in the future.

At another time Strong and Smalley were crossing the lake from Chimney Point in a canoe, and when near Sandy Point they saw something swimming in the water, which they at once supposed to be a deer, and gave chase. As they drew near they found it was an enormous black bear. This was a different affair, and a consultation was held. They had nothing but an axe, so it was planned that Smalley was to get into the wake of the bear and run the canoe bow on, while Strong, standing in the bow with the axe, was to knock Bruin on the head.

Smalley brought the boat up in good style and Strong, with all the force of a man used to felling the giants of the forest, struck the bear full on the head. The bear minded it no more than if it had been a walking stick instead of an axe, and instantly turning, placed both fore paws on the side of the boat and upset it, turning both men into the lake. Instead of following them the bear crawled up on the bottom of the boat and took possession, quietly seating himself and looking on with great gravity, while the men were floundering in the water. Smalley, who was not a very good swimmer, thought he might hold on by one end of the boat until it should float ashore, but no, Bruin would have none of their company; and they were obliged, each with an oar under his arms to sustain him, to make the best of their way to Sandy Point, the nearest shore. From here they had to go around the head of Bullwaga Bay, and north as far as Point Henry, where they found their boat, minus their axe and other baggage, and were very glad to come off so well.

One fall the bears were making destructive work in Strong's cornfield. He found where they came in and placed his trap in their road. The second morning he found his trap gone and plenty of signs that a large bear had taken it. Getting two of his neighbors, Kellogg and Pangborn, to go with him, they took three dogs, two guns and an axe. After following the track for some two miles they heard the dogs, and as they came up they found the bear with her back against a large stub, cuffing the dogs whenever they came within reach. The trap was on her hind legs.

Kellogg proposed to shoot the bear but Strong said he could kill her with his axe, rather than waste a charge of ammunition which was scarce and difficult to get. So taking the axe, and remembering his encounter on the lake, he turned the bit of the axe, intending to split her head open. He approached cautiously and when near enough gave the blow with tremendous force, but the bear, with all the skill of a practiced boxer, caught the axe as it was descending; with one of her paws knocking it out of his hand and at the same time catching him with the other. As she drew him up for the death hug she endeavored to grab his throat in her mouth. One moment more and he would have been a mangled corpse.

The first effort he avoided by bending his head close upon his breast; the second, by running his left hand into her open mouth and down her throat, until he could hook the ends of his fingers into the roots of her tongue. This hold he kept until the end, although every time the bear closed her mouth his thumb was crushed and ground between her grinders, her mouth being so narrow that it was impossible to put it out of the way. He now called on Kellogg for God's sake to shoot the bear, but this he dared not do for fear of shooting Strong, for as soon as he got the bear by the tongue she endeavored to get rid of him by plunging and rolling about, so that one moment the bear was on top, and then Strong.

In these struggles they came where the axe had been thrown. This Strong seized with his right hand, and striking the bear in the small of the back, severed it at a blow. This so paralyzed her that she loosened her hug, and he snatched his hand from her mouth and cleared himself of her reach. The men then dispatched her with their guns. His mutilated thumb he carried as a memento of the fight to his dying day.

Indians caused more fear than wild beasts, especially after the commencement of the Revolutionary struggle. Although through the policy of some of the leading men of the Grants the British had been induced to treat the settlers on the east side of the lake with mildness, and had forbidden the Indians to molest them, yet their savageness was ready to burst forth on the slightest provocation. So much was this the case that if a party of Indians appeared when the men were absent, the women allowed them to help themselves to whatever they liked.

At one time a party came in when Mrs. Strong was alone. They first took the cream from the milk and rubbed it on their faces; then rubbing soot on their hands, painted themselves in all the hideousness of the warpaint, and sang the war song with whoops and dances. Just as they were leaving, one of them discovered a showy colored short gown that her husband had just made her a birthday present of. This he took, and putting it on seemed greatly delighted, and with yells and whoops they departed.

One morning in June Mrs. Strong arose and went to the spring on the bank of the lake a few rods from the house. The birds had just commenced their morning matins. The air was laden with the perfume of wild flowers. Not a

breath stirred a leaf or ruffled the glass-like surface of the lake. As she stood listening to the birds she thought she heard the dip of a paddle in the water, and looking through the trees that fringed the bank, saw a canoe filled with Indians. In a moment more the boat passed the trees in full view. A pole was fastened upright in the bow, on the top of which was the scalp of a little girl ten years old, her flaxen ringlets just stirring in the morning air, while streams of clotted blood all down the pole showed it was placed there while yet warm and bleeding.

While horror froze her to the spot, she thought she recognized the hair as that of a beautiful child of a dear friend of hers living on the other side of the lake. She saw other scalps attached to their waist belts, and two other canoes farther out in the lake displayed these terrible signals at their bows. Upon seeing her the Indians gave the war whoop and made signals as though they would scalp her, and she fled to the house like a frightened deer. The day brought tidings that their friends on the other side had all been massacred and scalped, six in number, and their houses burned.

The morning before the taking of Crown Point by Burgoyne, Mrs. Strong was sitting at the breakfast table. Her two oldest sons, Asa and Samuel, had started at daylight to hunt for young cattle that had strayed in the woods. Her husband had gone to Rutland to procure supplies of beef for the American forces at Ticonderoga and Crown Point, when a daughter of Kellogg came rushing in with: "The Indians are coming and we are all flying! There are bateaux at the Point to take us off, and you must hurry!" And back she ran to help her own folks, her father then being a prisoner in Quebec.

Mrs. Strong was in very feeble health, totally unable to encounter hardship or fatigue — her husband away, her two oldest sons in the woods and no one to warn or seek them. There was no way but to try and save the children that were with her. She took her youngest, a babe of six months, and putting him in a sack with his head and shoulders out, fastened him on the back of her eldest daughter. Making up a bundle of the most necessary clothing for each of the other children, she started them for the Point, warning them not to loiter or wait for her, that she would overtake them. After putting out the fire she closed the house, leaving the breakfast table standing as it was when they first heard the news.

She traveled on as fast as she was able until she came to the north bank of Hospital Creek. Here, entirely exhausted, she sat down, when Spalding of Panton, who had waited to see all off, came riding at full gallop up the road. Seeing her sitting where she was he said: "Are you crazy? The Indians are in sight, the lake is covered, and the woods are full of them.!" She told him she could go no farther. He dismounted, placed her on the pillion, and putting his horse to his speed, arrived just as the last bateau, containing her children, was putting off. She was put on board, Spalding going on with his horse. That night they arrived at Whitehall (Skenesborough). Here the settlers scattered in many directions, some returning to Connecticut, and others going east. Zadock Everest and family, with other neighbors, went east and she went with them.

Asa and Samuel, as they returned towards night, saw by the columns of smoke coming up from every house, that the Indians must have been there. They hid themselves until dark and then, cautiously approaching, found their house a blazing ruin. Believing that the family had escaped, they retraced their steps and made their way east toward Otter Creek. At daylight they found themselves near Snake Mountain. Fortunately, when they left home the morning previous, they took a gun and ammunition. They shot a partridge and roasted it and saving a part for their dinner, pushed on. In about a week they found their mother and the rest of the children. They then hired a log house, the older boys working out, and each doing what they could for their support.

Hearing that Burgoyne had taken Crown Point, Strong left his cattle at

Brandon and hastened for his home. On coming within sight of the forts he secreted himself until night, then moved on cautiously. When he reached the center of a narrow ridge of land with a marsh on each side, a yell as demoniac as though the gates of the infernal regions had opened upon him, burst forth, and instantly he was surrounded by more than 200 savages, whooping and winging their tomahawks over his head. Instant death seemed inevitable.

A Tory was in command. Having heard that Strong was expected in with cattle, he had got the assistance of this band of Indians to intercept him. After a few moments he partially stilled the Indians and addressing Strong, asked: "Where are your cattle?" Strong answered: "Safe." This drove the Tory mad with rage and no doubt he would have sacrificed him on the spot if an old chief, who knew Strong, had not interposed. Strong then told them to take him to the fort, and whatever was proper for him to answer, he would cheerfully do. He was then bound and taken to the other side of the lake and placed in the guard-house until morning. When he was brought before the commanding officer, General Fraser, Strong explained who he was, the uncertain fate of his family, and his anxiety on their account. Fraser generously let him go on parole until the middle of November, when he was to be at Crown Point to go with the army and prisoners to Canada.

After thanking him, and just as he was leaving, he said: "General, suppose the army never returns, how then?" Fraser, smiling incredulously, said: "Then you are released from all obligation." And ordering him a supply of provisions for his journey, dismissed him. He now procured a boat and went to his house, which he found in ashes. After searching for any remains that might be left in case his wife and children had been burned in the house, he returned to the fort, where he procured a passage up the lake to Whitehall. Completely bewildered as to which way his family had gone, he was induced to believe they were in Connecticut, where he went but found they had not been there.

He returned and went in another direction, and after weeks of fruitless search had almost despaired of finding them.

One evening, weary and footsore, he called at a log house in Dorset for entertainment for the night. It was dark inside and a flickering light from the dying embers only rendered things more indistinguishable. He had just taken a seat when a smart little woman with a pail of milk came in and said: "Moses, can't you take the gentleman's hat?" That voice! He sprang towards her. "Agnes!" And she, with outstretched arms, "John, Oh John!" How quick the voice of loved ones strikes upon the ear, and vibrates through the heart!

That was a happy night in the little log house. The children came rushing in and each in turn received their father's caress. Smiles and tears mingled freely, for a father and husband was restored as from the dead.

VI. William Gilliland

THE flatlands and gentle hills of the Vermont side of the lake proved much more hospitable to the early settlers than the craggy western shore bordering the Adirondack wilderness. In time of danger the Vermont settlers could take comfort and refuge in the older New England settlements to the south and east, while northern New York remained a frontier yet to be conquered.

The earliest settler on the west shore was William Gilliland, an Irish soldier in the French and Indian War who obtained title to some 15,000 acres surrounding Willsboro. In 1765 he formed a company of settlers who left New York City in May and ascended the Hudson to Albany. From there part of the expedition fought its way up the rapids to Fort Edward in bateaux, and part drove 41 cattle overland to the head of Lake George, and from the foot of Lake Champlain to Crown Point, where they swam the channel to Chimney Point. Driven north on the Vermont side, they were ferried across the lake again beyond Split Rock and were there turned loose to browse in the forest.

The rest of the company arrived at the mouth of the Bouquet on June 8. After resting two days the pioneers ascended the stream to its first falls and there built a house 44 feet by 22, probably the first on the west shore between Crown Point and the border of Canada. After making a clearing they blazed a road to the mouth of the river, and with timber they had brought from the old French settlements to the south, constructed a sawmill powered by a wing-dam. "Game was abundant in the woods," notes Winston C. Watson, "the most delicious salmon thronged the stream . . . and beaver meadows yielded them sufficient hay for the winter."

Having married the daughter of a New York merchant, Gilliland was not destitute for funds. He went to Quebec for needed supplies, then in November returned to New York for the winter to make arrangements to bring his immediate family north the following spring. Those who remained at Milltown, as he called his new settlement, had trouble rounding up the cattle, which had become almost wild in the forests, but winter passed without undue hardship dragging logs to their mill and sawing them for the houses they intended to build. They drew their hay over the ice on the lake from a beaver meadow at Whallon's Bay (two miles southwest of Split Rock.) From there north to the Bouquet they built their cabins in the early spring.

Tragedy struck Gilliland near Stillwater on his way north in June; one of the bateaux carrying members of his family overturned and one of his daughters was drowned. Forging ahead with a heavy heart he arrived at Milltown and set to work at all the various tasks of an infant settlement — tending the sawmill, building a smithy, planting gardens, and, as proprietor, conducting the government of his far-flung estate. At its zenith it embraced some 30,000 acres and might have been further expanded to become a province had it not been for the advent of the Revolution and the departure of most of the settlers.

When they returned in 1784 they found that their fields, roads, and bridges had been reclaimed by the wilderness, and their houses laid waste by marauding war parties. Having originally spent large sums planting his colony, Gilliland now bore the burden of beginning anew without the funds to do it. Claims from antagonists seeking identical patents from the new government to lands he had purchased under the old forced him to sell additional lands to pay for the litigation.

Before long the once wealthy proprietor was reduced to poverty. Rebuffed by many who once sought his support and counsel, he became partly deranged and wandered into the forest. As he struck this way and that his hands and knees became deeply lacerated, his strength ebbed away, and the gloomy wilderness which he claimed, instead claimed him. Thus departed the pioneer of Essex County.

VII. A Traveler's Impressions

(Edited from *Travels Through North America*, 1796, by Isaac Weld)

WE set off about one o'clock, but from the channel being very narrow, it was impossible to make much way by tacking. We got no farther than six miles before sunset. We then landed and walked up to some farm houses on the Vermont shore to procure provisions, for the boatman had told us it was quite unnecessary to take in any at Skenesborough, as there were excellent houses close to the shore the whole way where we could get whatever we wished.

At first we went to a comfortable log house. Neither bread, nor meat, nor milk, nor eggs were to be had; the house was crowded with children of all ages and the people, I suppose, thought they had but little enough for themselves. At a second house we found a venerable old man at the door reading a newspaper, who civilly offered it to us for our perusal and began to talk upon the politics of the day. We thanked him for his offer and gave him to understand that a loaf would be much more acceptable. Bread there was none; we got a new Vermont cheese, however.

A third house now remained in sight and we made a third attempt at procuring something to eat. This one was nearly half a mile off but alas! It offered still less than the last; the people had nothing to dispose of but a little milk. With the milk and the cheese, therefore, we returned to our boat, and adding some biscuits and wine which we had luckily on board, the whole afforded us a frugal repast.

The people at the American farmhouses will cheerfully lie three in a bed rather than suffer a stranger to go away who comes to seek for a lodging. As all these houses were crowded with inhabitants we felt no great inclination to ask for accommodation at any of them, but determined to sleep on board our little vessel. We accordingly moored her at a convenient part of the shore, and each of us having wrapped himself up in a blanket we laid ourselves down to sleep.

The boat was decked two thirds of her length forward and had a commodious hold, but we preferred the cabin or after part, fitted up with benches and covered with a wooden awning, under which a man could just sit upright provided he was not very tall. The benches, which went lengthwise, accommodated two of us, and the third was obliged to put up with the cabin floor. But a blanket and a bare board out of the way of mosquitoes were luxuries after our accommodations at Skenesborough; our ears were not assailed by the noise even of a single one the whole night, and we enjoyed sounder repose than we had done for many nights preceding.

The wind remained nearly in the same point the next morning, but the lake being wider, we were enabled to proceed faster. We stopped at one house to breakfast and at another to dine. At neither of these, although they bore the name of taverns, were we able to procure much more than at the houses where we had stopped the preceding evening. At the first we got a little milk and about two pounds of bread, absolutely the whole of what was in the house; and at the second a few eggs and some cold salted fat pork; but not a morsel of bread was to be had. The wretched appearance also of this last habitation was very striking. It consisted of a wooden frame, merely with a few boards nailed against it, the crevices between which were the only apertures for the admission of light, except the door. The roof was so leaky that we were sprinkled with the rain even as we sat at the fireside.

That people who have the necessaries and conveniences of life within their reach, as much as any others in the world, can live in such a manner is really most astonishing! It is, however, to be accounted for by that desire of making money which is the predominant feature in the character of the Americans in general, and leads the farmer in particular to suffer numberless inconveniences. If he can sell the produce of his land to advantage, he keeps as small a part of it as possible for himself and lives the whole year round upon salt provisions, bad bread, and the fish he can catch in the rivers or lakes in the neighborhood. If he has built a comfortable house for himself he readily quits it as soon as finished, for money, and goes to live in a mere hovel in the woods till he gets time to build another. Money is his idol, and to procure it he gladly foregoes every self-gratification.

From this miserable habitation we departed as soon as the rain was over, and the wind coming round in our favour, we got as far as Ticonderoga that night. The only dwelling here is the tavern, a large house built of stone. On entering it we were shewn into a spacious apartment crowded with boatmen and people that had just arrived from St. John's in Canada. Seeing such a number of guests in the house we expected nothing less than to be kept an hour or two till sufficient supper was prepared for the whole company, so that all might sit down at once together, which is the custom in the country parts of the United States. Our surprise therefore was great at perceiving a neat table and a comfortable little supper speedily laid out for us, and no attempts made at serving the rest of the company till we had quite finished.

This was departing from the system of equality in a manner which we had never witnessed before, and we were at a loss for some time to account for it;

but we presently heard that the woman of the house had kept a tavern for the greater part of her life at Quebec, which resolved the knotty point. The wife is generally the active person in managing a country tavern, and the husband attends to his farm, or has some independent occupation. The man of this house was a judge, a sullen demure old gentleman who sat by the fire with tattered clothes and dishevelled locks, reading a book, totally regardless of every person in the room.

53. *A romanticized view of the ruins of Fort Ticonderoga, about 1820.*

The old fort and barracks of Ticonderoga are on the top of a rising ground just behind the tavern. They are quite in ruins and it is not likely that they will ever be rebuilt, for the situation is very insecure, being commanded by a lofty hill called Mount Defiance.

Early the next morning we left Ticonderoga and pursued our voyage to Crown Point, where we landed to look at the old fort. Nothing is to be seen there, however, but a heap of ruins; for shortly before it was given up by the British the powder magazine blew up, by which accident a great part of the works was destroyed. Since the evacuation the people in the neighborhood have been continually digging in different parts in hopes of procuring lead and iron shot. The vaults, which were bomb proof, have been demolished for the sake of the bricks for building chimneys. At the south side alone the ditches remain perfect; they are wide and deep, and cut through the top with different kinds of shrubs, have a grand and picturesque appearance. The view from this spot of the fort, and the old buildings in it overgrown with ivy, and of the distant mountains beyond the lake, is indeed altogether very fine.

Particularly beyond Crown Point the scenery is extremely grand. The shores are there beautifully ornamented with hanging woods and rocks, and the mountains on the western side rise up in ranges one behind the other in the most magnificent manner. It was on one of the finest evenings possible that we passed along this part of the lake, and the sun setting in all his glory behind the mountains spread the richest tints over every part of the prospect. The moon also appearing nearly in the full shortly after the day had closed, afforded us an opportunity of beholding the surrounding scenery in fresh though less brilliant colours.

Our little bark was now gliding smoothly along, whilst every one of us remained wrapt up in silent contemplation of the solemn scene, when suddenly she struck upon one of the shelving rocks. Nothing but hurry and confusion was now visible on board, everyone lending his assistance. At last she stuck so fast that for a short time we despaired of being able to move her. At the end of a quarter of an hour, however, we again fortunately got her into deep water. We had before suspected that our boatman did not know a great deal about the navigation of the lake, and on questioning him now, it came out that he had been a cobbler all his life, till within the last nine months, when he thought proper to change his business, and turn sailor. All the knowledge he had of the shores of the lake was what he had picked up during that time, as he sailed straight backward and forward between St. John's and Skenesborough. On the present occasion he had mistaken one bay for another, and had the waves been as high as they sometimes are, the boat would inevitably have been dashed to pieces.

The humble roof of another judge, a plain Scotch labourer, afforded us shelter for this night. It was near eleven o'clock, however, when we got there, and the family having retired to rest we had to remain rapping and calling at the door for half an hour at least before we could get admittance. The people at last being roused, opened their doors, cheerfully got us some supper, and prepared their best beds for us. In the morning, having paid our reckoning to the judge, he returned to his plough, and we to our boat to prosecute our voyage.

We set off this day with a remarkable fine breeze, and being desirous of terminating our voyage as soon as possible we stopped but once in the course of the day, and determined to sail on all night. A short time after sunset we passed the boundary between the British dominions and the United States. Here we were brought to by an armed brig of twenty guns under English colours, stationed for the purpose of examining all boats passing up and down the lake. The answers which we gave to the several questions asked being satisfactory, we were accordingly suffered to proceed. Since the surrender of

the posts, pursuant to the late treaty with the United States, this brig has been removed and laid up at St. John's.

When night came on we wrapped ourselves up in our blankets and laid down upon the cabin floor, where we might possibly have slept until we got to St. John's, had we not been awakened at midnight by the loud hollers of the sentinel at the British fort on Isle aux Noix. On examining into the matter it appeared that the boat had been driven on shore while our sleepy pilot enjoyed his nap at the helm. The sentinel, unable to imagine what we were about, seeing the boat run up close under the fort, and suspicious of some attack, had turned out the whole guard, by whom we were finally dismissed. We now took command of the boat upon ourselves, for the boatman was so sleepy that he could not keep his eyes open. Relieving each other at the helm, we reached St. John's by day-break, one hundred and fifty miles distant from Skenesborough.

VI

The Rising Passions of Trade.

❦

The Redcoats Come Again.

THE trickle of settlers to the North became a freshet. By 1810, 143,000 malcontents seeking cheap land and free air had bundled up their goods in the older states and pressed through the forests, over the ice, or through the waves to the shores and hinterlands of the Champlain Valley — the majority of them to the Vermont side.

Among the promising communities north of Whitehall (then rising from the ashes of Skenesborough) was Vergennes. By 1800 blast furnaces, forges, a wire factory, a rolling mill and fulling mill clustered around the falls at the head of navigation seven miles up the Otter. Much of the ore came from a mountain north of Crown Point.

Another bustling center of water power was Ira Allen's at the lower falls of the Winooski. During the late 1780's he built two saw mills there, one at each end of his dam; a grist mill, and two forges with a furnace for the manufacture of anchors and bar- and mill-iron. On the mill dam Allen's ferry shuttled back and forth between Colchester and Burlington, and below the falls he built a flat-bottomed schooner for trade with Quebec.

The river was so full of salmon, which came all the way from the Atlantic, up the St. Lawrence, Richelieu, and the lake to spawn, that they were caught at the falls with scoop-nets and barreled for export. Deer, beaver, muskrat, sable, and a few stray wolves from New York roamed a dense pine forest between the river settlement and that to the west at Burlington Bay. Early settlers killed three bears at the crest of the hill given by Allen for the establishment of the University of Vermont, and it was some time before their brethren ceased their wanderings across the rutted road between the settlements at the river and the Bay. Unexpected arrivals were rats from St. Jean aboard "Admiral" Gideon King's horse boat.

In February, 1790 Horace Loomis, one of Burlington Bay's early citizens, arrived with his family and their goods over the ice in five sleighs — having stopped the previous night near Crown Point.

"After waiting about half an hour for some *flip*," he recalled, "we took up our residence in a log house . . . on what is now Pearl Street, where we lived until the latter part of the same year, when we moved into the house occupied by Edward C. Loomis (on the corner of Pearl and Williams) which was raised on July 8th of the same year. All the people that could be got from Shelburne, Essex, Colchester, and Burlington were present at the raising; we had a good time, plenty of St. Croix rum, a barrel of which my father brought from Sheffield."

At this time only four buildings perched at the edge of the woods on the lake. A few logs fastened to the bank served as the first dock, but most lakemen anchored in deeper water, rolling their barrels of molasses overboard and floating them ashore.

The beginnings of any large city are almost exclusively of interest to its own citizens, unless some remarkable event interrupted the pedestrian events of the day. One of these, reported by Loomis, was the visit of Prince Edward, the father of Queen Victoria, in 1793.

He came in February from Quebec, where for some time he had command of a regiment. His trip through the country was accomplished in carryalls and sleighs. His first stopping-place in the states was at Chazy or Champlain in New York — thence on the ice to the Grand Isle, where he stopped the night preceding his arrival at Burlington, a courier having been sent there to make the necessary preparation for his accommodation.

There were not over seven framed houses in the whole village at that time, the forest being almost unbroken, except on Water Street, and the road leading easterly to the falls through what is now Pearl Street, and to the north. There was but one house of sufficient size to accommodate so large a company, the large oak-framed two-story dwelling just completed, and occupied by Phineas Loomis and family.

The Prince arrived in the afternoon with thirteen carryalls and sleighs, and left the third day after before noon. He had two aids and two body guards, a cook and a lady. His body guards slept by his door, and his cook prepared the provisions which they had brought with them. He parted with his lady or mistress at this place, she going to New York and he to Boston. They always conversed in French. He was very kind in his attention to her in parting; she was fixed nicely in the sleigh with an abundance of fur robes, the Prince tucking up the robes and placing the large dog at her feet. They parted very affectionately, to meet, as was understood, in the West Indies.

A little incident occurred in the passing of the Prince and his lady from the house to the sleigh, which illustrates somewhat the character and personality of the Prince. An awkward but stout fellow was standing in the path, not readily giving room for the prince and his lady to pass. The prince advanced, and taking him up bodily, set him on one side in the snow. He changed his teamsters at this place, dismissing those who brought him from Canada. He seemed quite worried while here, but it was a common saying of those who carried him to Boston that he was a jolly companion, enjoying the pork and beans and nutcakes and cheese as well as any of them.

Among the early settlers of the town was Col. Stephen Keyes, a gentleman of the old school, who wore a cocked hat, kept a hotel on Water Street, and was collector for the district of Vermont. He proposed to pay his respects to the Prince, and with several young gentlemen of the village made a call in the evening. Col. Keyes introduced himself to the prince, and then stated that he had brought with him some young gentlemen who wished to pay their respects to him. They were severally presented and the prince respectfully bowed to each; but what must have been their dismay when the prince and his aids informally and abruptly retired to their own apartments without deigning an apology or an explanation. The colonel could not brook this, and in unmeasured terms and unchosen phrases vented his indignation, and among the mildest of his expressions said the prince was "no gentleman."

At the risk of making the colonel instead of the prince the hero of the tale, an anecdote of the colonel should be told, which will illustrate the effect which this rebuff was likely to produce. Two or three British officers, with their dogs, stopped at the hotel kept by the colonel. It was a humble house, but its best and largest north room, kept in the nicest order with its clean sanded floor, was not an uninviting place for British officers to dine, and particularly on such a dinner as the colonel never failed to set for gentlemen. The officers with their dogs went in to dinner, and they soon began to feed them on the floor. The colonel looked upon it as an indignity, and bringing in a brace of loaded pistols, laid them formally on the table, and denouncing the conduct of the officers, swore he would protect the respectability of his house and was ready to do it.(Whether or not he did seems to have been left to the imagination of the reader.)

The granting in 1791 of the first patent in the United States (signed by George Washington and Thomas Jefferson) to Samuel Hopkins of Burlington for a process of making potash, served notice that the people were preoccupied, if not obsessed with, lumbering. Homesteaders were as likely to burn the wood from their pastures for potash, as to sell it for masts or for building. The value of first-growth white and Norway pine and oak flanking the rivers all the way to the mountains and blanketing the horizons, was incalculable, and the means of floating it to Canada was almost made to order. The Revolution had been fought, the umbilical cord to Canada and England had been severed, yet geography still decreed that the settlers in the Champlain Valley face to the north. The lake and their livelihood flowed that way.

The first raft of oak was floated to Quebec by Stephen Mallet of Colchester in 1794, and the first of Norway pine two years later by John Thorp of Charlotte. From that time until almost the last accessible tree had fallen, Champlain became a sluiceway of wood. Nearly a year was often required to assemble a raft. The trees had to be drawn to the river banks in winter, floated to the mills in the spring, processed in the summer, gathered in the fall as masts of logs, rough or square-hewn, and bound together to await spring high water in the Richelieu.

Parapets were erected on top of the rafts and loaded with staves and saw lumber, tents or a log cabin, and provisions for the crews. To prevent setting fire to their conveyance, clay for the foundation of cooking hearths was pounded down over the staves. Driven by sweeps or crude sails, the large undulating platforms at last began their tedious voyage to Quebec. Since each raft represented a large investment which might be lost in the spring flood over the Richelieu rapids, rafting was physically and financially a hazardous venture. Other than the elements, the lumbermen were at the mercy of Quebec middlemen, the relentless laws of supply and demand, inflation, and the scarcity of hard cash.

In a study of the economic bondage of the Champlain Valley and Canada between 1760 and 1815, H.N. Muller relates the rafting adventures of Guy Catlin of Burlington, who made "a full, if not entirely scrupulous, use of the troubled times of the embargo and the War of 1812 to make a fortune." In the spring of 1805 he left Burlington for St. Jean to supervise the passage of a Lamoille River raft during its critical descent of the Richelieu rapids and its delivery and sale at Quebec. Under the guidance of a hired pilot at St. Jean, the raft safely passed the rapids but "stove one crib of oak timber" when a west wind drove it against an island below them. It next ran afoul of another raft, and then of a "pious officer" who forbad Sunday labor — a problem "settled by one of the hands giving him a severe glazing." The swift-flowing St. Lawrence drove the raft against an island beyond Quebec, and Catlin waited weeks before he finally sold it.

Walter Crockett quotes the fantastic description in a New York newspaper of May, 1808 of huge rafts gathered on the lake at the boundary. "One was said to be nearly a half-mile long, carried a ball-proof fort, and was supposed to carry a cargo of wheat, potash, pork and beef, valued at three hundred thousand dollars or upward, being the surplus produce for a year. Moreover, this great raft was said to be manned by five hundred or six hundred armed men, prepared to defy customs officials. This report not only was untrue, but was absurdly untrue."

At least it served to dramatize the scope of the large northward trade in lumber and other commodities, and the frequent collision of presumably irresistible federal policies with the at-all-times movable objects of trade. In the light of self-preservation, the negotiations of the people of the Champlain Valley with the British, and their ceaseless smuggling regardless of the regulations of Washington, Quebec, or London, became credible if not strictly defensible.

It was a public and private affliction. During the Revolution Ethan and Ira Allen expropriated their brother, Levi, for being a Tory, yet after the war a brisk trade developed between Levi, who settled across the line in St. Jean, and Ira at Onion River. (In December of 1785 Levi contracted to deliver for Quebec firms 20,000 cubic feet of square oak timber, 10,000 of white oak pipe staves, and 150,000 square feet of white pine boards from the Champlain Valley.)

Haldimand, the governor-general of Canada, called the "Vermontese" a "profligate banditti" and so they were, if by that he meant individuals determined to guard their options at almost any cost. Guarding them required adroit footwork. In the three decades after 1783 the governments of the United States, Canada, and Britain vacillated between free trade and no trade and various stages between: winking at trade while ostensibly forbidding it, licensing some to conduct it while penalizing or convicting others; permitting it with Quebec but not for transshipment to England, or only for transshipment to England.

Many settlers chose to ignore these laws and to sell all the timber, pot- and pearl ash, horses, cattle, sheep, fish, cheese, grain, and tobacco they could on the Canadian market, in return for salt and manufactured goods from Europe. The most persistent smuggler, a non-resident but frequent visitor, was John Jacob Astor, whose traffic in furs became the foundation of his fortune. His

Burlington agent, "Admiral" Gideon King, fitted his 30-ton sloop, *Lady Washington*, with a false bulkhead, behind which an invaluable amount of illegal or semi-legal contraband escaped the eyes of the authorities.

Jay's Treaty of 1796, stipulating that the duties on goods entering Canada be no more than those for the same goods imported from England (with corresponding provisions for the United States) at first caused near panic on Lake Champlain, but after adjusting to it Yankees thrived, much to the dismay of the British. Merchandise that never sailed over the border before now enlarged the traditional list, and when the lake was frozen sleighs piled with goods from as far away as Boston crossed to Canada on the ice.

No customs house monitored or restrained this traffic before 1787, but the value of goods (at least those brought to the attention of the authorities) was recorded thereafter. In 1798, two years after the lifting of a Canadian embargo on furs imported directly to the United States, almost 10,000 pounds sterling worth of beaver, muskrat, martin, otter, racoon, deer, bear, fox, and mink traversed the Richelieu and the lake. By 1800 the figure rose to 32,000 pounds sterling and seven years later to 75,000. By this time many commodities other than lumber were flowing in the opposite direction: iron supplied by 23 forges in the Champlain Valley, paper from five mills, and wool and cotton of every description. By 1807 trade on the lake had risen to 200,000 pounds sterling.

The impressment of American vessels and their crews by the British and their repeated insults to American sovereignty induced President Jefferson to invoke the Embargo of 1807 which, with the inland provisions of March, 1808, prohibited any intercourse whatever with Canada. It struck the Champlain Valley like a twister, raising cries of outrage from St. Jean to Whitehall. Threatened with financial ruin, the people dealt with the Embargo (and subsequent measures to modify and reinstate it) in the usual manner; despite vigorous attempts at enforcement they largely ignored it.

The most convulsive event prior to the War of 1812 involved the clash of customs officers with the crew of a notorious smuggling vessel called the *Black Snake*. Its cargo, that precious substance yielded by the ashes from trees settlers burned to clear their lands, kept body and soul together during the critical interval before they could grow and sell their crops. A lively market for potash had developed in Canada and it arrived there despite every impediment. In remote places it traveled to the nearest "ashery" on the backs of the settlers, but near the lake it found a direct and convenient means of shipment. It was also the most important substance of politics. While Republicans were hobbled with Jefferson's Embargo, the farmers could count on Federalists to ignore their smuggling, hence their growing power in the Vermont legislature.

The lake's forested points and coves admirably served the potash traffic, and the open-decked *Black Snake,* 40 feet long, fourteen wide and four and a half deep, with seven oars on each side and a powerful and desperate crew to man them, became a peerless evader of the law. She had originally served as a ferry between Essex and Charlotte and was also equipped with a mast and sail, and with a rudder to maneuver her sharp prow and square stern. She had never been painted but was smeared with tar, hence her name. Her capacity of 100 barrels of potash earned her five or six hundred dollars a trip, at that time a most lucrative pay-load. To avoid trouble on the broad lake, her course lay along the east shore of St. Albans Bay to Maquam Creek. By shifting her load to smaller boats one and a half miles up that stream, she could float through a narrow straight to Charcoal Creek, and from there to the Missisquoi. The journey from the mouth of the river across Missisquoi Bay put her in Canada.

On one of her trips she was surprised by a customs officer who boldly stepped aboard and commanded her crew to surrender. The captain instead ordered his crew to bend their oars for Canada, with the result that the customs man arrived there with the ashes. After suffering this humiliation the district customs officer, Jabez Penniman (husband of the widow of Ethan Allen) put a prize crew aboard the revenue cutter, *Fly,* with orders to seize the *Snake* at all costs. At this time she was owned by two Canadians who had hired a tough navigator named Truman Mudgett to command her. He paid his crew ten dollars a trip and armed them with guns, three-foot clubs, large stones, pike-poles to fend off the revenue boats and, to cope with the worst of emergencies, a blunderbuss 8 feet 2 inches long carrying fourteen bullets in a barrel an inch and a quarter in diameter.

On the first of August, 1808 Daniel Farrington and his detachment of a sergeant and twelve privates learned that the *Snake* had left Canada the night before. Instead of the usual route, it had hugged the east shore of North Hero, hiding in a bay during daylight and proceeding in the darkness to Joy's Landing on the Onion River three miles from Burlington. Grounding the *Snake* about 60 rods above this place, Mudgett ordered that the guns be cleaned and oiled. (The crew, no doubt, also became well lubricated with a two-gallon jug of rum they had brought with them.) Mudgett then left to get provisions and ammunition. Upon his return at nightfall two men arrived with word that the *Fly* was coming and consequently they could not trust the *Snake* with their load of potash. When Mott showed them the blunderbuss, they offered ten gallons of rum for the capture of the revenue boat. Over the objections of two of his crew (now increased to ten by the enlistment of two others named Sheffield and Ledgard) Mudgett ordered that the night be spent "running bullets."

News of the *Fly's* arrival was no rumor. Having spent the night at the southern end of Hog Island west of Swanton, she was passing the Heroes when hailed by a man waving a handkerchief on shore. Revealing all the names of the smugglers aboard the *Snake,* he declared she had recently passed that way en route to Onion River. And that was where they found her, one end tied to some bushes on the bank and her crew on shore, armed to the teeth.

As she hove into view Mudgett warned her not to land but could not scare Farrington, who brought her alongside the *Snake.* "Don't lay hands on that boat," shouted Mudgett, retreating a few steps on shore and waving his gun. "I swear by god I will blow the first man's brains out who lays hands on her!"

With the *Fly's* brave crew proceeding, nonetheless, to board the *Snake,* Samuel Mott, one of Mudgett's men, rested the heavy barrel of the blunderbuss in the crotch of a tree and pointed it at Farrington. "Come on, boys," he cried. "Parade yourselves! You are all cowards! They are going to carry the boat off!" At the same time, according to later testimony, one of the *Snake's* two new recruits called out "in a Methodist tone of voice": "Lieutenant, prepare to meet your god! Your blood shall be spilt before you get out of the river!"

Despite this the revenue men kept rowing both boats, the smugglers following along the shore. Opposite Joy's Landing a gun was fired, and then a second, its bullet passing through the stern of the *Fly* within six inches of Farrington's legs. Several more salvos followed, and as Ellis Drake, one of Farrington's men, stepped back to take the *Fly's* tiller he was struck by two bullets and died instantly.

Farrington ordered his men not to return the fire but to run to the shore. Here he was met by Captain Jonathan Ormsby, a nearby resident, who demanded to know why Farrington did not arrest these outlaws. The two officers had just climbed the bank when Mott discharged the load of fourteen bullets, slugs, and buckshot from the blunderbuss. Pierced by five of them, Ormsby cried out: "Lord have mercy on me! I am a dead man!" So was Asa Marsh, one of Farrington's soldiers, who received two shots in his breast. Farrington fell gravely wounded with one shot through his left arm, another through his right shoulder, and a third grazing his forehead and lodging in his hat. Sergeant Johnson's men now rushed upon the smugglers and overpowered all of them except Mott and Josiah Pease, who escaped but were

TO THE PEOPLE OF VERMONT.

FELLOW CITIZENS,

IT IS DONE ! The cup of guilt is full ! Treason, rebellion and murder stalk abroad at noon-day ! Our land has been stained with the blood of our citizens, acting in defence of the government and laws of our country. By whom ? A foreign foe ? No : but, (horrid to relate !) by the bloody hands of domestic traitors.

Capt. JONATHAN ORMSBY, a respectable farmer, belonging to Burlington ; Mr. ELLIS DRAKE and Mr. ASA MARSH, two respectable young men, belonging to Capt. Pratt's company of militia, stationed at Windmill Point, were all killed at Burlington on Wednesday the 3d inst. about noon, in a most wanton and barbarous manner, by a party of insurgents, employed in smuggling potash into Canada, in violation of the laws. The Collector detached Lieut. Farrington, a sergeant and twelve men, in pursuit of a boat, which had gone up Onion river after a load of potash.—The Lieutenant found the boat and took possession of her, notwithstanding the insurgents threatened to blow out his brains if he attempted to meddle with her. The Lieutenant dropped down the river, with the cutter and the boat he had taken, about half a mile ; when the insurgents fired upon him and killed Drake. The Lieutenant then ordered both boats to be rowed on shore, near the place whence the fire proceeded : he landed with his men, and ascended the bank of the river ;—immediately the insurgents discharged a large gun, called a wall-piece, the barrel of which is eight feet in length, and was loaded with sixteen ounce balls, and some buck shot—which carried instant death to Captain Ormsby and Mr. Marsh, severely wounded the Lieutenant in the head, the left arm, and slightly wounded him in the right shoulder. Capt. Ormsby had been laboring in his field during the forenoon, near the fatal spot, was on his return to dinner, had just reached the place where the government troops entered the road, when the murderous discharge took place, which, at the same instant, sent two souls companions into eternity.

If any thing can add to the horror of this, too horrid scene, it is the observation of certain federal characters of the vicinity, who even lay claim to the name of high respectability, tending to screen the assassins, and throw the whole weight of guilt on the part of the government.——Says one, *The men were sent here by Penniman to steal an empty boat, and died like fools*—Says another, *I hope to God Penniman will be hung for it*—Says another, *I should care but little about it, if I did not fear it would influence the ensuing election*—Says another, on hearing of the melancholy event, *I am glad of it, if they are republicans who are killed*.——Such was the current of expression which poured from the mouths of federalism, while the blood was still gushing from the weltering bodies of our countrymen, murdered by federal hands at mid-day, within the boundaries of that town which boasts itself of being the strong hold of federalism, and some of whose principal merchants furnished the insurgents with powder and ball, for the express purpose of performing this bloody work.

The federalists now begin to lengthen their faces, and pretend to feel regret for the transaction ; but their hypocritical tears will not avail them. This horrid deed has been done by their procurement ; they are partners in the guilt of the perpetrators, and they are accountable to their country and their God, for all the blood that has been shed.

When a large body of men, and more especially those in the higher walks of life, who arrogate to themselves all the virtue, all the talents, and all the religion of the country, combine together for the purpose of opposing the laws of their country ; when they openly and publicly, by printing and speaking, treat the government and the officers of the government, from the President of the United States down to the lowest executive officer, with abuse, ridicule and contempt ; when they trample on the laws of their country, by daily exciting, both by precept and example, the violation of those laws by force and arms ; when they exult at the success of the insurgents in every act of treason they commit ; when they

bid defiance to government, and threaten the officers with assassination if they attempt to do their duty ; when with more than savage barbarity they exult over the bleeding bodies of our murdered citizens ; and when they even insult the faithful soldier while oppressed with grief at the loss of his beloved comrades :—then is the cup of guilt full ; then is it time TO ROUSE IN DEFENCE OF YOUR COUNTRY AND YOUR LIVES.

This is no ordinary contest. It is not a simple question, who shall be governor and councillors ; but it is a struggle for the existence of your government ; for the protection of those rights purchased with the blood of your fathers ; and for the protection of your lives. Should that faction whose hands are still reeking with the blood of your brethren, come into power, what have you to expect ? If they have done these things in the face of law, in the face of authority, what will they do when clothed with power ? This bloody scene is but an opening wedge to the measures they would pursue. The tragedy of Robespierre would be reacted in the United States ; and every distinguished character, who is a friend to his country, might expect to be sacrificed to the malice of an unprincipled and vindictive faction.

Fellow citizens, on you depends the fate of your country—by your suffrages at the approaching election, you will decide, whether you deserve the name of freemen ; whether you are worthy of your fathers ; whether you will defend the government of your country, and protect your wives, your children, and your own lives ; or whether you will tamely give up your dear bought rights, and submit your necks to the axe of the guillotine.

By supporting our present patriotic governor and councillors, you will perpetuate the existence of our government, and transmit to posterity the blessings we now enjoy.

By neglecting to attend the poll, or by voting for the federal ticket, you will entail on your country all the horrors of slavery, oppression and murder.

MONITOR

54. *Volcanic political scene is conveyed by a broadside of the "Black Snake" affair.*

later picked up. Cyrus Dean was recaptured soon after escaping through the window of the Burlington jail.

The violence of this drama in front of a flammable political backdrop caused consternation in this easy-going region. Smuggling may have been one thing but murder under any circumstances was a monstrous act. The funeral of the three men, attended by an excited crowd, served only to exacerbate the political warfare, the Republicans calling the Federalists protectors of the assassins, and the Federalists castigating the government for a raw display of force.

On August 23 the state supreme court assembled at Burlington, the eminent Chief Justice (and playwright) Royall Tyler declaring ". . . that some were ready to condemn the accused unheard, while others, perhaps were disposed to excuse, and if not to excuse, to palliate." He advised the grand jury that ". . . if, in some moments of levity, any of you have thought that the primary laws of society made for the preservation of human life ought on this occasion to be relaxed, and to be accommodated to certain supposed exigencies of the times, purify yourselves from these prejudices."

The grand jury returned a bill of indictment for murder against Mott, Mudgett, Dean, Pease, and four others. A political miasma suffused the trials, which resulted in verdicts of murder against Mott, Dean, and Sheffield, but in Dean alone being sentenced to be hanged on October 28. After a respite of two weeks granted by the governor, he was conducted to the court house to hear a sermon, and then to the crest of the hill, where 10,000 people had gathered around the scaffold. Displaying "a hardihood and careless uncon-cern perhaps never equalled in this part of the country" he breathed his last at 3:00 p.m.

Since the jury could not agree in the case of Mudgett he was discharged. Mott and Sheffield were granted new trials. Convicted of manslaughter, they were sentenced to stand one hour in the pillory, to receive 50 lashes on their bare backs, and to be confined 10 years in the state prison. Ledgard received almost the same sentence but the governor saw fit to pardon him three years later — and, subsequently, both Sheffield and Mott.

The *Black Snake* affair demonstrated that trade can be mightier than the pen and the sword. If Jefferson's Embargo was an act of national desperation it was also one of futility; nothing short of a cordon of troops all the way from Lake Memphremagog to the St. Lawrence could plug the vast sieve of the Canadian border.

Consider Missisquoi Bay, part of which lies in Quebec. The embargo of course had nothing to do with vessels passing from one Canadian port to another, but if they sailed from the northern shores of Missisquoi Bay to St. Jean they had to enter the United States, thus presenting smugglers with a loophole as big as all outdoors. Not that they had to bother with circuitous routes. Anchoring just south of the boundary, smugglers would abandon ship and then cut her cable, allowing their contraband to drift over the border by itself, so that only nature could be caught in the act. Friendly Canadian hands would see to it that the boat reached its destination.

Nicholas Muller writes that "John Banker, Jr., an enterprising New Yorker, was alleged to have obtained a commission to fit out a privateer on Lake Champlain. A small sailboat armed with only three muskets, the phony privateer *Lark* would wait just off Rouses Point near the border and 'over-power' vessels laden with cargoes for the Canadian market. The property, forcibly captured by an armed privateer, came under the authority of international law, legally beyond the reach of revenue officers. A prize crew then sold the cargoes in Canada at a price pre-arranged by its original owners. Mr. Banker returned the money to the owners, reserving a percentage for himself."

Wharves were purposely built astride the boundary so that Americans could unload their goods in the United States, and Canadians, out of reach of the U.S. Customs, reload them on their boats docked in Canada. Although all merchandise imported legally or otherwise was presumably recorded in Quebec, much of it must have escaped their ledgers, for it often passed over back roads or through the woods even more readily than on the water.

In the winter of 1808 and '09, 100 sleigh loads were said to have crossed through Swanton to Canada every day for fifteen days. Cattle driven to the border ambled over it by themselves with a little inducement. The name Smuggler's Notch, Mount Mansfield's remote and awesome ravine, was not bestowed in a flight of fancy; untold contraband, four-legged and otherwise, traversed it in both directions. In the year of the Embargo, trade passing through St. Jean, then the only inland port of entry to Canada, increased 31 percent over 1807. It more than doubled in 1809 and gained another 41 percent in 1810. Even during the embattled years that followed, the Richelieu continued to deliver to the St. Lawrence Valley a king's ransom in spars and planks, while by land cattle were described as pressing through the forests like herds of buffalo.

In this manner local Americans and their Canadian neighbors tried to adjust — if smuggling could be called that — to a growingly ominous international scene. Yet events would again prove that they could no more maintain their course than their sloops in the teeth of a northeaster out of the Canadian maritimes. France had gone to war with Austria in 1791, and two years later, with her ancient adversary across the channel. England in turn had descended upon America's fledgling fleet of traders to the French West Indies. Jay's Treaty temporarily restitched some old wounds, but with Britain determined to prevent neutrals from trading with France the family feud again burst forth. By electing Federalists New Englanders thought they could loosen the Republican tourniquet on their seacoasts, but as it turned out no local or national antidote or party palliative could prevent an unwanted war, which was declared on June 18, 1812, principally as the result of a tightened British blockade of American shipping. Actually the government had but three options: to allow maritime New England to atrophy by keeping its ships out of the Indies, to swallow the country's pride by letting them trade and risking their loss to the British Navy, or to declare war.

Although the Champlain Valley historically had the most to lose by invasion, the position of the local Federalists was to keep on trading and to fight only if the Redcoats actually sailed up the lake. In 1813 Vermonters elected a Federalist legislature by the narrowest of margins, and a governor, Martin Chittenden, committed to walking a tightrope perilously suspended between local autonomy and national monomania. The spectacle of wilful Federalist libertarians feeding the British army with Vermont and New York beef and supplying oak and pine spars for British ships hardly attested to their patriotism. Neither did the intransigence of the New England states, all of which (except Vermont) joined in the Hartford Convention to consider secession from the Union. Only in terms of the rampantly individual and sectional loyalties of the day does such behavior become rational. The adhesive of nationalism may have been applied, but would take a long time to set.

Since there were as many or more old fashioned Republican patriots as there were Federalists in the Champlain Valley, it became almost hopelessly fractured in its preparation for war. While the governor-elect of Vermont was determined to have as little as possible to do with it, his own brother-in-law, Colonel Isaac Clark, an Eleventh U.S. Infantry colonel known as "Old Rifle," appeared in Burlington in 1812 to purchase for the federal government 10 strategic acres on the bluff as a headquarters for the northern army, and for the defense of the harbor.

History repeated itself on September 12 of that year when Thomas Macdonough, an already distinguished 28-year-old naval veteran, arrived on horseback from Portland, Maine to supervise the building of a fleet (it had been only 36 years since Benedict Arnold had shouldered the same burden). Nor did Macdonough have much more than his predecessor to work with: two small gunboats built in 1809, which he found rotting with wide-open seams at Basin Harbor, near the mouth of Otter Creek. While fitting out two of the lake's sloops, the *Hunter* and *Bulldog* as gunboats, he seems to have commandeered a third, the *President,* as a flagship. Later he acquired a fourth sloop, *Rising Sun,* which he renamed the *Preble,* and a steamboat on the stocks, the *Ticonderoga,* which he refitted as a schooner — a "forlorn looking squadron" he called it as he sailed into Shelburne Harbor for the winter.

In February fifteen ship carpenters arrived from New York. As soon as the ice melted, gun carriages, carronades, and ammunition from New York were forwarded to Shelburne from Whitehall, enabling the *Growler* and *Eagle* (renamed from *Hunter* and *Bulldog)* to sail out of the harbor armed with a total of 38 guns. Meanwhile troops had collected at Burlington and at Plattsburgh, which for three decades had been the western shore's chief port. An advance from Plattsburgh to the Canadian border in the fall of 1812 had ended ignominiously when Americans mistakenly attacked each other. General Henry Dearborn then marched his 5,000 troops across the ice to spend the winter on the bluff in Burlington. The sallies of Zebulon Pike, one of his officers, against civilian and even military smugglers appear to have availed him little. These people, despaired the explorer, were "void of all sense of honor or love of country."

The Valley's first skirmishes took place in June of 1813 when, against Macdonough's advice, his deputy, Lt. Sidney Smith, chased three gunboats down the Richelieu. After finding the enemy fortifications at Isle Aux Noix too strong, his sloops turned around to beat their way back against a swift current and strong wind. They were now at the mercy of the British land battery, which after firing several hours, succeeded in putting one 24-pound shot through the *Eagle's* bow and hull, sinking her in shallow water, and another through the *Growler's* mast. The sloops' entire complement of 112 men, one of whom was killed and nineteen wounded, was shipped off to Montreal and Halifax. Despite taking considerable punishment themselves the British emerged from this encounter with the two American sloops, which were repaired and renamed, for the third time, *Broke* and *Shannon.*

Meanwhile Macdonough, whose good judgment it had been to avoid entrapment in the Richelieu, had the misfortune of grounding the *President* in the lake. Although he managed to free her and return her to Burlington with two gunboats, he could thus far claim little progress in complying with orders from the secretary of the navy that he was upon no account "to suffer the enemy to gain the ascendancy on Lake Champlain."

The gravity of an almost defenseless lake in the path of a British army in

Canada rumored to number 6,000 now finally began to dawn on the people of the valley. Fifty-seven of Burlington's most prominent citizens organized themselves into a corps commanded by two captains, one of whom, interestingly enough, was Guy Catlin, the veteran trader with Quebec. Troops from in and out of state continued to arrive at the battery, which was fortified with a parapet containing thirteen embrasures. By the first of August over four thousand men were bivouacked there under the command of General Wade Hampton (grandfather of the Confederate army officer). By this time Macdonough had acquired three more sloops to replace the *Growler* and *Eagle*, and was beseeching New York for armament and for seasoned sailors, whom Arnold had found just as hard to find in 1776.

Protected by the guns on the battery Macdonough's sloops were still being fitted out when, at the end of July, the British crossed the border with 1400 troops and marines aboard 47 bateaux, three gunboats, and the two captured sloops, *Broke* and *Shannon*. After destroying a blockhouse, arsenal, and armory near Plattsburgh and sacking other public and private storehouses

55. Although the British were expected to invade the New York side of the lake, troops were also stationed on the Vermont border. View on the Tyler farm, Highgate, was painted in 1814.

56. Macdonough by Thomas Lincoln (after Gilbert Stuart).

worth more than $200,000, they started for Burlington. When they appeared on August 2 and began a cannonade a mile and a half from shore, only one of Macdonough's sloops and two small gunboats were ready for duty, but these joined the guns on the battery in an answering salvo. The British then withdrew to the south, destroying four small sailing vessels and returning to Canada with two ferryboats and a small sloop loaded with flour. On their way they landed in Swanton and burned the barracks built along the green for troops (absent at the time of the raid) who had been enforcing the revenue laws.

Macdonough was now invited, if not commanded, by General Hampton to accompany the army in an attack against St. Jean which (with the loss of the *Growler* and *Eagle* starkly in mind) he declined to do for the time being. Rather, he spent his energies at Burlington beefing up his fleet. By October it comprised, other than the flagship *President,* four other well-armed sloops and four gunboats. Although it still hardly qualified as a fleet it was all he had to reinforce Hampton's fruitless sorties against the forts in the lower Richelieu late in the fall.

The year 1813 must certainly have been viewed in New England and on Lake Champlain with something less than pride. While Americans in the West were winning notable victories on land and water, particularly that of Captain Oliver Perry on Lake Erie, the local scene was one of stagnation. Smuggling continued unabated, and the forays of the regular army across the border and back reflected upon their generals an ineptitude bordering on the farcical. The third brigade of the third division of the Vermont militia had hardly crossed the lake to help shore up defenses north of Plattsburgh than Governor Chittenden ordered them home on the grounds that they had left Vermont's own frontier, in his words, "exposed to the retaliatory incursions and ravages of an exasperated enemy." He declared that Vermont's military forces should be reserved exclusively for its own defense "excepting in cases provided for by the Constitution of the United States, and then, under orders derived *only* from the Commander-in-Chief."

To which the indignant officers of the Third Brigade in Plattsburgh wrote a stinging rejoinder, calling his "insidious" proclamation "a gross insult to the officers and soldiers in the service," and "unwarranted stretch of executive authority issued from the worst motives, to effect the basest purposes. It is in our opinion a renewed instance of that spirit of disorganization and anarchy which is carried on by a faction to overwhelm our country with disgrace."

They declared it their duty, when ordered into the service of the United States, to march to any section of the Union. "We are not of that class who believe that our duty as citizens or soldiers are circumscribed within the narrow limits of the Town or State in which we reside, but that we are under the paramount obligation . . . to the great Confederation of States." Therefore they declared they would not obey his order to return, but would continue in the service of their country until legally and honorably discharged. There was nothing the governor, who was convinced that peace ought to replace "a protracted, expensive, and destructive war," could do about the defiant brigade, which remained until cold weather ended the threat of an invasion in 1813.

The northern army then returned to its winter encampment around the Burlington battery, occupying also the main four-story building of the University of Vermont. As usual winter proved more sinister than the enemy; over 2300 soldiers fell sick and 74 died.

To escape frigid northwest winds sweeping across the harbor off 25 miles of broad lake, Macdonough's squadron sailed south to take refuge below the falls at Vergennes, seven miles up the winding Otter Creek, where the British could not easily pursue him. After ice sealed the river below the sheltered basin he became less preoccupied with defense than with forging there in the spring the foils to drive the British lion back to the furthest reaches of his northern lair.

✿❦❧✿

1814 began as ominously as 1777, the year of Burgoyne's visit. There was little question that as soon as the ice vanished under the climbing sun the British would be back again. And all that stood in their way was Macdonough's covey of sloops beneath the Vergennes waterfall. That a new fleet could be conjured up in a few months was a most visionary assumption, yet on January 28 President Madison ordered that fifteen gunboats, or a ship and three or four gunboats be built as quickly as possible. Although Macdonough had served before the mast of navy ships and merchantmen since he was sixteen and learned as much about them in and out of battle as any admiral, it must have seemed to him that Washington's instructions bordered on fantasy.

His task seems a little less preposterous if "nature's handmaid to industry," the falls of the Otter, even then serving a surprising cluster of waterwheels, are taken into account. Charcoal and iron ore for the furnaces and forges were as plentiful as lumber for the up-and-down sawmills. Shipwrights were not, but Macdonough succeeded in securing one of the best, Noah Browne of New York, who agreed to launch at Vergennes a 24-gun ship in no less than 60 days. Since construction could not begin until early spring, and the ice would not leave the lake's Narrows perhaps until April, many supplies would have to come by land, despite all but impassable roads.

Somehow the supplies did come — 80 heavily-loaded transport wagons in one consignment alone from Troy. Others freighted with shot (adding to the 177 tons that the local forges managed to produce) arrived from Boston, as did a single anchor weighing 3,000 pounds. General Alexander Macomb, the new commander at Burlington, sent 400 Vermont militia, few of them of much use at the shipyard. In five and a half days after March 2, however, 110 men felled and forwarded to the basin enough lumber for three ships. On March 7 they laid the keel of the 734-ton brig *Saratoga* and launched her 40 days after her timbers were standing in the neighboring woods!

Since news of such activity could not be kept secret, the shipyard became vulnerable, not to British raids upriver, but to the sinking of ships loaded with

57. Mid-nineteenth century view of the basin at Vergennes which had changed little since Macdonough built the American fleet there in 1814.

rocks at the entrance to the channel. General Macomb therefore prevailed upon Governor Chittenden to call out 1000 more local militia for the river's protection. As soon as a battery was erected at its mouth, regular troops arrived from Plattsburgh to replace the militia, except for a Panton company which was ordered to rally to an alarm of three heavy guns fired in quick succession from the battery.

This precaution was taken none too soon. On May 9 Captain Daniel Pring sailed out of the Richelieu on His Majesty's 16-gun brig, *Linnet,* accompanied by five sloops and thirteen galleys. As word of his presence raced through the valley citizens gathered to run bullets and do whatever else they might for their protection. Fifty artillerymen were rushed from Burlington to help defend the Otter Creek battery, where naval lieutenant Stephen Cassin stood ready with an assortment of troops manning seven 12-pounders on ship carriages that Macdonough placed there.

As it approached Charlotte on its way up the lake one of the smaller vessels of the British squadron passed near the home of Charles McNeil, the owner of the Essex ferry. He is reported to have "called to the captain and asked if he was about to fire on unarmed and defenseless people, to which question no attention was paid. McNeil then directed his family and neighbors to lie down, which they did. A charge consisting of twelve 2-pound balls was fired. The height of the bank and the proximity of the vessel to the shore compelled the British gunner to aim so high as to carry the balls over McNeil's house, although they grazed the top of the bank and cut off a small poplar over the heads of the prostrated spectators. The balls were found in his meadow at the next haying. Two other charges were fired, one of which went through his horse barn. The drunken commander, being put under arrest by the commander of the flotilla, excused his brutal assault upon women and children on the pretense that he saw soldiers in uniform on the bank."

Arriving two and a half miles off the mouth of the Otter on May 14, the British fired on Fort Cassin for an hour and a half, upending one of its guns and injuring two men. By the time some of Macdonough's ships had arrived downriver from the basin, the battery's defenders apparently had inflicted enough damage on several British galleys so that the whole enemy squadron withdrew to the Four Brothers Islands. From there, after being joined by two galleys that had tried unsuccessfully to raid a gristmill on the Bouquet River, they departed for Canada.

Few doubted that this was just a sample of what was to come, and preparations ashore and afloat now went forward in earnest. On May 26 Macdonough was able to leave the shipyard with his new 26-gun *Saratoga*, the 120-foot-steamboat-turned-schooner, *Ticonderoga*, sixteen guns, the sloop *Preble*, nine guns, and six gunboats each with two guns. The previous flagship *President* and the sloop *Montgomery*, with ten and six guns respectively, and four more 75-foot gunboats joined the fleet later. On August 11 a second large brig, the *Eagle*, was launched an astounding seventeen days after her keel was laid at Vergennes.

A comparison of the size of these brigs, excelled only by a few vessels of the class of the *Constitution*, indicates the magnitude of Macdonough's feat. Charles H. Darling, a Burlingtonian and assistant secretary of the navy early in this century, confirmed that the *Eagle* was "substantially the same size as Perry's flagship on Lake Erie, while the *Saratoga* was much superior to Perry's largest vessel. The time in which Perry built his ship has often been mentioned in praise and wonder, but Macdonough's ships were not only of larger tonnage but were built and completed in a shorter time."

At St. Jean the British were also building a fleet in an atmosphere as contentious as that which plagued them during the French wars and the Revolution. Least among their difficulties was a dearth of troops; no less than

15,000 veterans of Wellington's illustrious army arrived in Canada during the summer, joining as many more already under the command of Lt. General Sir George Prevost. Unlike Burgoyne's grandiose invasion to subdue the northern states, Prevost's mission was to insure the protection of Canada by destroying American naval power on the lake. Simultaneous campaigns by land and water would be necessary, and therein lay his dilemma. As Waldo F. Heinrichs observes in his study of the British side of the war, there was trouble with the navy.

In order to produce ships Prevost had to do business with the admiralty, which was jealous of the army and vice versa. Although Prevost outranked the commanding naval officer in Canada, the approval of Captain Sir James Yeo was needed for naval requisitions. Yeo claimed that his own problems on the Great Lakes had priority. Therefore his local deputy, Captain Daniel Pring, could not start a shipbuilding program at St. Jean until February of 1814. Lack of coordination cost Prevost and Pring an irretrievable opportunity to capture the American fleet in May when it was still on the river at Vergennes. Instead, Pring had merely fired on Fort Cassin from a distance and withdrawn. That, Pring asserted, was Prevost's idea; his own plan had been to destroy Macdonough's fleet, but Prevost had wanted to wait until the British squadron was large enough to accompany his troops. Nonsense, declared Prevost, Pring had just bungled the mission. And so it went.

When the *Saratoga* appeared on the lake the British realized they were behind in this "race with the adze," and that they needed a ship of the same class, or better. To complement the *Linnet,* Pring had been counting on the frame of a brig shipped from England, but when it arrived he found it would draw too much water for shallow bays — a blunder exposed in the House of Commons as one of the most extraordinary in the annals of naval affairs. At later than last minute Pring began construction at St. Jean of a 37-gun frigate, the largest then (or ever) on Lake Champlain. Despite a shortage of shipwrights and trained seamen (because of the demands of Yeo's naval program on Lake Ontario) Pring managed to scrape together 200 sailors by the time the *Confiance* was launched, and 70 soldiers to fill her complement of 270.

Although the *Confiance* was still unfinished when Captain George Downie arrived on September 1 to command the British squadron, he set valiantly to work completing her fittings, a task he could not have hoped to accomplish without the masts, spars, and tar supplied by Vermont smugglers. At the end of June two spars were seized as they floated toward the border, presumably destined to become the foremast and mizzenmast of the *Confiance;* and three weeks later, a large raft loaded with planks, spars, and 27 barrels of tar.

Although the raft was impounded a mile from the border, and its crew turned over to the authorities for trial "on charge of furnishing succor to the enemy," the British managed to secure the spars by sending out detachments of marines from Isle Aux Noix. Largely on the strength of help from the smugglers, General Prevost decided to invade New York rather than Vermont. So much for the "traitorous and diabolical" smuggling traffic, as the *Burlington Sentinel* called it.

Just as callous, however, was the action of the War Department in Washington. With a British army of 10,000 ready to cross the border any minute, 4,000 of the American troops defending Plattsburgh were ordered to the Niagara frontier, despite the warning of General George Izard (who had replaced Wade Hampton) that everything north of Plattsburgh would be in enemy hands within three days of his departure. Little wonder the British thought they had nothing to fear from a succession of vanishing American generals. Warnings of the consequences of Washington's game of military musical chairs went unheeded and Izard marched away, leaving only 1500 regular troops to defend the west shore of the lake. No sooner had he left than the British occupied the town of Champlain just as he predicted. Thus the American cause rested more than ever with Macdonough's instant navy, then patrolling the northern New York shore.

A captivating glimpse of life on the *Saratoga* during the lull before the storm appears in the account of John H. Dulles, a Yale student from Philadelphia who had received from a Burlington friend a note of introduction to Macdonough.

My letter being delivered to the commander of the squadron, I received an invitation to dine and spend the day on board the flagship on the following Sunday. That was the 4th of September, a week before the battle of Lake Champlain. At the appointed hour the Commodore's gig was ready at the landing, and I found a companion for the trip, the chaplain of the army stationed at this military post, but who, for very obvious reasons, preferred to exercise his function aboard the ship rather than among the soldiers. At noon divine services were performed, the commander and officers being seated on the quarter-deck, the chaplain at the capstan, and the crew, about 300 men, occupied the room from midships to the bow. All was orderly, and not only the officers, but the crew, showed such marked attention that I expressed my surprise to the Commodore. He replied, "The men do behave well, but you must not be deceived by an inference that it is from pious feelings altogether," adding with a smile, "there are other considerations controlling their conduct."

I passed some time with the younger officers nearer my own age, and was struck with the palpable evidence of the one pervading spirit of a master mind that ruled in that mass of volatile young men and the rude, man-of-war sailors. The cock, so celebrated in the history of the battle for flying up to the yard-arm and crowing lustily throughout the engagement, attracted my attention while he paraded the deck. To my simple question addressed to a little group of midshipmen, "What do you think about the coming battle?" a young fellow replied, very modestly, "We know the British force to be superior to ours, but we will do our duty." There was at that fearful moment a calm, resolute composure in every word and on every face that assured me that all would be well.

Retiring to the cabin, Commodore Macdonough conversed with the singular simplicity and with the dignity of a Christian gentleman on whose shoulders rested the weightiest responsibility that bore on any man in that period of our history. The conflict, inevitably to occur within a few days, was to decide the most important issues of the war. With the destruction of the American squadron on Lake Champlain, the British army was sure to make its way unobstructed to Albany, possibly to New York, and probably dictate the terms of an ignominious peace. That army, composed of 14,000 picked soldiers, fresh from victories in Spain and at Waterloo, commanded by a picked officer, the governor general of Canada, was on its march southward, supporting and being supported by the naval force on the lake.

M'DONOUGH's SHIP

Macdonough was then 31 years of age, but seemingly several years younger, of a light and agile frame, easy and graceful in his manners, with an expressive countenance, remarkably placid ... The confidence of his officers and men in him was unbounded, and such as great leaders only can secure. While awaiting the dinner hour he entered into conversation on religious services in the navy, and, among other things, remarked that he regarded the Epistle of St. James as peculiarly adapted to the sailor's mind; the illustrations drawn from sea life — such as "He that wavereth is like a wave of the sea driven with the wind," and "Behold the ships, though so great, are turned about with a very small helm. . . ."

At dinner a blessing, being invited, was offered by the chaplain, and it appeared to be no unusual thing. A considerable number of the officers attached to the other vessels were present by invitation, as I was told, given in rotation. In the midst of the meal the Commodore, calling attention, said, "Gentlemen, I mean the sailor gentlemen, I am just informed by the commander of the army that the signs of advance by the British forces will be signalled by two guns, and you will act accordingly."

He retired from the table early and the conversation became more unrestrained, and when one of the lieutenants enforced some remark with an oath, an officer sitting near him immediately exclaimed, "Sir, I am astonished at your using such language. You know you would not do it if the Commodore was present." There was a dead pause, and a seeming acquiescence in the propriety of the rebuke, severe as it was. At the close of the day the strangers were brought on shore and the men of the squadron left in hourly expectation of a battle.

The invasion of Isle La Motte by a vanguard of British gunboats on September 3 met the conditions under which even hard-core Federalists declared they would fight. Except for out-and-out Tories, Vermonters of every stripe abandoned their fields and counting houses and headed for the lake, crowding aboard anything that would float.

To reach Plattsburgh more quickly, volunteers from St. Albans, Georgia, and Milton forded the sand bar from the latter town to the islands. Sheldon responded with a company organized and led by a minister. In Middlebury a public appeal for $295 provided ammunition for three detachments. Shoreham blacksmiths worked night and day to equip a cavalry company. The September 9, 1814 *Burlington Sentinel* apologized for a one-page issue on the grounds that every able-bodied male had gone to war.

Just getting there proved half the battle for some of the volunteers. Rather than cross St. Albans Bay, Jonathan Blaisdell, a house-builder, and two companions, Gadcomb and Walbridge, set out on horseback for the sand bar to South Hero. Blaisdell complained he did not like going to sea on horseback, but after bolstering their nerve at Fox's Tavern on the Milton side, the three started for the long bar.

"The wind blew strong from the north," Blaisdell recalled, "but Gadcomb thought he could cross without difficulty, though the swells ran so high and dashed so upon the shore. We urged our horses in without difficulty and proceeded till we saw a light upon the opposite shore, which we supposed had been lighted to pilot us across. About half way over, the water began to deepen, the swells from the north rolling hard against us, till our horses, drifting off the north side of the bar, were afloat. Gadcomb undertook to swim his horse forward to the shore. Walbridge, behind, said his horse wanted to turn round and go back. My horse stood right up and down — in no swimming condition."

At this point the last two horses decided that discretion was the better part of valor and returned their riders to the shore where they entered. "We repeatedly hallooed, and receiving no answer from any quarter, supposed Gadcomb was drowned, and started to go back to the tavern, but on our way through the swamp, we heard somebody halloo, and answered. The halloo was kept up back and forth till we found it was Gadcomb, who had swum ashore on the point below us and landed in the most dismal part of the swamp. We waited till he came up to us, when we all returned to the tavern wet as water could make us, and remained about two hours till the moon was up and about a hundred had collected to cross; so that when we crossed, which at length was nicely done, the line of them reached clear across the bar.

"After we got over we went up to the old landlord who kept a tavern on South Island, where we stayed the remainder of the night. The landlord stated he hoped we should get whipped by the British, and that all would get off the bar who attempted to cross. This raised my ideas, and I told him we should hear no such talk on our route, that we were going to Plattsburgh to fight for our country, and we could fight before we got there, if necessary. The effect was enough to stop that Tory's noise. We went down the next morning and waited for a sloop to take us across. About 2 o'clock p.m. the sloop arrived and took us over to Plattsburgh. This was Wednesday."

Two days later, on September 10, General Samuel P. Strong of Vergennes (the son of the Revolutionary veteran) informed Governor Chittenden that 1812 Vermont militia had reported to him at Plattsburgh. Twenty-four hours later a total of 2500 had arrived, more than the regular troops and the New York militia combined. Even so, the British land forces, consisting of 10,467 officers and men (9,500 of them infantry) still outnumbered the Americans two to one. Having covered the 22 miles between the border and Plattsburgh against minor opposition, this formidable army had stopped at the Saranac River where, on an elevated plain above the opposite bank between the river and the lake, General Macomb's determined and well-deployed Yankees awaited a dubious fate.

With the exception of Champlain's battle with the Iroquois and Arnold's desperate encounter at Valcour, the events of September 11, 1814 proved more fateful than any in the history of the lake, and almost as crucial to the destiny of the Union. Because of the wider use of the printing press and the reporting of every small detail by participants, the Battle of Plattsburgh appears in fuller dimensions than its predecessors. Peter Palmer in his history of the lake, and Admiral Mahan and Theodore Roosevelt, among others, in their tactical analyses have explored every aspect ashore and afloat. It is enough to stress in this narrative that the fate of two vastly unequal land armies depended primarily upon the strength of their navies.

Like Macdonough with his *Saratoga* and *Eagle,* the commander of the British fleet had performed a near-miracle in getting the *Confiance* ready for battle — or at least more nearly ready. Since carpenters were still at work on her magazine when she left St. Jean on September 7, she had to tow a bateau loaded with powder. Pitch oozed from the green planking of her decks. Carronade gun locks had to be fitted to her long cannon, since their firing mechanisms had not arrived from Quebec. When she emerged from the Richelieu after grounding briefly on a shoal, 25 carpenters were still at work fitting belaying pins, cleats, and breaching bolts. As late as the 9th she was still taking aboard marines and soldiers who, as it turned out, had just one day to learn their battle stations. Cryptic messages passing between Prevost and Downie, the former demanding the flotilla's immediate assistance and the latter sparring for more time, affirm that the army and admiralty were still indulging in their own prerogatives.

But despite their reverses the British had produced the stronger fleet: sixteen vessels aggregating 2402 tons, manned by 937 and carrying 92 guns, compared to the Americans' 2244 tons, 882 men, and 86 guns. These totals do not include the sloops *President* and *Montgomery,* which Macdonough was not able to use (the former had been damaged in a storm and the latter had to serve as a troop transport). The disparity between the largest ships was critical; the 1200-ton *Confiance* outweighed the *Saratoga,* and, excelled in fire power with her gun-deck of a heavy frigate carrying 27 long 24-pound guns, four 32-pound carronades, and six 24-pounders. The other British ships were the 350-ton brig *Linnet,* the two large sloops (originally *Hunter* and *Bulldog)* captured from the Americans the previous year (renamed for the fourth time, *Chubb* and *Finch)* and seven gunboats. Macdonough's sole advantage consisted of the combined batteries of the *Saratoga* and *Eagle,* which outweighed those of the *Confiance* and *Linnet.*

When the British rounded Cumberland Head in a modest northeast breeze on the clear cool Sunday morning of September 11 and saw the American flotilla anchored in a northeasterly line across Plattsburgh Bay about one mile from the American army on the heights, it must have occurred to Downie that Macdonough was no novice. Having all but bottled-up the harbor, he had correctly calculated that for the British to get into position to fight they would first have to face the wind that had brought them around the point, and then lose part of it in the lee of Cumberland Head. The southern entrance to the harbor was restricted by the shoals off Crab Island, and that to the north inside

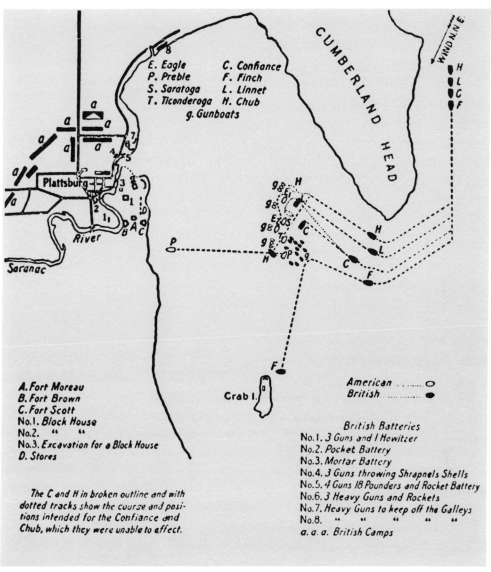

E. Eagle   C. Confiance
P. Preble   F. Finch
S. Saratoga   L. Linnet
T. Ticonderoga H. Chub
     g. Gunboats

A. Fort Moreau
B. Fort Brown
C. Fort Scott
No. 1. Block House
No. 2. "   "
No. 3. Excavation for a Block House
D. Stores

*The C and H in broken outline and with
dotted tracks show the course and posi-
tions intended for the Confiance and
Chub, which they were unable to effect.*

American ....○
British ....●

British Batteries
No. 1. 3 Guns and 1 Howitzer
No. 2. Pocket Battery
No. 3. Mortar Battery
No. 4. 3 Guns throwing Shrapnels Shells
No. 5. 4 Guns 18 Pounders and Rocket Battery
No. 6. 3 Heavy Guns and Rockets
No. 7. Heavy Guns to keep off the Galleys
No. 8. "   "   "   "   "
a. a. a. British Camps

58. Admiral A.T. Mahan's diagram of the battle in Plattsburgh bay.

the two-mile-long promontory of Cumberland Head was protected by the
Eagle. South of her lay the *Saratoga,* anchored from the bow, stern, and
amidships with springs on separate lines attached to the anchor chains, so that
she could be turned to fire in any direction. Similarly anchored next in line to
the south were the *Ticonderoga* and *Preble.* The eleven gunboats protected
gaps in the column.

After pausing to await the arrival of his own gunboats and to plan his attack, Downie moved slowly toward the American fleet. It was 9 o'clock. In an eerie silence Macdonough, surrounded by his officers, knelt and prayed for their success.

The *Eagle* opened fire with a shot that fell short of the *Confiance*. While passing to the northern end of the American line, the *Linnet* fired a broadside of 12-pounders, all falling short but one, which hit the chicken-coop on the *Saratoga's* deck releasing the game cock the sailors had brought on board. Unharmed, the cock flew into the rigging, flapped his wings and, to the laughter and cheers of the crew, crowed defiantly. That, they thought, was a good omen.

Macdonough bided his time until the *Confiance* came within range. Then, sighting one of the *Saratoga's* long 24-pounders himself, he fired. With startling accuracy the ball passed through the hawse-hole of the *Confiance* and crashed through the entire length of her deck, killing and wounding several of her crew and shattering her helm. Managing at last in a contrary wind to bring her about, 350 yards away, Downie let go a thunderous broadside from sixteen

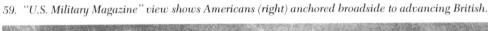
59. *"U.S. Military Magazine" view shows Americans (right) anchored broadside to advancing British.*

24-pounders, each firing double shot. They went straight to their mark, shaking the *Saratoga* from stem to stern. Among the 40 sailors knocked flat by this salvo, some were killed and many wounded. While sighting a bow gun a second lieutenant was struck dead by part of a quoin without having his skin broken.

The battle now erupted everywhere. The *Eagle* had also been struck, and now the *Linnet* shot her springs away, forcing her to take refuge between the *Saratoga* and *Ticonderoga*. But the damaged flagship was having enough trouble defending herself. Twice she was set on fire by heated shot from the *Confiance's* special furnace. A severed spanker boom had fallen on Macdonough's head, knocking him unconscious for several minutes. He was again knocked down by the severed head of one of his gunners, which came hurtling across the deck. One by one the *Saratoga's* guns fell silent until only a single carronade, or short gun, remained in action on her starboard side. Then that broke loose from its moorings and plunged down the main hatch with its carriage. Still, the flagship did not strike her colors. Letting go her stern anchor and cutting her bow cable, Macdonough worked feverishly to turn her around with spring lines so that he might bring her port battery to bear on the *Confiance*.

If hope remained for the Americans during this desperate interval it was that the enemy's prospects seemed equally hopeless. Not long after the *Saratoga* had shot away the port bower anchors of the *Confiance* a new barrage dismounted a gun behind which Captain Downie had been standing and killed him instantly. Wreckage covered her decks, and with all but four of her guns on one side out of action, efforts were made to bring the fresh battery on the other side to bear on the *Saratoga*. But even if her anchors had not been shot away, there had not been enough time to prepare for winding her around, as Macdonough succeeded in doing with the *Saratoga*. Battered with new broadsides, the *Confiance* surrendered at about 11 o'clock.

The *Saratoga* now concentrated on the *Linnet*, which fought gallantly despite splintered masts and tangled rigging. To escape by cutting her cable was out of the question for Captain Pring, who after a new barrage, was forced to haul down his brig's colors. Having suffered a similar pounding, the *Chubb* drifted helplessly down the American line. Upon receiving one more shot from the *Saratoga*, she also surrendered.

The *Preble*, pursued in the meantime by four British gunboats, had been run ashore, while Downie's crippled *Finch* drifted on to the rocks off Crab Island. The British gunboats then concentrated on the schooner *Ticonderoga*. Walking her decks in a blizzard of shot, Lt. Cassin, her commander, ordered that

60. Her rigging in shreds, Saratoga *fires port battery on* Confiance.

her guns be loaded with canister and bags of musket balls. When Midshipman Hiram Paulding found he could not discharge those under his supervision because of faulty matches, he resourcefully touched them off by firing his pistol at them. Thus the *Ticonderoga* was able to hold her end of the line. Providentially for the Americans, the greater number of British gunboats fled early in the battle. (Their commander subsequently escaped before his court-martial and was cashiered from the service.)

After a thunderous and bloody cannonade of two hours and twenty minutes, His Majesty's guns fell silent and his officers surrendered their fleet. An eye witness, Rev. H.B. Bogue, reported upon their demeanor and Macdonough's reception, which he described as a grand display of restraint.

"They came under convoy guard directly from the flagship, *Confiance,* and as they stepped upon the deck of the *Saratoga* they met Commodore Macdonough, who kindly bowed to them, while they, holding their caps in their left hands and their swords, by the blades, in their right, advanced toward him and, bowing, presented their weapons. The Commodore bowed and said: 'Gentlemen, return your swords into your scabbards and wear them. You are worthy of them. And having obeyed the order, arm in arm, with their swords by their sides, they walked the deck of their conqueror."

Macdonough sent a gig ashore with a dispatch to the Secretary of the Navy saying that "The Almighty has been pleased to grant us a signal victory on Lake Champlain in the capture of one frigate, one brig, and two sloops of war of the enemy." The Commodore had reason to be grateful; the devastation was as profound on his own ships as on those he had vanquished.

"The havoc on both sides is dreadful," declared Midshipman Lee of the *Confiance*. "I don't think there are more than five of our men out of three hundred, but what are killed or wounded. Never was a shower of hail so thick as the shot whistling about our ears. Were you to see my jacket, waist-coat and trowsers, you would be astonished how I escaped as I did, for they are literally torn all to rags with shot and splinters; the upper part of my hat was also shot away. There is one of our marines who was in the Trafalgar action with Lord Nelson who says it was a mere *flea-bite* in comparison with this."

In his biography of his father, Rodney Macdonough states:

Not a mast in either squadron would bear to make sail on and the lower rigging, being nearly shot away, hung down as though just thrown over the caps. The *Saratoga* had 55 round shot in her hull. Most of the enemy's fire, at least from the *Confiance,* passed well over the *Saratoga's* deck, and at the close of the action there were not twenty whole hammocks in the nettings. The guns of the *Confiance* were leveled at point blank range, and as the quoins were loosened at each discharge and were not properly replaced, her guns became more and more elevated and their shot went over instead of into the *Saratoga*. Bad as was the condition of the latter, that of the *Confiance* was infinitely worse. Her spring and rudder had been shot away and her "masts, yards and sails so shattered that one looked like so many bunches of matches and the other like a bundle of old rags . . . and her hull like a riddle." She had received over 105 round shot in her hull, many of them between wind and water, and was almost foundering when she struck. The outside of her was literally covered with small shot which failed to penetrate her stout oak planking. Her decks, strewn with the dying and dead, were

> *Red, from mainmast to bitts,*
> *Red, on bulwark and wale,*
> *Red, by combing and hatch,*
> *Red, o'er netting and vail.*

The *Linnet,* too, had been so often hulled that the water was nearly a foot above her lower deck at the end of the fight. As the *Confiance* and *Linnet* were in a sinking condition, men were sent at once to their pumps and the gunboats towed them into shallow water.

One of the eye-witnesses of the engagement was Senator Phelps of Vermont, who was then a boy living on his father's farm near the shore of the lake. He used to relate how, after the British had surrendered, he took a boat and pulled out to the *Saratoga*.

When he climbed up on deck he found it slippery with blood and almost covered with the wounded and the dead. He saw a man walking quickly back and forth on the quarterdeck, his cap pulled down over his eyes and his face and hands almost black with powder and smoke. Upon asking who the man was a sailor replied, 'That's Commodore Macdonough.''

⁂

The downfall of the British fleet left General Prevost and his army of 10,000 stranded on the banks of the Saranac. Confident of the victory of His Majesty's superior fleet, he had ordered his troops to cross the river at three points. Sheer numbers should have guaranteed their success, but the Yankees, fighting for their homelands from behind bunkers and trees, gave those who managed to cross a hot reception.

Blaisdell, the St. Albans carpenter who had crossed the sand bar to South Hero and from there to Plattsburgh four days previously, recalled that "they forded the river and advanced into the pine plains, where the Vermont and New York volunteers were distant about 80 to 100 rods. The woods were full of Vermont and New York volunteers, every man fighting for himself, all on the Irishman's own hook, and we were so hard upon them that they were compelled to retreat, and we pursued them like a band of bloodhounds back to the river, their dead and wounded scattered along the way."

As soon as he learned the awful word that Downie's fleet had surrendered, Prevost decided that the jig was up and at once turned the backs of his large army on Plattsburgh and started for Canada, leaving behind many weapons, tons of biscuits, and hundreds of gallons of rum.

In his volume of Dr. D.S. Kellogg's memoirs of the battle, Allen S. Everest recreates the atmosphere of a county infested with British soldiers. Upon their arrival Nathaniel Platt, for whose family the town was named, refused to leave his homestead, saying he had never turned his back on the British and never would. "He liked to annoy the officers by asking them, 'Why don't you take these Yankee forts and not wait for your fleet?' 'Well, Captain Platt, we are in no hurry about it. We will take them at the same time when the fleet comes.' The Captain was sitting on the piazza in front of the house when the British came in. A young lieutenant came ahead and said, 'Well, old man, who are you?' The old gentleman, who was quite infirm, rose up slowly and said, 'Young man, I'm Captain Platt and be damned to you!' The British general, coming up immediately, said to the lieutenant, 'You are well answered. You ought to be more respectful in addressing an old gentleman.'"

61. *The American victory is proclaimed by a commemorative broadside.*

Simeon Doty, a soldier in Captain Reynolds' Alburg company, stated: "At the time of the battle of Plattsburg(h) I was in Captain Joseph Hazen's company in North Hero. Our captain went over first on Sunday and we could not go then. We went over on Monday. On our way we saw the fleet. We went to Crab Island. I helped bury the dead there. They were broken up and smashed up a great deal. I went on to the fleet in a skiff. I saw the British Commodore (Downie), his aide and his *Miss,* all dead. The colors were laid over them. My brother fainted when he saw the blood and the dead.

"We landed on the north part of Crab Island. There were two hospitals there made of plank. The dead were carried off southward and were buried in trenches without coffins . . . Redcoats and bluecoats were put together. One hospital was a long plank building, planked on both sides, and the roof was made of plank. The wounded were laid in two rows. A man was walking along between them, the wounded were groaning and taking on terribly and calling for the doctor. The rows were as long as from here to the barn (five rods). . . ."

The burial of the 143 killed on both fleets took place at the north end of the island, a cortege of the dead officers, wrapped with the flags of their vessels, arriving to the booming of minute guns. After the wounded were evacuated, Macdonough's attention was directed to the salvage of both fleets. He saved the *Confiance,* now an American ship-of-war, by inclining her to one side to keep the shot holes on the other out of water.

The worst was over. Now came glory for the victors, and for the British army and navy, a period of mutual recrimination. (Deprived of his command, Prevost died within a year, a week before his court-martial.) News of the British retreat passed quickly among the Vermonters gathered on hilltops along the eastern shore. The booming of cannon had resounded 25 miles across the water to Burlington where, on the afternoon of the battle, a messenger rode in with the good news. That night every house was lighted, bells rang, and guns thundered from the wharf and the battery.

Twelve days after the battle, following a banquet at Plattsburgh, Macdonough and General Macomb were triumphantly ferried to Burlington and conducted from the wharf to the Coffee House in an elegant coach by a band and officers of the army and navy. The next morning a crowd from the surrounding towns gathered on the green to witness a parade to the meeting house of the cavalry, two bands, citizens, civil authorities, judges of the county court, officers of the army and navy, the committee of arrangements, the clergy, and finally Generals Macomb and Strong, Commodore Macdonough, and the Governor.

No less than 21 toasts were offered after the service: "The 11th of Sep-

62. *After the battle Macdonough sailed his fleet to the head of navigation at Whitehall. Years later it was still to be seen at its permanent mooring in East Bay.*

tember, 1814 — the day on which our naval Hercules came of age; the Union of the States — our happiness in peace, our security in war; the government of the United States — may the headwinds of party spirit no longer prevent them from laying their course directly for the port of public prosperity; American Sons of the Ocean, Nature's Noblemen. . . ." To the honored dead, to George Washington, to the Vermont and New York militia and all the combatants, to the heroes of the Revolution, to agriculture, commerce, and manufactures, to peace upon just and honorable terms. Finally, that evening, a ball was held in a chamber festooned with evergreen and flowers and with the gold letters: "T. Macdonough, the Hero of Champlain."

He became a national monument. Congress ordered that a gold medal be struck, and promoted him to captain. (Although he had long been called Commodore, his previous rank had been Master Commandant.) Vermont gave him 100 acres overlooking the scene of the battle, and New York, a handsome sword and a thousand acres in Cayuga County; Connecticut, a pair of gold-mounted pistols; Delaware, a sword and silver service; Albany, the freedom of the city, and New York City, the same in a gold box. The Staffordshire works in England manufactured for export an elegant dinner and tea and coffee service bearing a description of the battle. Such an outflow of praise and celebration seems less overwhelming when it is recalled that they loved their heroes in those days, and that prior to the Battle of Plattsburgh the war's outcome was in doubt. After it Britain gave up hope of a settlement on its terms. Advised by the Duke of Wellington that nothing was to be gained by further fighting, Prime Minister Liverpool instructed the peace delegation at Ghent to agree to the mutual restitution of conquered territory that the Americans demanded. The treaty was signed on Christmas eve.

In view of Macdonough's skillful defensive strategy, "his readiness of resource and indomitable pluck," Theodore Roosevelt considered him the foremost naval figure down to the Civil War. Admiral Mahan emphasizes that this was Champlain's second naval engagement with critical consequences for the still fragile Union — another key, like that at Valcour Island in 1776 — to liberty. While other events of paramount importance transpired elsewhere, the Eagle, like the cock that crowed in the rigging of the *Saratoga*, flapped his wings most vigorously over Lake Champlain. It is curious that two of the terms that have come to be identified with the national being, "Yankee" and "Uncle Sam," sprang from the Northcountry. Originally a meat inspector who stamped the initials "U.S." on barrels of salted meat for the northern army in the War of 1812, Uncle Sam was genially regarded by soldiers, if not by Federalists in Vermont and New York who, despite its favorable outcome, regarded the war as a mistake. Cartoonists eventually began to clothe Uncle Sam in Stars and Stripes and in 1861 Congress recognized him as a national symbol.

With fall coming on, Macdonough temporarily repaired his enlarged fleet so that it could sail to Whitehall's East Bay, there to be laid up for whatever eventuality. But as it turned out, a salute to Burlington as the *Saratoga* and *Confiance* sailed by on October 2 was the last time big guns ever spoke on Lake Champlain.

VII

The Waterborne Era: A Panorama of Transport.

I N an era crowded with inventions it is difficult to understand why it took centuries just to harness the steam in a vessel of boiling water to drive a reliable engine. Even after Thomas Newcomen and James Watt developed the first practical cylinder, piston, and separate condenser, the steam engine was not yet ready to go to sea. The river banks of Europe and America became graveyards of the efforts of de Gary, Ramsaye, Papin, Hulls, Fitch, Rumsey, Henry, Jouffroy, Symington, Ormsbee, and Morey before Robert Fulton's 100-foot *North River* of Clermont made her historic voyage to Albany in 1807.

The next year John Winans, an enterprising Quaker who owned a shipyard at Poughkeepsie, and James, his younger brother, pilot of the *North River*, moved to Lake Champlain to build what they hoped would become the first successful steamboat on any lake in the world. The hull of their vessel took shape at Burlington Bay under an oak tree (previously a whipping post) just west of John Winans's new house at the corner of King and Water streets. One hundred and sixty-seven tons in burden and 8 feet in depth, the new boat exceeded the length of the original *North River* by 25 feet and cost Winans and his associates the then large sum of $20,000. Launched sideways, she stuck in the mud but was floated on a freshet of rum.

Fulton had had to import his engine from Boulton and Watt in England. But Winans was able to find one second-hand on the Hudson, horizontal in design with a side lever bell crank, a balance wheel 10 feet in diameter, a

20-inch cylinder with a 3-foot stroke, and a boiler developing all of 20 horsepower. Extremely Spartan in appearance the *Vermont,* as she was christened, resembled a long narrow canal boat with a bare deck except for a small elevation amidships, a smokestack, two masts for sails to help her along in a favorable wind, paddlewheels hung over the side with little protection, and apparently some sheathing forward that served as a pilot house and shelter for the crew. Below deck, other than the engine and boiler compartment, was one large room 25 feet by 18 feet, for eating and sleeping, with berths on one side.

As she prepared to depart on her maiden voyage in June, 1809, almost exactly 200 years after Champlain discovered the lake, Captain Winans stood in the bow in his Quaker suit and, to the cheers of the spectators, shouted orders through wood smoke and hissing steam to the engineer and to the helmsman holding the rudder in the stern. The expectations of the wind-and-canvas fraternity that she would fail were dashed. Despite her slow speed of 5 miles an hour when the wind wasn't blowing she succeeded as emphatically as the *North River,* for she had to breast Champlain's heavy winds and large waves, whereas Fulton's boat traveled on a relatively sheltered river. The implication was clear: if a steamboat could succeed on a large lake, so might it even on the ocean.

The *Vermont* was supposed to cover her 150-mile route from Whitehall to St. Jean in 24 hours, and usually did despite frequent breakdowns. Although Gideon King's sailing packets often beat her they failed to put her out of business, since they were at the mercy of adverse winds or none at all. Soliciting passengers who wished "to pass Lake Champlain with safety and despatch" she met the Troy and Montreal stages at St. Jean and Whitehall, thus connecting with the New York-bound *North River* at Albany to provide the world's first regular service largely by steamboat between two widely separated cities.

Leaving St. Jean Saturday mornings at 9 o'clock and arriving at Burlington at 8 in the evening and Whitehall at 9 the next morning, she was advertised to start north on Wednesday after a several day layover, thus appearing to have settled for two trips a week, at least at the outset. In the absence of docks at intermediate ports small boats had to take on her passengers and freight. The pilot, often guiding her in total darkness with nary a navigational aid, must have lived as precariously as the engineer, who stood ready with a pot of molten lead to pour into cracks that developed in his boiler and engine. To keep her on an even keel heavy barrels were rolled back and forth across the deck.

Strangely enough, few observations survive of the *Vermont* in action. In "The Theater in Burlington in 1808," an extract from *Retrospections in America*, John Bernard considered her "the most delightful conveyance I have ever tried, although I was exceedingly annoyed by an old lady on board who was continually at my elbow, inquiring if I thought 'all was safe' or knew 'how hot they kept the furnace.' After enumerating with painful minuteness how many cases had occurred during the past year of boilers bursting, and how many lives were lost on each occasion, she always concluded with assurance that were the engine to give way in the present instance, we must all infallibly perish, our only choice being whether we would die by hot water on deck or cold water below."

During the war, which interrupted the *Vermont's* service to St. Jean, her first pilot, Hiram Ferris, appears to have doubled as navigator for Macdonough's flagship *Saratoga*. On one occasion the steamer nearly fell into the hands of the British who lay in ambush at Providence Island, their gunboats camouflaged with bushes. But a smuggler awaiting nightfall on the island overheard their plot and warned the *Vermont* by intercepting her in a rowboat. Several kegs of powder were subsequently placed in her hold; Winans evidently considered blowing her to perdition preferable to her capture by the British.

On a number of occasions during the war she served as the first steamboat in history to carry troops, but her proudest day came in 1814 when she ferried Commodore Macdonough and General Macomb to the celebration in Burlington after their victory at Plattsburgh. Resuming her schedule to St. Jean, she had almost completed six seasons of service when, on October 15, 1815, three miles north of the border on the Richelieu, her connecting rod detached itself from the crank and punctured her hull before the throttle could be turned off. Torpedoed from within, as it were, she lingered about 30 minutes until Winans could put her passengers and freight ashore, and then settled to the bottom.

Where the Winanses led, entrepreneurs were sure to follow. Between 1814 and 1832 four companies, a partnership, and an individual built ten new steamboats: the *Phoenix* (1815), *Champlain* (1860), *Congress* (1818), *Phoenix II* (1820), *General Greene* (1825), *Franklin* (1827), *Washington* (1827), *Macdonough* (1828), *Water Witch* (1832), and *Winooski* (1832). There would have been another, the *Ticonderoga*, in 1813 had Macdonough not appropriated her hull in Vergennes and completed her as a schooner for his fleet.

The *Phoenix I* became the most famous of these vessels for the unfortunate reason that her departure in flames was among the earliest and most dramatic

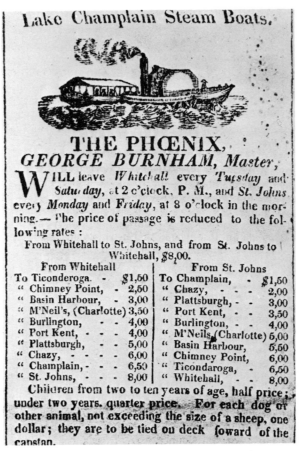

63. Doomed Phoenix *traversed the lake twice a week.*

on American waterways. Larger and more elaborate than the *Vermont,* the 146-foot *Phoenix* was originally driven by a second-hand engine from the *Perseverance,* which had been laid up on the Hudson as an unsuccessful challenger to the Fulton-Livingston monopoly. Jahaziel Sherman, her captain, obtained from them the exclusive right to operate steamboats on Lake Champlain and accompanied the *Perseverance's* precious engine and boiler to Vergennes.

The main deck of the *Phoenix* differed from the *Vermont's* in that it was protected by a canvas awning abaft the smokestack. Just behind the 25-foot guards around the paddlewheels were suspended small boats for boarding or debarking passengers, except at main ports. They were entered by way of ladders to the deck. A housing protected a staircase down to the gentlemen's and ladies' cabins, decorated with the most stylish furniture. A small state-

*Charming view of Basin Harbor in the early 1800's. Courtesy Basin Harbor Club.
Below: Timber raft on Lake Champlain, from an English engraving (1831) after a painting by T. Cole.*

Night packet boat on the Champlain Canal.

Between the opening of the Champlain Canal in 1823 and the railroad's arrival at Whitehall 25 years later, passengers traveled from there to the Hudson River on horse-drawn packets. The above views were reproduced from lantern slides colored with bits of glass and semi-precious stones. Courtesy the Liberty Eatery, Whitehall.
Right: Cargo-carrying canal boats at Burlington around the turn of the century. From a postcard, courtesy Special Collections, Bailey Library, University of Vermont.

Steamer Ticonderoga *leaving Basin Harbor in 1952. By R.N. Hill. Below: Falling mercury raises steam around Burlington-Port Kent ferry, laid up for the winter. By Stuart Perry.*

Old stone warehouse at Larrabee's Point wharf,
typical of those at Benson's Landing and Chipman's
Point in the Narrows; Victorian Van Patten cottage
at Cedar Beach (bottom) and Webb's manorial
Shelburne House (right) present lively contrasts
in lake architecture. By R.N. Hill.

room, smoking and baggage rooms, a barbershop, kitchen and pantry, captain's stateroom and separate office, and an area stacked with cord wood, competed for space with the boiler and engine. Like the *Vermont*, the *Phoenix* had no pilot house or any passenger facilities on deck other than a railing to keep them from falling off. After a year of service she received a new engine which increased her speed to 8 miles an hour.

Shortly after midnight on September 5, 1819 she was beating her way down the moonlit lake past Colchester Reef in the teeth of a fresh northeast wind. Having just finished a midnight snack, members of her crew apparently left a candle burning between the shelves of the pantry, for a few minutes later the entire galley was in flames. John Purple Howard, a Burlington hostler on his way to Montreal as a messenger for the Bank of Burlington with $8,000 in a carpet-bag, discovered the fire and rushed through the cabins arousing the 46 passengers and crew.

At this time Captain Jahaziel Sherman was at home with a fever and his 21-year-old son, Richard, commanded the boat. Having been up all the previous night with his new responsibilities, he had just retired, but immediately appeared on the afterdeck trying to quiet the passengers. Although Howard had secured the carpet-bag with the $8,000, there was more money in the captain's office. His son, steward of the boat, and the captain tried to get it by climbing over the wheelhouse, but the fire had spread to the oil around the engine, had broken through the deck, and now, fanned by the north wind, enveloped the entire center of the boat.

When it became obvious that it was beyond control the passengers charged for the lifeboats. Forced to restrain them with a gun in each hand, the young captain loaded the starboard lifeboat with the women, to whom the stewardess had brought their things from the cabin, and with enough men to fill its capacity of twenty — among them Howard's son, who had been entrusted with the carpet-bag and who shared with an older man the responsibility of ferrying the passengers to nearby Providence Island. Fourteen others now climbed into the larger port lifeboat, but before it could be filled someone cut the lines and it drifted astern, leaving eleven persons on the flaming deck, among them the stewardess who had made one more trip to the cabin.

Accounts of these desperate moments vary. Some said that John Pierson cut the lines; others declared it was MacVane, the engineer, who abandoned the machinery while it was running, forced his way into the lifeboat and, after setting it adrift, refused to return to save those who were left. When others in the boat insisted upon going back he threatened to "knock the first man overboard who should rise to make the attempt." The pilot, according to another account, "exhibited a singular turn of mind. . . . he rushed into the throng of passengers proposing to the captain that all hands go ashore on two pieces of wood he had picked up and held in his hands and loudly insisting that they would make a sufficient raft to support and save everybody upon."

All agreed that the youthful captain was magnificent. Upon the departure of the second lifeboat he strapped some of the remaining passengers to planks and threw chairs and benches over for others to cling to. One man hung to the rudder until part of it burned off, whereupon he took refuge on that. When all the others had left the *Phoenix* the captain took to the water on a table-leaf. He was discovered unconscious near Stave Island over two hours later and picked up by one of the lifeboats which had landed its passengers on Providence Island and then returned for those floating near the wreck. Six, including the stewardess, were lost in the waves off Colchester Reef, over which the *Phoenix* drifted, burned to the waterline, and finally sank.

What of the carpet-bag? It had reached Providence Island safely in the hands of Howard's son only to disappear during the rescue operations when he entrusted it to others. Since he and a Colonel Thomas, navigators of the lifeboat, were the only ones willing to return in it to rescue those left near the wreck, he could not take the carpet-bag with him. In the confusion during the night an Irishman rifled it and early in the morning crosssed to Grand Isle in a small boat and then made his way to Bell's Ferry, hoping to reach Plattsburgh before he was discovered.

In the meantime another son of John Howard had arrived from Burlington, where the fire had been plainly seen. Directed by his father to find the money, he learned the identity of the culprit and caught up with him near the Grand Isle ferry. Rather than surrender, the thief brandished two large knives, whereupon Howard, seizing a stake from a nearby fence, ordered him to capitulate. He finally did.

The burning of the *Phoenix* might have discouraged prospective passengers had they not understood that the fire was caused by candles in the pantry, which could have happened to any building on land. Whatever their doubts about setting forth in a floating teakettle, they did so in increasing numbers on progressively larger boats.

True to its mythical heritage, at least part of the *Phoenix*, the engine, arose from the wreck to serve on the *Phoenix II*. The boilers of the larger *Franklin* of 1827 were placed on the outside guards of the main deck (instead of in the hold), the theory being that if they blew up they wouldn't carry the deck and passengers with them. Shielded from stem to stern with a covered promenade, the main deck contained the ladies' cabin, while the dining room and gentlemen's cabin remained below — an obvious improvement over the earlier boats where both sleeping areas crowded the hold.

The confusion on the older boats had indeed become such that the Lake Champlain Steam-boat Company was forced to post a set of regulations, serving notice that the back cabin was exclusively reserved for ladies and children (servants to sleep on the deck). Gentlemen passengers were admitted to the forward cabin in the order in which they paid their fare. They were not allowed to remain in the washroom over ten minutes, and if there were not enough berths, were expected to sleep on sofas or cross-lockers.

"As the comfort of all persons must be considered, cleanliness, neatness, and order are necessary; it is therefore not permitted that any person shall smoke in the ladies' cabin, or in the great cabin, under penalty, first, of one dollar and a half, and half a dollar for each half hour they offend against the rule; the money to be spent in wine for the company. It is not permitted for any person to lie down in a berth with their boots or shoes on (with the same penalties). A shelf has lately been added to each berth, on which gentlemen will please put their boots, shoes, and clothes. Hitherto the cabin table has been much encumbered from gentlemen throwing their small garments on it. . . . In the ladies' cabin and in the great cabin cards and all other games are to cease at 10 o'clock at night, that those persons who wish to sleep may not be disturbed.

"Gentlemen are not permitted to sing or whistle the tunes of *Clinton's March* or *Burgoyne's Defeat* as it may prove offensive to some of the company."

Since Champlain steamboats provided the only convenient link from New York to Montreal they became vehicles of the great and near-great. Two years before she burned, the *Phoenix* carried President Monroe and the next year, the remains of General Montgomery, who had fallen in the siege of Quebec in 1775. The Revolution was still a recent memory and Montgomery remained a lamented casualty. Having attended to his burial, the overseer of works of the garrison of Quebec also supervised his removal 43 years later (upon which the musket ball that had killed him rolled out of his skull). The General's nephew accompanied the remains to St. Jean, where they were carried aboard the *Phoenix*, draped in mourning, her colors at half-staff. The voyage from Whitehall to St. Paul's churchyard in New York City continued with great solemnity.

Aboard the *Congress* in September, 1819 Professor Benjamin Silliman of Yale steamed past the weathering survivors of the Battle of Plattsburgh, which were anchored stem to stern in East Bay at Whitehall. "As we passed rapidly by, a few seamen showed their heads through the grim portholes from which five years ago the cannon fire poured fire and death. . . . Sparless, black, and frowning, these now dismantled ships looked like coffins of the brave and will remain as long as worms and rot will allow them, sad monuments of the bloody conflict."

That he might avoid the dampness and bustle on deck Silliman sat in his carriage during the 25-mile passage to Ticonderoga. How strange he remarked, that a fortress once clustered with armies should now be reduced to a solitary wisp of smoke curling from a stone chimney in its half-fallen walls.

During his triumphant tour of the northeast hinterlands in 1825 General Lafayette arrived in Burlington from Windsor in an open barouche drawn by four gray horses to lay the cornerstone of the new building at the University of Vermont, to attend a public dinner, and later a private reception at the brilliantly illuminated governor's mansion, Grasse Mount. Toward midnight the official entourage proceeded to the wharf where the General boarded the *Phoenix II*, resplendent with American and French flags. The *Congress* also stood by, her cabin windows illuminated, her stern adorned with a full-length transparent portrait of George Washington, and her bow and sides bearing the inscriptions: "Friend in need is a Friend indeed" — "A Nation's gratitude, June 28, 1825" — "Brandywine, 1777" — and "Yorktown, October 19, 1781." After a salute of 13 guns from the *Phoenix* the two steamers weighed anchor for Whitehall, where the General disembarked the next day under a canopy of flags between two lines of girls who scattered flowers in his path.

Lest the impression be gained that the early steamers earned unvarying acceptance, particularly among the British navy, consider the complaints of Captain Basil Hall about his trip in 1827:

Our route lay along Lake Champlain in a very crowded steamboat filled with tourists on their return from the north. The machinery was unusually noisy, the boat weak and tremulous, and we stopped, backed, and went again at no fewer than eleven different places, at each of which there was such a racket that it was impossible to get any rest. If a passenger did manage to doze off under the combined influence of fatigue and the monotonous sounding of the rumbling wheels, which resembled eight or ten muffled kettle drums, he was sure to be awakened by the quick "tinkle! tinkle!" of the engineer's bell or the sharp voice of the pilot calling out, "Stop her!" or he might be jerked half out of his berth by a sound thump against the dock or wharf.

If these were not enough, the rattle and bustle of lowering down the boat was sure to banish all remaining chance to sleep. In the cabin there was suspended a great staring lamp, trembling and waving about in a style to make a sailor giddy — while

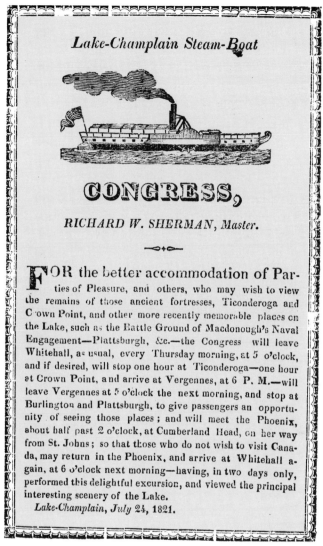

Lake-Champlain Steam-Boat

CONGRESS,

RICHARD W. SHERMAN, Master.

FOR the better accommodation of Parties of Pleasure, and others, who may wish to view the remains of those ancient fortresses, Ticonderoga and Crown Point, and other more recently memorable places on the Lake, such as the Battle Ground of Macdonough's Naval Engagement—Plattsburgh, &c.—the Congress will leave Whitehall, as usual, every Thursday morning, at 5 o'clock, and if desired, will stop one hour at Ticonderoga—one hour at Crown Point, and arrive at Vergennes, at 6 P. M.—will leave Vergennes at 5 o'clock the next morning, and stop at Burlington and Plattsburgh, to give passengers an opportunity of seeing those places ; and will meet the Phoenix, about half past 2 o'clock, at Cumberland Head, on her way from St. Johns ; so that those who do not wish to visit Canada, may return in the Phoenix, and arrive at Whitehall again, at 6 o'clock next morning—having, in two days only, performed this delightful excursion, and viewed the principal interesting scenery of the Lake.
Lake-Champlain, July 24, 1821.

64. *Historic sites were already advertised in 1821 broadside.*

underneath its rays stretched numberless weary passengers, some on mattresses spread on deck, others on the lockers or on the bare planks — the very picture of woe, like the field of battle after the din of war has passed. Among these prostrate objects of compassion various stray passengers might be seen picking their way, hunting for their bags and clothes, and talking all night in utter disregard of the unhappy wretches cooped up in the sleepless sleeping berths around them. At every stop or stopping place fresh parties either came on board or went away, or both, so that the overcrowded cabin was one scene of buzz buzz during this very long night.

Too often history has been woven from the endless skeins of war and politics, leaving the tapestry bare of the more enduring vignettes of everyday life. Part of the void has been a lack of understanding or acceptance of what constitutes history; and part, perhaps, has been that the observations of people in high places, above the sights, sounds, and smells of the times, are clouded by matters they think more important.

The reputation on Lake Champlain of Captain Gideon Lathrop, a native of Stockbridge, Vermont, induced the largest steamboat association in the world to secure his skill in the management of the impressive *North America* on the Hudson — since, according to a newspaper, "Captain Lathrop retains the simplicity of a youth allied to the character of a finished gentleman." Lathrop kept a diary of his trials and pleasures during his steamboating years, and his entries from 1827 to 1835, while engaged in towing and as a master of the *Congress* on Lake Champlain, offer an enticing smorgasbord of inland water life. The captain acted occasionally as a doctor and undertaker, and even as a policeman to quell the panic when a man on his boat came down with the cholera, said to have been the first local case in the epidemic of 1832.

April 19 (1827)—A fit of ague and fever this day. Had a light attack last Sunday.

April 23—Puked and purged at no small rate. Towed Mr. Boardman's and Mr. Bate's rafts from Mallet's Bay to Law's Island and lay at the mouth of river Lamoille at night.

May 17—Bought Plutarch's *Lives,* 6 volumes for $14.50.

June 14—. . . . Squall of rain and wind from the northwest. The mast of a skow in tow struck by lightning and much shivered.

June 15—1 a.m.—water all out of the boiler. Gale of wind from N.W. Came to anchor and raft drifted ashore at Elm Point . . . . Mr. Douglass' raft much damaged and about 20 large logs lost.

June 17—. . . . Another attempt to stop the leak in the boiler—without success.

June 24—Come to at Cedar Mountain. Another attempt by McVini and Lee to stop leak in boiler. Without success . . .

June 25—Unusual bad weather this tow—leaky boiler and south wind.

July 3—Went to Middlebury as evidence in Fisher trial. Swore that no person exchanged money on board *Congress* when Fisher was passenger to my knowledge . . . . Returned with Judge Haightcart.

July 4—Celebrated by hard work and 48 guns . . . .

July 9—. . . . Come to 6 hours at A. Island to stop leak in boiler.

July 11—Come to with strong south wind. Found on Point Rush (au Roche) a Mr. Moore, aged 67. One of the most jolly old souls I ever met with. He treated us with cider and stories of the Revolution to our hearts' content.

July 18—Fine day. At sunset off Fort Ticonderoga. Arrived in Whitehall with whole tow at 12 o'clock noon. This completes the towing for this season and may Heaven grant me a more pleasant livelihood the remainder of my steamboating than that of towing rafts.

August 6—From St. Johns. An Irish woman delivered of a son on deck.

August 9—An unpleasant dispute with an old man concerning a dog on board. Damn the dogs and such ungenerous fellows.

August 15—Went to Montreal with my sister and returned same day. $3.00 expense.

August 25—Went to Lake George with my mother. 26th to Saratoga Springs, 27th to Whitehall. A very pleasant time and mother seemed to enjoy the trip. At Ticonderoga fell in company with a gentleman and his daughter. Very pleasant company but damned talkers.

August 30—Rec'd from Mr. Cotton of Boston 1 Vol Athaneum and Friendships Offering $3.50. $4.00 acknowledged by a passenger for a dispute on the 9th for his dog.

October 5—Broke part of hand gear off St. Johns. Went to Wards, Montreal, to repair.

November 21—Broke ice from Four Channels to Chimney Point.

November 27—Dismantled our boat and stored furniture in Mayo and Follett's store.

December 30—Settled with N. Webb on account of goods damaged . . . . think it too much but am glad to get clear of his sarcastic looks.

January 1 (1828)—Pleasant dance at Mr. Mott's for N. Year . . . . Found the Indians very merry on New Years and want every stranger to join with them in dissipation . . . . A visit to the Nunnery . . . . The Nuns glad to see Company.

January 26—Launched from the shipyard, Shelburne, the steamboat *(Franklin)* at 11 A.M. by the signal of a gun . . . . By assistance of jack screws we moved her about 20 feet at 3 P.M. . . . . she started and went off in fine style to the tune of *Hail Columbia* and firing guns on board and on shore with many cheers . . . .

February 11—Arrived at Albany at 9 P.M. Steamboats running to New York. The people all wrapped in melancholy at the sudden death of De Witt Clinton.

February 13—The funeral of Governor De Witt Clinton occupied this day. All business suspended. The stores and shops closed. The town crowded with the military and different societies, forming into companies. Half past 2 the procession left the house of the deceased and marched with great regularity and solemnity, the band playing the German hymn and other tunes suitable to the occasion.

February 21—From Troy unusual hard travelling & rainy. Rode all night and arrived at Poultney at sunrise.

December 26—Fisher had no trial. The jurors were more or less prejudiced.

March 4 (1829)—Rainy day and 95 guns for Andrew Jackson's presidential inauguration.

March 22—To the Harbor with Mayo and Cady's wagon. Broke down.

March 23—Drowned off Bacon's Hill Mr. Lattimer, an engineer from N.Y. We succeeded in hooking him up at sundown in 60 feet of water.

April 1—My birthday—23 years of age. Fine weather.

April 29—Fine dance at Howards, bill $2.63. Rather high price for a little tea and cold cuts handed around.

July 4—Dislike towing rafts. Independence in my own mind.

July 15—At 10 o'clock taken unwell and 2 P.M. in violent pain.

July 16—Arrived and was carried immediately home and Doctor Moody employed. He flattered me my complaint was light and would soon be able to resume my occupation, but a short time convinced him and my friends the complaint was of a serious nature and at the termination of five weeks I for the first time left the room after suffering everything save death with the bilious fever but kind Heaven saw fit to restore my health and I continued to gain remarkably fast. I received pointed attention and kindness from the good people . . . . and the best of physicians and nurses. May I never forget their attention to me but cherish the recollection with gratitude and ever be ready to assist the needy and repay their goodness by doing as we would be done by.

September 21—At Port Kent dock ran foul of the *Franklin* . . . . damaged *Franklin* in water wheel . . . . spoiled our billet head and signal lamp on bowsprit.

October 31—Aground at St. John's dock one hour. Left 2 P.M. Aground at Champlain 1½ hours. Commenced snowing and rain at dark. Wind north east and blowing fresh. About 7 p.m. struck the reef at Pt. Fair (au Fer). We carried an anchor astern and by sounding found from 7 to 11 feet water one cable length to windward and at 11 o'clock succeeded in getting afloat after the most uncomfortable 4 hours I or my vessel ever felt from thumping on the rocks and icy weather. Come to anchor, totally dark.

December 1— . . . . Run our vessel under Crab Island and put away for the Head. Found sea much heavier than anticipated, obliged to put back in dock as we broke the horn or iron that connects the block to rudder and drifted a few minutes without a helm. Succeeded in steering up under the Island again with our tiller, when we were all thunderstruck with the cry "Tiller gone!" Heavens, what next. A vessel adrift in the height of a gale without one possibility of steering to a harbor, but can anyone describe the happiness we were now destined to enjoy in seeing the noble boat steer up to the wind without the assistance of one feeble hand (save the great kind Providence that seemed to direct her) we succeeded in getting under Crab Island and let her anchor go. It held well, but kept steam all night to guard against dragging. After a consultation we hit upon the simple plan of lashing the blocks to the rudder . . . . Thank Heavens we lay well all night.

April 1 (1832)—Age 27 years. In good health. Weigh 144 pounds.

April 16—I have given $15 to buy mourning dresses for Mary and Harriet Bennett—poor orphans, they have lost their only parent by the untimely death by suicide. I have paid Mrs. Johnson's passage to Vergennes and back to attend the funeral, $2.00.

April 10—I have taken William Seddle . . . . as an apprentice until he arrives at the age of 21 years on the 4th day of June 1842. On that day I am to give him one common suit and one holiday suit and $100 in cash.

April 23— . . . . May Heaven bless us with a favorable season and continue to shield us from the rude storms—and teach our weak minds to steer a course that will bring us to the desired haven at last.

☙❦❧

No sooner had steamboats conquered the lake than a further development altered trade and travel. Pioneers had dreamed of a canal around the Richelieu rapids to the St. Lawrence and the sea. As early as 1783 Ira Allen had extolled the benefits of such a canal to General Haldimand in Quebec. A survey proved it feasible, and had it not been for Canadian merchants who stood to lose as middlemen if ships sailed directly from the St. Lawrence into the lake, it might have been built in the 18th century.

As it happened, the first canal led not to Canada but to the south. Although there had been talk in New York about canals west and north from the Hudson, and companies had been incorporated to build them as early as 1791, little was done prior to the administration of Governor De Witt Clinton, under whose tireless leadership a new survey was made in 1817 and construction begun from Waterford on the Hudson to Whitehall. The distance was 64 miles, 46½ of which became an artificial channel (the Hudson was used for 11 miles and Wood Creek for six-and-a-half). Seventeen ascending and descending locks were necessary, three of them at Whitehall to raise vessels 16 feet above the lake. A dam on the upper Hudson 900 feet long and 28 feet high fed water to the canal's summit.

The Champlain Canal was completed in 1823 (along with the Erie) and the first boat to navigate it, the *Gleaner,* hailed from St. Albans Bay. Leaving there in September with a load of wheat and potash she passed easily and triumphantly through the entire canal, only to wait several days at Waterford for the completion of the locks to the Hudson. A flotilla of boats decorated with flags and streamers accompanied her to Troy. Saluted with a volley of artillery, her owners repaired to the Troy House for a public banquet and testimonials. At Albany, Hudson, Poughkeepsie, and New York City "The Barque of the Mountains," as a prominent poet called her, drew widespread attention.

When the canal opened it was as if some great force had suddenly tipped the lake to the south, emptying into Whitehall the goods that had always gone to St. Jean. Any previous trade passing through the southern port had

had to be transshipped to Troy and Albany on trains of wagons which, however, could not haul quantities of heavy products like the iron ore found at several places on the New York shore. (Although early settlers had taken advantage of the Cheever Bed near Crown Point and built forges at Skenesborough, Vergennes, and Onion River, production had gone mostly to local markets. The large Winter Bed was discovered in Clinton County in 1800 and nine years later, the superior Arnold Bed, which yielded ore in great demand by manufacturers at Hudson River ports. As early as 1822 a large deposit in the Adirondack foothills of Moriah was feeding a small blast furnace below them at Port Henry.)

New horizons for iron and other products appeared limitless, and the stirrings in the mines anticipated what would become the lake's second most important industry. First was lumber; the canal ushered in its second golden age almost overnight. Even the promoters of "Clinton's Ditch" could not have predicted the galvanic stimulus of its northern spur upon the sawmills that cropped up everywhere along the fringes of the Adirondack and Green Mountain forests in the quest of trees that had not previously been floated to Canada. From a modest 46 thousand dollars in 1824, total revenues from tolls on the canal rose to 72 thousand the next year and 107 in 1828. Doubling every eight years from 1828 to 1842, they represented an immense traffic in terms of the purchasing power of 19th century dollars.

The revolution was nowhere more apparent than in the springing-up of home-grown shipyards for the construction of boats designed to fit the locks. During the early years of the century some 30 large sloops operated by or in behalf of "Admiral" Gideon King had monopolized travel and trade on the mountain-bound lake. The first of them had been built on the Winooski River by Benjamin Boardman, a sea-captain, and a Connecticut shipwright named Wilcox. Five others were launched at Burlington Bay before 1800, among them the 25-ton *Dolphin* and *Burlington Packet,* and the 30-ton *Lady Washington* and *Maria,* the latter two the handiwork of Richard Fittock (whose principal claim to posterity was a trade sign on his waterfront tavern bearing George Washington's portrait on one side, and to be safe, Admiral Nelson's on the other). The rest of King's sloops were built after 1800, the majority at Essex and Whitehall.

When steamboats took all of his passengers and some of his freight the "Admiral" chose the time-honored alternative of joining the opposition. Far from threatening the steamboat passenger business through the lake the canal stimulated it, if anything, while bringing an unexpected windfall to sailing vessels carrying heavy products to Whitehall for transshipment to tide-water.

65. *Canal packets competed with Troy and Whitehall stagecoaches.*

Bearing such names as *Daniel Webster, Henry Clay, Montgomery, Lafayette,* and *Hercules,* some of the schooners and sloops now constructed to supply the canal boats weighed as much as 200 tons. The canal simultaneously generated its own fleets of barges owned by the Northern Transportation Line, the Six Day Line, and others. The most enterprising of these companies (in league with Troy businessmen) soon expanded their domains to vessels on the lake and the Hudson, in order that cargoes might make the whole trip under the flag of one company.

A further change took place about 1845 with the advent of sloop-rigged canal boats. These could load on the lake, step their masts at Whitehall (in order to pass under the canal's many low bridges) and, towed by steam tugs on the Hudson, swiftly reach their destinations by avoiding two transfers of their cargoes at the northern and southern ends of the canal. In order to save further time in transit for such perishable commodities as cheese and butter, steam tugs began to receive tows at both ends of the canal, and by mid-century the lake's large fleet of sailing vessels began to dwindle. The so-called "long boat" system was perfected and dominated, as had been the sloop-rigged canal boat, by the Merchant's line of Burlington, managed by Timothy Follett, John Bradley, and later by Thomas H. Canfield among others. With 40 boats in business it maintained its headquarters in a four-story stone building at the corner of Maple and Water (Battery) streets, and an office at Coenties Slip in New York City.

Since neither wind nor steam were useful on the narrow and shallow canal, animals had been employed to tow the boats from the beginning, mainly teams of mules plodding the hard-beaten tow path to the next "station" several miles away, where fresh teams took up their burden. As durable as the animals they drove, the "mule-skinners" became a breed apart, dwelling in shacks near the mule barns in Whitehall and squandering their meager wages on rum and black-strap molasses in the saloons that lined the streets along the canal. Even tougher were the pugilists whom canal boat captains hired to improve their chances of beating other vessels into the locks.

Whitehall, the vortex of this activity, became the most boisterous canal town in the northeast — its melange also including streams of steamboat passengers en route to New York or Montreal. Until the arrival of the railroad

66. Larrabee's crossing ferry, with the ruins of Fort Ticonderoga in the background.

their only means of travel from the Hudson to the lake were by stagecoach over the ruts and potholes to Troy, or by canal packet. Pulled by horses rather than mules, these hulking vessels fitted out with sleeping cubicles and dining areas became a world of their own as they threaded their way by day and night through the fields, forests, and ledges of Wood Creek and beyond.

On a nice day passengers sitting on the deck were afforded a lofty view of the countryside and of canal life so near at hand that when they passed a tow headed in the opposite direction the two vessels almost touched. Traversing the swamps on rainy or sticky days amidst clouds of Whitehall mosquitoes proved less rewarding, as did lowering buckets over the side for morning "ablutions." Their reveries on deck interrupted every few minutes by a horn announcing their arrival at a lock, or by cries of "Low bridge!," New York ladies and gentlemen counted the hours until they could board the comparatively sumptuous river and lake steamboats at the ends of the canal.

Since there were no bridges on the lake, ferries crossing and recrossing at numerous points added another dimension to the long waterway's diverse flotilla. William Gilliland's mention of New Englanders transporting his cattle from "Cloven Foot" to "Cloven Rock" (obviously Split Rock) in 1765 was the first of an east-west ferry. Three years later at least one vessel was carrying freight between Ticonderoga and Larrabee's Point (then called Shaw's Landing). Others unquestionably operated in that vicinity prior to the construction of the military bridge between Ticonderoga and Mount Independence.

In 1788 Gideon King was sailing "cutters" from Burlington to Essex and Plattsburgh, and in 1790 running two converted war schooners to St. Jean. Soon after the turn of the century ferries were crossing from Chipman's Point to Wright's, Orwell to Port Marshall (later called Montcalm Landing, below Mount Defiance), Chimney Point to Crown Point and Port Henry, Arnold's Bay to Bessboro (Westport), Basin Harbor to Rock Harbor, and Charlotte to Essex.

In the Narrows, floats of cedar logs pinned to stringers with a railing containing oarlocks sufficed, or the raft might be propelled by setting poles or by sweeps. Passengers crossing the broad lake had to depend on sails and shifting winds. In 1819 a Mr. B. Langdon of Whitehall patented a horse-powered sidewheel ferry which presently appeared at several crossings on the lake and the Hudson. A traveler in 1820 at first thought this invention to be hard on the horses, "but this," he concluded, "is an illusion as it seems very immaterial to their comfort whether they advance with their load, or cause the basis on which they labour to recede."

He found the boat to be "of the most singular construction. A platform covers a wide, flat boat. Underneath the platform there is a large horizontal solid wheel which extends to the sides of the boat, and there the platform or deck is cut through and removed so as to afford sufficient room for two horses to stand on the flat surface of the wheel, one horse on each side, and parallel to the gunwale of the boat. The horses are harnessed in the usual manner for teams, the whiffle trees being attached to stout iron bars fixed horizontally at a proper height into posts, which are a part of the fixed portion of the boat. The horses look in opposite directions, one to the bow and the other to the stern; their feet take hold of channels or grooves cut in the wheels in the direction of radii; they press forward and, although they advance not, any more than a squirrel in a revolving cage or than a spit dog at his work, their feet cause the horizontal wheel to revolve in a direction opposite to their own apparent motion. This, by a connection of cogs, moves two vertical wheels, one on each wing of the boat. . . . The horses are covered by a roof furnished with curtains to protect them in bad weather and do not appear to labour harder than common draft horses with a heavy load."

The "superior Horse-Boat *Eagle*," probably of this type, was running three trips a day between Basin Harbor and Westport in 1841. Six horses drove another between Charlotte and Essex between 1821 and 1827, but this was of a different design since three horses, yoked together on each side of the deck, transmitted their power directly to the wheels through treadmills. This was the arrangement employed on the *Gypsy*, running from Chimney Point to Port Henry. As with the Langdon method where the horizontal wheel trod by the horses was geared directly to both paddle wheels, the treadmills provided uncertain navigation, for if the horses on the left treadmill walked faster than those on the right the ferry was bound to veer to starboard regardless of what the helmsman might do. One ingredient of a straight true course was the long whip of the "engineer" who sat usually in one of the passenger's buggies and applied encouragement to one team or another, depending on which was lagging. The owner of the ferry, Asahel Barnes, all but overcame this difficulty by importing some even-gaited Canadian ponies.

On his return to New England from Niagara, the most able spokesman of this era, Nathaniel Hawthorne, chanced to cross the lake at Larrabee's Point. Tarrying on the veranda of the Greek Revival hotel near the landing, he observed that the stores close by the wharf "appeared to have a good run of trade foreign as well as domestic; the latter with Vermont farmers and the former with vessels plying between Whitehall and the British Dominions. Altogether this was a lively spot. I delighted in it, among other reasons, on

67. *United States Hotel (left) dominated the small but busy landing at Larrabee's Point.*

account of the continual succession of travelers who spent an idle quarter of an hour in waiting for the ferry boat; affording me just enough time to make their acquaintance, penetrate their mysteries, and be rid of them without the risk of tediousness on either side."

Hawthorne painted a broader and more vivid canvas when he crossed to Burlington on a walking tour in the summer of 1835. As the son of a sea captain he could hardly be expected to describe fresh water without a note of derogation, but his account in the *New England Magazine* remains the best on the lake in the early flush of the waterborne era, and of life at its principal port.

Not that we had come that morning from South America, but only from the New York shore of Lake Champlain. The highlands of the coast stretched north and south, in a double range of bold, blue peaks, gazing over each other's shoulders at the Green Mountains of Vermont. The latter are far the loftiest and, from the opposite side of the lake, had displayed a more striking outline. We were now almost at their feet, and could see only a sandy beach, sweeping beneath a woody bank, around the semicircular bay of Burlington. The painted light-house, on a small green island, the wharves and warehouses, with sloops and schooners moored alongside, or at anchor, or spreading their canvas to the wind, and boats rowing from point to point, reminded me of some fishing town on the sea-coast.

But I had no need of tasting the water to convince myself that Lake Champlain was not an arm of the sea; its quality was evident, both by its silvery surface, when unruffled, and a faint, but unpleasant and sickly smell, forever steaming up in the sunshine. One breeze from the Atlantic, with its briny fragrance, would be worth more to these inland people than all the perfumes of Arabia. On closer inspection, the vessels at the wharves looked hardly seaworthy — there being a great lack of tar about the seams and rigging. . . . I observed not a single sailor in the port. There were men, indeed, in blue jackets and trowsers, but not of the true nautical fashion, such as dangle before slop-shops; others wore tight pantaloons and coats preponderously long-tailed — cutting very queer figures at the mast-head; and, in short, these freshwater fellows had about the same analogy to the real "old salt," with his tarpaulin, pea-jacket and sailor-cloth trowsers as a lake fish to a Newfoundland cod.

Nothing struck me more, in Burlington, than the great number of Irish emigrants. They have filled the British provinces to the brim, and still continue to ascend the St. Lawrence, in infinite tribes, overflowing by every outlet into the States. At Burlington, they swarm in huts and mean dwellings near the lake, lounge about the wharves, and elbow the native citizens entirely out of competition in their own line. Every species of mere bodily labor is the prerogative of these Irish. Such is their multitude, in comparison with any possible demand for their services, that it is difficult to conceive how a third part of them should earn even a daily glass of whiskey, which is doubtless their first necessary of life — daily bread being only the second. Some were angling in the lake, but had caught only a few perch, which little fishes, without a miracle, would be nothing among so many. A miracle there certainly must have been, and a daily one, for the subsistence of these wandering hordes. The men exhibit a lazy strength and careless merriment, as if they had fed well hitherto, and meant to feed better hereafter; the women strode about, uncovered in the open air, with far plumper waists and brawnier limbs, as well as bolder faces, than our shy and slender females; and their progeny, which was innumerable, had the reddest and the roundest cheeks of any children in America.

While we stood at the wharf, the bell of a steamboat gave two preliminary peals, and she dashed away for Plattsburg, leaving a trail of smoky breath behind, and breaking the glassy surface of the lake before her. Our next movement brought us into a handsome and busy square, the sides of which were filled up with white houses, brick stores, a church, a court-house, and a bank. Some of these edifices had roofs of tin, in the fashion of Montreal, and glittered in the sun with cheerful splendor, imparting a lively effect to the whole square. One brick building, designated in large letters as the custom-house, reminded us that this inland village is a port of entry, largely concerned in foreign trade, and holding daily intercourse with the British empire. In this border country, the Canadian bank-notes circulate as freely as our own, and British and American coin are jumbled into the same pocket, the effigies of the king of England being made to kiss those of the goddess of liberty. Perhaps there was an emblem in the involuntary contact. There was a pleasant mixture of people in the square of Burlington, such as cannot be seen elsewhere, at one view: merchants from Montreal, British officers from the frontier garrisons, French Canadians, wandering Irish, Scotchmen of a better class, gentlemen of the south on a pleasure-tour, country squires on business; and a great throng of Green Mountain boys, with their horse-wagons and ox-teams, true Yankees in aspect, and looking more superlatively so by contrast with such a variety of foreigners.

The lake's naval battles had nothing on the steamboat war. Dominated by the Champlain Transportation Company, founded in 1826, it became a text-book case of competition and the elimination thereof.

As a starter the company built the longer and faster *Franklin,* and as its adversaries began to founder, it absorbed or engulfed, one way and another, the Lake Champlain Steam-boat Company (owner of the *Champlain, Congress,* and *Phoenix II),* the Champlain Ferry Company *(General Greene* and *Winooski),* the St. Albans Steamboat Company (the *Macdonough),* and the Messrs. Ross and McNeill and Captain Jahaziel Sherman, owners respectively of the *Washington* and *Water Witch.*

Retiring some of these boats and arranging the schedules of others to yield the maximum flow to their coffers, the directors of the Transportation Company decided in 1836 to adorn their monopoly by building at their Shelburne Shipyard the world's finest steamboat. And so it turned out to be, according to the eminent and usually acerbic viewer of things American, Charles Dickens.

There is one American boat — the vessel which carried us on Lake Champlain, from St. Johns to Whitehall, which I praise very highly, but no more than it deserves, when I say that it is superior even to that in which we went from Queenstown to Toronto, or to that in which we travelled from the latter place to Kingston, or I have no doubt I may add, *to any other in the world.* The steamboat, which is called the *Burlington,* is a perfectly exquisite achievement of neatness, elegance and order. The decks are drawingrooms; the cabins are boudoirs, choicely furnished and adorned with prints, pictures, and musical instruments; every nook and corner of the vessel is a perfect curiosity of graceful comfort and beautiful contrivance. Captain Sherman, her commander, to whose ingenuity and excellent taste these results are solely attributable, has bravely and worthily distinguished himself on more than one trying occasion; not the least among them, in having the moral courage to carry British troops at a time (during the Canadian rebellion) when no other conveyance was open to them. He and his vessel were held in universal respect, both by his own countrymen and ours; and no man ever enjoyed the popular esteem who, in his sphere of action, won and wore it better than this gentleman.

By means of this floating palace we were soon in the United States again, and called that evening at Burlington; a pretty town, where we lay an hour or so. We reached Whitehall, where we were to disembark, at six next morning; and might

68. *The* Franklin *represented a long step forward in design.*

have done so earlier, but that these steamboats lie by for some hours in the night, in consequence of the lake becoming very narrow at that part of the journey, and difficult of navigation in the dark. Its width is so contracted at one point, indeed, that they are obliged to warp round by means of a rope.

If any allowance is made for such lavish praise it is that Sherman's pro-British outlook in no way diminished his stature in the eyes of an arch-Englishman like Dickens. Nor, on the other hand, did a captain who dared carry troops to crush the Canadian Rebellion endear himself to the natives, many of whom supported the Canadian cause.

Never, according to the editor of the *Burlington Sentinel,* was "a greater or more reckless outrage committed upon the feelings of the American people by any of the citizens of Vermont, than was coolly perpetrated by the captain of the Steam Boat *Burlington* — and probably under orders of the Directors of

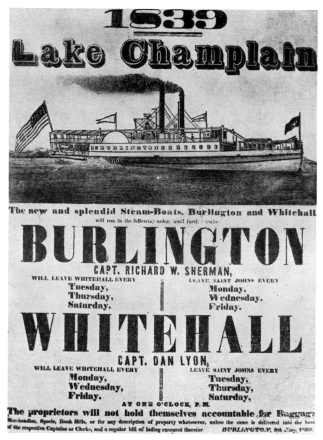

69. *The elegant* Burlington *was the prototype for her successors.*

the Company." Asserting that the rebellion of the Canadian Patriots could not have been put down if the *Burlington* had not landed six or eight hundred Redcoats with artillery and ordinance behind their lines south of Isle Aux Noix, the editor cried: "Is there a man, who has a drop of American blood, or one spark of American feeling, that will not blush for his Country's flag, that will not feel indignant that any of his countrymen should have profaned and disgraced it by making it subserve the purposes of British tyranny? Let then the voice of the American public be heard in such a manner that it will make this soulless corporation and their minions tremble!"

Nor was Sherman's reputation improved by his persistently aristocratic bearing. Even such a distinguished passenger as President Van Buren at first declined to meet him, saying: "No, I know Sherman. He thinks the world is a steamboat and he is the captain."

But his vessel continued to gain universal praise, Sir James Lucuzthn, the Provost of Glasgow, declaring: "The interior decorations are so truly splendid that you might fancy yourself in the drawing room of a ducal palace. The cleanliness of the vessel is the admiration of all strangers. There is no unpleasant shouting or noise. All orders are given by bell signals from the officers on deck; no brawling to the engineer, 'stop her,' 'turn ahead,' 'two back strokes,' and such vulgar expressions as you hear aboard our steamers on the Clyde. . . . The men are all trained to their particular duties — every one at his post — and the discipline equal to that on board a ship-of-war. The arrangements at meals are excellent and the greatest attention paid to the passengers by the stewards, who are numerous and all dressed in neat, clean, fancy uniforms."

At the time Sherman was building the *Burlington* a cloud bigger than a

70. *Steamboat war turned the lake into a raceway.*

71. Richard ("Dandy Dick") Sherman, captain of the Burlington.

man's hand in the form of an opposition vessel arose on the Whitehall horizon. Its promoter, Peter Comstock, the energetic owner of a line of passenger packets on the canal had, so the Champlain Transportation Company thought, been well "rewarded" when it absorbed the Champlain Ferry Company, of which he had also been a director.

Deciding with considerable wringing of hands that the *Burlington* must not have Comstock as a competitor, the directors of the Transportation Company voted to pay him a lump sum of $20,000 for his unfinished steamer, to elect him to their own Board, and to hire him for a thousand dollars a year as their "agent" in Whitehall, provided he promise not to build, directly or indirectly, any more boats — a contract to which Comstock bound himself in writing.

They then completed his boat, which they called the *Whitehall*, and in 1838, the summer after the launching of the *Burlington*, put her on line run to St. Jean. (Four years later they also completed a smaller vessel, the *Saranac*, to replace the *Winooski* as the Burlington-Port Kent ferry.) No sooner had they again established their supremacy than they received the distressing news that residents of New York had chartered the New York and Lake Champlain Steamboat Company, apparently with plans to build a new opposition boat.

Gravely digging into its till once more, the monopoly paid off the directors of the new company and elected three of its members to its own Board.

This deal had no sooner been made than the eight-year contract with Peter Comstock ran out. Resigning as a director, he let it be known that he was about to take to the warpath with a new steamboat, again expecting, no doubt, to be bought off by the monopoly. The hand-wringing resumed, more anguished than before, in the face of rumors that some of the Champlain Transportation's own directors were backing Comstock, with the prospect of sharing his melon — rumors, however, that were never verified. Having had enough blackmail, the directors voted to call his bluff and, if necessary, to fight.

Comstock may have been bluffing but also proved ready to build another opposition boat, the swift *Francis Saltus*. Launched at Whitehall in 1844 she served for years as the white hope of the public and the nemesis of the monopoly. Retaliating at once, the Transportation Company placed the equally fast and more elegant *Burlington* on the same run and cut the previous fare through the lake from five to three dollars. With the *Burlington's* superior accommodations there should have been no contest, but Captain Sherman's posturing annoyed the local people, while Comstock's image as an independent fighting the greedy monopoly greatly attracted them. So did the popular captain of the *Saltus*, H.G. Tisdale, whose fraternity of schooner and sloop captains placed every obstacle in the path of the *Burlington* and at each landing accosted her master with impudent variations of this ditty:

> *Dick Sherman is so very slick*
> *The fops all swarm around him thick*
> *As humbugs 'round a pot of honey;*
> *So Dick's cologne brings him the money.*
>
> *Oh, Dicky is a gallant lad,*
> *He makes the ladies very glad;*
> *He smiles and flirts with great parade,*
> *And then makes love to the cabin maid.*
>
> *The* Saltus *and the* Montreal
> *Will drive him from the lake next fall.*
> *Ha, Ha, Ha. That's the fun*
> *For Dandy Dick of the* Burlington.

After some months of humiliation and dwindling revenues, the monopoly established a night-line served by the *Burlington* and *Whitehall* and, for day-line competition with Comstock, entered the newly lengthened *Saranac*

72. *The veteran opposition boat was a perennial embarrassment to the monopoly.*

under the command of the popular P.T. Davis. With its night-line boats making up the loss, the monopoly could afford a further reduction of the *Saranac's* fare to fifty cents — its purpose, of course, being to starve Comstock out of business.

The outcome now depended on speed, and various stratagems were adopted to increase it, among them throwing pitch pine into the boilers to raise their pressure, and tying down their safety valves. Far from objecting to pressures beyond those for which the boilers were designed, passengers lined the decks egging on the captains and engineers, placing bets, and fighting in the bars as the steamers raced neck-and-neck up the lake. When not a single additional revolution per minute could be coaxed out of their engines the captains began to skip landings, with the result that passengers who had been lured aboard one boat or the other could never be sure where they would get off.

In his summary of these hectic years during which he himself played a central role in the robust development of local and national transport, Thomas H. Canfield calls attention to the lawless "runners" who all but abducted passengers at Whitehall.

"We should do great injustice did we fail to give Whitehall the credit of first bringing forward these ubiquitous men to public notice, and of afterwards being the nursery school of their training and education. Their business was to await the arrival of stages, packets, steamers, and then to accost the passengers, expatiating upon the superior comforts and facilities which their respective lines afforded — and by the most ingenious arguments and eloquent appeals, which were peculiar to themselves, to induce the travelers to believe that each line was the best: 'got through to Troy first,' 'was the mail line,' 'was the opposition to the monopoly,' was the line 'which went right straight through,' with a variety of other phrases, all expressive of the superior facilities of each. By some these agents were voted a nuisance, by others as great friends to the traveler. Conspicuous among them, and we may truly say the founder of the system, was Augustus Reed, Esq., a man of good address, great energy, and withal possessing such powers of eloquence as to convince even the most skeptical that the 'wrong route were the right.' Under his instruction at Whitehall a large number of these agents graduated for years, who were employed in different sections of the country, being regarded for a time almost indispensable, until the through system of ticketing and checking baggage, adopted by the railroads, dispensed with their services."

The war between Comstock and the monopoly might have resulted in a boiler explosion had it not been preceded by a financial one. Try as he would, Comstock could not make ends meet with a fare lower than a dollar, while the monopoly further decreased the *Saranac's* to twenty-five cents. This proved ruinous and Comstock capitulated. But the *Saltus* did not, for her ownership passed to a group of his backers, Troy businessmen with fresh resources and every expectation of success in the wake of his failure.

By continuing the *Saranac's* ridiculously low fare, Champlain Transportation directors expected the new owners of the *Saltus* to wilt like Comstock. But they did not. Deciding that something had to be done to stem their alarming losses, the monopoly in 1844 presented an olive branch to the Troy consortium, suggesting that receipts of the two boats be divided between the opposing parties.

When this offer was refused indignantly the monopoly changed its tactics. With the sole purpose of "beating the *Saltus*" it laid down at the Shelburne shipyard the 240-foot keel of a new boat intended to be finer and faster even than the *Burlington*. As the butt of the steamboat war, Captain Sherman, supervisor of her construction, was only too happy to oblige. On her trial run in the spring of 1847, the new vessel logged 19 miles an hour, over two knots faster than anything on the lake. The innovation of staterooms on her second deck was bound to become a further attraction.

Early one morning the citizens of Burlington saw a bright new sidewheeler opposite the *Saltus* in their harbor, her milk-white sides accenting the proud letters of her name: *United States.* Billows of smoke arose from the two boats' four stacks, and by sailing time a crowd had gathered. Just before the appointed hour, the water boiled under the wheels of the *Saltus* as she burst away from the dock. From the center window of the pilot house of the still-dormant *United States* appeared the side whiskers of Captain William Anderson as he studied the widening breach of the *Saltus.*

Satisfied that he had allowed her a decent lead, he reached for the bell-pull, and a moment later the walking beam plunged with a surge of power. Standing before his gleaming machinery the engineer seized the throttle and pulled it down as far as it would go. The *United States* literally hurtled to life. Pandemonium reigned on shore and on the decks. At first the breach between the *Saltus* continued to widen, then it stayed the same, then grew smaller. Steadily the *United States* gained until the quickening revolutions of her wheels brought her to the *Saltus's* stern, then broadside. As whistles roared above the passengers' hoarse shouts, she forged ahead, leaving the *Saltus* to thump shamefacedly along in her wake.

A race requires a winner, even if it is a monopoly. As the summer waned it became obvious that it was not the *Saltus.* Day by day she yielded more of her patronage to the crowded decks of the new queen of the lake. The next season the threadbare opposition decided it had had enough and the *Francis Saltus,* with the hull of another contender on the stocks, the *Montreal,* came as did all things, under the control of the Transportation Company.

So far, so good (or bad, for the public). But if the directors of the monopoly could have read the future of the *Saltus* in a crystal ball, their victory would have afforded little jubilation. The resignation of Richard Sherman as a director and captain might have served them as an omen. Refusing to use a cut-off he had invented for the engine of the *United States,* they appointed the more popular William Anderson master of the new vessel, the last straw for the proud Sherman.

Moreover, a new kind of adversary was entering a game in which the monopoly had previously called all the shots. During the four decades after 1807 passenger travel between New York and Montreal had progressed from sloop and schooner, horseback and stagecoach, to steamboat and canal packet. Now the iron horse was galloping toward the lake from the east and south. In December 1849 the dignitaries of the Rutland and Burlington, which won the race with the Vermont Central only by a few hours, pronounced "the union of the waters of Lake Champlain and the Atlantic" and good wishes for the health of Timothy Follett, merchant, canal, and steamboat functionary,

73. Railroad Station House and steamboat landing near the border at Rouses Point.

and now the Rutland's first president. While the main line of the Vermont Central did not enter the port because of the opposition of shipping interests, the right of way of the Rutland, whose directors obviously enjoyed an inside track with those of the Transportation Company, led directly to its Burlington wharf.

In 1848 a railroad to connect the Hudson River and Lake Champlain steamboats was completed from Saratoga to Whitehall, outflanking the stage lines from there to Troy and scuttling the canal packets. To the north two years later, the tracks of the Champlain and St. Lawrence connected Rouses Point with Montreal. While the arrival of railroads elsewhere severely affected or eclipsed the patronage of water routes, they at first acted as an elixir to Champlain steamboats. Although Montreal-bound passengers could, after May 1852, choose between the steamboat and rail lines from New York to Albany and Troy, and proceed north from the latter city by train via the Rutland and Burlington and Vermont Central, the railroad connections were as fractured as the relationships among their highly competitive promoters. The better option, therefore, was to travel by train on the Saratoga and Washington to Whitehall, board the steamboats for Rouses Point, and the train from there to Montreal.

As far as east-west traffic was concerned, the lake long presented an impasse to ambitious railroad men who dreamed of through routes from Portland, Maine, or Boston to the west. Cornelius Vanderbilt had preempted the pass along the banks of the Mohawk, and there was no other nearly as feasible all the way north to the Canadian border. For most of its 120 miles, the lake was too wide to permit railroad bridges, and where it was not, the towering foothills and craggy peaks of the Adirondacks presented the unfriendliest of barriers.

The north-south railroads thus at first served the boats as feeders. While they made the basin at Whitehall busier than ever, the arrival of the first train from Montreal to Rouses Point turned historic St. Jean into a ghost port. Thomas Canfield relates the story of Jason Pierce, whose previously thriving business as a forwarder at St. Jean vanished overnight. A former resident of Vermont who had been taken prisoner by the British at the Battle of Plattsburgh, Pierce was widely known around lake as an honorable, gentlemanly and forward-looking businessman with high aspirations for St. Jean. Upon the completion of the Ogdensburg and Lake Champlain railroad, the line from St. Jean to Montreal (built largely through the efforts of Pierce) had no option but to connect with the west-bound road at Rouses Point — by-passing St. Jean in the process.

"Mr. Pierce at once saw that an operation of this kind must change the whole business from St. Jean to Rouses Point . . . . For a quarter of a century or more he was the prominent man of the place . . . and believed it was to remain in the future as in the past the great entrance to the 'King's highway.' When he saw it was to be shorn of its prominence by the extension of the railroad to Rouses Point, and instead of being the head of business to be a mere way-station upon the road, he became so much annoyed and his mind was so much affected by it that his health began to fail. And as the time approached when the steamboat was to discontinue her trips there he became worse, and on the 6th of September, 1851, the same day that the steamer *Whitehall* took her departure for the last time from St. Jean's, the spirit of Jason C. Pierce took its departure from this world of care and trouble."

As St. Jean languished, the hamlet and port of Rouses Point awoke to prodigious activity. Just after it became the thriving northern terminus of trains and boats a traveler wrote:

Late in the evening the steamer landed us at the end of water communication of Lake Champlain at a very extraordinary place named Rouses Point within one mile of the boundary line of the U.S. and Canada; it requires some little detail to convey . . . the enormous extent of bustle, confusion, business and pleasure all brought into focus upon an immense wharf or pier of wood, running the length of some hundred feet into the lake itself. Upon the entire length of this pier is erected a large hotel, with warehouses and stores adjoining. The bedrooms are in the higher regions, whilst, underneath, the railway terminal and offices communicate with the hotel on the right wing; then the steam and other boats plying alongside either pier, receiving and discharging merchandise or passengers, add greatly to the business-like character of the place. Here the Yankee is in his glory, although the confusion and noise beat even that of Broadway in New York. This was another occasion on which the weary traveler had little chance of a night's rest, surrounded as he is by the hissing engines, both from boat and rail, the noises of the cranes and bustle of hundreds of passengers with their heavy baggage.

The stakes by water and rail were now enormous and the Champlain Transportation Company, however tightly and resourcefully controlled by local directors in the past, had become the pawn of a much expanded struggle. One of its central figures was Oscar Alexis Burton, an energetic and avaricious trader from St. Albans Bay, of whom it was said: "He seemed to realize that money was a great power, he wanted it and determined to get it." Starting out in the potash business, he dreamed of controlling all the trading, and therefore the shipping, at the Bay. To do so he and his brother built a dock alongside that of the established merchant, N.W. Kingman, fully expecting the steamboat to land there, but on the day their dock opened for business the boat steamed right past to Kingman's, leaving Burton white-lipped and empty-handed.

By means of close-fisted transactions in lumber, horses, sheep, land and merchandise, the interlopers gained the leverage to buy out Kingman. Upon the death of his brother of erysipelas, Oscar paid his sister-in-law only half her share of the business, saying "a young widow with $5,000 is about as well off as she would be with $18,000." Eventually, with the help of none other than the notoriously fraudulent New York manipulator, Daniel Drew (the inventor of "stock watering," who plied his livestock with salt, then slaked their thirst just before they were weighed and sold), Burton established a bank in St. Albans.

His next target was the Champlain Transportation Company, which he and Drew acquired in the summer of 1849 by buying controlling interest from some of its directors. At its first meeting his captive board declared a dividend of $15 a share and a special compensation to Burton of $10,000 which, with subsequent emoluments, enabled him to purchase in Burlington an impressive house with iron lions guarding the entrance.

Among the measures taken by Burton and Drew to line their purses was one that also happened to improve the lot of travelers — a through passenger and freight line from New York to Montreal connecting with Drew's steamboats on the Hudson. This enabled passengers to travel between the two cities in 48 hours with only one ticket. Whatever advantages accrued to through traffic, the local public was disgusted with the latest machinations of the monopoly, and before long rumors drifted down the lake of a new opposition boat at Whitehall.

Having learned from Comstock's experience with the *Francis Saltus* (taken over by the monopoly) that speed was the key to a successful challenge, the builders of the new vessel, the *R. W. Sherman,* exerted every effort to make her the fastest on the lake. The newspapers expended a springtide of ink in her behalf, quoting her master, Captain Chapman as declaring,"'O.A. Burton or any other old-line director cannot have the directing of her business, and she will sail as an opposition boat — opposition to the old line, opposition to his prices and slow-sailing steamers.' . . . We certainly like the tone of his manifesto and the news falls among the old-line directors with the effect of a 24-pound shot. . . . "

Failing to scuttle the new boat by injunctions and other devices Burton had the impertinence, asserted Captain Chapman, "to circulate a report that he (Burton) had purchased the *R. W. Sherman* so that the public would think it was owned by the monopoly and not patronize it, with resultant damage to the independent owners . . . a base and contemptible falsehood. Anyone who

74. R.W. Sherman *(later the* America) *established all-time speed records on the lake.*

is acquainted with O.A. Burton knows that truth to him is stranger than fiction! Mr. Burton does not own the *Sherman,* he has not bought me."

At last dawned the day of the *Sherman's* maiden voyage.

"In due time the gallant *Sherman* took us aboard, and as the superb and graceful boat moved from the wharf, hearty cheers arose from the animated crowd assembled to greet her, while the *Saltus,* crowding steam, was creeping along the eastern shore of the Lake, some three miles ahead of the *Sherman,* like a suspected codfish, and in vain hope of reaching Burlington first, by virtue of having made but one landing since leaving Whitehall, while the *Sherman* had made all. But the *Sherman* swept into her course, and gallantly passed the *Saltus* . . . and who can measure the hearty cheers that greeted the noble steamer and her popular commander as she approached and left our wharves — all the while 'sonorous blowing martial sounds' under the management of the Whitehall and Burlington bands."

The Burlington Free Press was transported:

"She passed the *Saltus* this morning . . . as easy as though that boat were going the other way — and if any responsible man has a seedy sort of hat . . . we are prepared to wager one of Barnum's 'ne plus ultras' that she will make mincemeat of the *United States* on the first opportunity."

Alas, the exuberance of public and press proved short-lived. In a breathless series of transactions calculated to reap enormous profits in 1852, Burton and Drew sold the entire Champlain Transportation Company — the *United States, Francis Saltus, Burlington, Whitehall,* and *Montreal* (still unfinished) together with their shipyard, everything except their charter, to the Rutland and Burlington Railroad. Unlike the Vermont Central which had achieved a connection between Boston and Montreal by way of a railroad bridge on pilings at Rouses Point, the Rutland line, also with connections to Boston, ended at Burlington. By purchasing the steamboat line it gained control of most of the water traffic from the south and, at the same time, a connection at Rouses Point with the railroad to Montreal.

The retention of their charter was the key to the next move of Burton and Drew. While they now had no steamboats, they knew where they could get one — the fastest on the lake. "A few days ago," mourned the press, "it became a matter of public note that certain persons, composing a majority of the board of directors . . . in express violation of the articles of association, and without consultation with the stock holders, leased the (*Sherman*) to the aforesaid monopoly, commonly called the Champlain Transportation Company for a sum not sufficient to pay expenses . . . thereby making the stockholders liable for the balance of the expenses; hoping in a short time (after

75. *Fireworks celebration was slated, curiously enough, for August.*

playing this diabolic and treacherous game) to compel the stockholders in the new company to sell their interest at a price to suit the convenience of its above-mentioned directors. . . ."

Burton acquired not only the *Sherman* but also another vessel on the stocks at Whitehall, the 260-foot *Canada* launched in 1853. Having eliminated the opposition with this single stroke, he then placed these two vessels in competition with the railroad to which he had sold his older and slower vessels. After a little over two years of competition, the Rutland and Burlington resold to the monopoly, at less than one-third of their purchase price, the vessels it had so recently acquired — all, that is, except that elderly trouble-maker, the *Francis Saltus*. The Rutland and Burlington had sold her to the Plattsburgh and Montreal railroad, which had developed a new connection to Montreal. (Another smaller boat, the *Boston*, was retained by the Rutland and Burlington as a ferry.) Try as they would, Burton and Drew could not regain control of the *Saltus*, which was carrying much of their Plattsburgh traffic to Burlington for transshipment by rail. After exhausting legal and semilegal means, they launched a program of simple piracy. The Supreme Court might have untangled the legal implications of the action that followed, but what it all boiled down to was that possession was nine points of the law.

At the apex of the struggle ownership of the *Saltus* passed to a Mr. Price, a director of the Plattsburgh and Montreal Railroad. An agreement was reached whereby Burton would pay him $25,000 to lay up the *Saltus*, allowing the monopoly to handle lake traffic for the railroad. Price took the cash and retired the *Saltus*.

About six weeks later — on June 10, 1856 — one of Burton's own men, Captain Chamberlin, former master of the *Saltus*, crossed the lake at night with a prize crew. Boarding the steamer, binding up the watchman and setting him ashore, they fired the *Saltus's* boilers and steamed out of Plattsburgh harbor into the broad lake. Captain Chamberlin's excuse, fabricated no doubt by Burton, was a claim on the *Saltus* for repairs he had once made on her.

A law suit was hastily filed against Chamberlin and the monopoly, not by Price who had been well compensated, but by one of his backers, a Mr. Cook. After much agitation the court awarded custody of the *Saltus* to Cook, and the old company had to surrender it. This failed to discourage Burton. A little later, while the *Saltus* was docked at St. Jean, Captain Chamberlin with another prize crew seized her again (on the same technicality of a claim for repairs, but this time under Canadian jurisprudence) and sailed her up the lake to Shelburne Harbor. There they beached her, removed some of her machinery, and hid it in the bushes. Then they opened the seacocks on the steamer *Whitehall* and sank her directly astern of the *Saltus*.

A few days later the sloop *Hercules* from Plattsburgh sailed into the Bay, her deck crowded with 100 seamen. Hot for a fight, they had come to retrieve the *Saltus* by force. As they rounded the point they saw their quarry with the *Whitehall* sunk at her stern, and completing the semi-circle around her, the *United States* and *Canada* with full heads of steam, their crews standing by. As the 100 seamen drifted closer the situation seemed even more hopeless, for the *Saltus* was chained with heavy links to a tree on shore, while "Henry Campbell sat on the chain, a revolver in his hand and dared anyone to remove the cable."

When it seemed as though there must be an explosion of some kind, Sheriff Flanagan of the invading forces drew a revolver on Judge Smalley of the defenders, but the judge didn't scare a bit. At last the frustrated crew of the *Hercules* turned about and sailed bitterly back to Plattsburgh without its quarry — and with a gloomy report for Mr. Cook. But the courts again found in his favor, the result being a familiar one in the annals of the monopoly: it again purchased the *Saltus,* together with a release for claims and damages. The veteran opposition boat had caused too many sleepless nights over the years, so it was with grim satisfaction in 1859 that the directors ordered her dismantled and sunk.

❧✵❧

By the mid-nineteenth century a lake tucked away in the northern mountains had become a major artery of the great stream of interstate commerce.

So many barges choked the Champlain canal that the iron industry at Port Henry, which floated 140,000 tons of ore to tidewater in 1864, had to secure an additional outlet by rail at Burlington. Since the local manufacture of iron was preferable to clogging the canal with ore for manufacture on the Hudson, the barges that went south returned that year with 103 thousand tons of coal to fuel the furnaces of Essex and Clinton counties. It was first-come first-serve at the locks, and a boatload of iron ore had to jockey for position with one of lumber, or hides, or logs. In 1867 hundreds of thousands of bushels of potatoes, and tannery cargoes worth a million dollars passed through the canal.

Throughout the nineteenth century and well into the twentieth Port Henry remained the center of the west shore's iron industry, the Victorian mansions of its two major barons, George Sherman and J.G. Witherbee, overlooking their dockside furnaces and mills. The port's high-grade magnetic ore had originally come 7½ miles from the rich Mineville deposit in heavily braked wagons descending a steep plank road built of four-inch hemlock 8 to 10 feet in length. A railroad was later built to haul ever-increasing loads down to the eight furnaces, twenty forges, and three rolling mills flanking the wharf. Several hundred boats, covering an acre or two, often waited there for a tow, their barefoot "captains" shouting orders to the "dock-wallopers" who loaded their boats with wheelbarrows. Two barges each with 100 tons of ore were often filled by a gang of four of these men in a single day.

76. Bird's-eye view of part of the Burlington waterfront in the early 1870's shows the changes wrought by the third lumber boom. The Central Vermont Railroad dock and station appear at left, while the next to last pier at the right served the Rutland terminal. Slip at far right facilitated piling lumber directly from canal boats. Pioneer Shops' varied industries composed the aggregation of buildings at upper left. During this period the port was handling 170 million board feet of lumber a year.

As highly visible on and near the lake were the millions of tons mined and manufactured each year by the Port Henry Iron Company, the Witherbee-Sherman, and Crown Point works (and those at Iron Mountain of the Chateaugay Iron Company in the township of Dannemora) their value was exceeded by the seemingly endless outpouring of logs from the northern forests — no longer New York or Vermont logs, but Canadian. They arrived by way of a second canal called the Chambly, built around the twelve-mile rapids of the Richelieu between St. Jean and the Chambly basin.

Its completion in 1843 heralded the last of three great migrations of lumber (first, that to the north of the valley's virgin timber, then to the south by way of the Champlain canal) and now to the south by way of the Chambly and to the Atlantic seaboard by railroad. No sooner had the Rutland line (and the Vermont Central by way of a spur) connected Burlington with Boston than enterprising merchants, led by Lawrence Barnes, visualized a vast new market in metropolitan New England.

From forests on the Ottawa, Three Rivers, and other Canadian streams, barges carrying 80,000 board feet sailed singly or departed in tows for the Richelieu where they were hauled single-file through the Chambly canal, then to the lake. At Burlington their cargoes were stacked and transshipped by freight cars to Concord, Manchester, Hartford, Boston and New Bedford.

Of the 40 million board feet Burlington was handling by 1860 a lumberman wrote that no one dreamed the port would be "lumbered up with boards and planks on their distant voyage to Europe, South America, California, and the far isles of the Pacific, but such is the fact . . . . If a ship at Boston, bound for Australia, needs a cargo of lumber, it is put into the cars at the planing mill, carried to Boston and unloaded direct from the cars to the vessel. If one for the West Indies calls for a load, it can be supplied with a cargo of rough boards with the same facility and dispatch. Every demand for pine lumber or any of its manufactures, whether rough, dressed, tongued and grooved, made into doors, sash, blinds, or boxes, or even houses, ready made, can be furnished to order upon short notice."

By 1868 thirty acres around the wharves were stacked with lumber brought there by some 400 vessels, American and Canadian — many of them "pin-flats," the Quebec version of the sloop-rigged canal boat. These eventually yielded to steam tow boats, each occasionally handling a cluster of barges carrying as many as three million board feet of pine and spruce. At the height of the boom 1,021 steamers, ships, and canal boats, manned by crews numbering 3300 were registered in the Champlain district.

In the vintage year of 1873 when it was the third largest lumber port in the

77. Turn-of-the-century view of downtown Whitehall near the canal's entrance to the lake.

United States, Burlington received 170 million board feet; a decade later the mill of one firm alone was planing 40 million feet a year. The mills spawned a host of satellite industries and as many fortunes, spent by lumber barons on opulent mansions on the hill. Cheap immigrant labor abounded; the prospect of a minimum wage had not yet warmed the heart of the wildest reformer.

Lumbermen had reason to expect their bounty would pour indefinitely from the Canadian cornucopia, but such was not to be the case. For more than a century the forests had not been so much cut as mined; already a movement was afoot to conserve the last great stands on the Adirondacks' eastern slopes. At the same time newly tapped forests in the American west were saturating the market. To fend off cheap foreign lumber Congress was induced, in 1893, to place a duty of $2.00 for every thousand feet of lumber imported from Canada, with the result that within a few years the lake's third age of lumber was reduced to ashes.

The commercial fleet declined with it, although many canal boats found other cargoes like grain and marble from the islands, shavings from the local woodworking industries for the bedding of New York City's horses, pulpwood, and, unlikely as it may seem, boatloads of Canadian eels in holds specially constructed to ply them with a constant supply of water. So confident were the people of the Champlain and Hudson valleys of the continued usefulness of the southern canal that in 1905 New York began a costly program to strengthen and deepen it to twelve feet, and to enlarge the locks so that they could admit longer and wider vessels carrying from 300 to 600 tons.

Completed in 1916 the so-called Champlain Barge Canal continues an unbroken heritage of a century and a half of inland water transport with barges carrying millions of gallons of oil and gasoline from the Hudson to be stored at various depots on the lake when navigation ceases during the winter.

No way of life, other than the steamboatmen's, belonged more intimately to the lake than that aboard the traditional canal boat. It died hard, lingering into the first two decades of the twentieth century. Hauled by powerful tugs bearing such names as *Brilliant, Defender, Peerless,* and *Protector,* as many as 60 boats often huddled in a single tow, each with its own living quarters in the stern, a floating village of families and individuals, French and polyglottal Americans, bound together for a century by the imperatives and traditions of the northern waterway.

> *Now all good wood-scow sailor-mans*
> *tak warnings by dat storm.*
> *go marry wan dam nice french girl*
> *and leev on wan dam beeg farm.*
> *den spose de win shes blow lak hurricane*
> *and bimeby shes blow some more*
> *you can't get drown on Lac Champlain*
> *so long as you stay on shore.*

Within a year of the passing of the *Francis Saltus* and the steamboat war, the devious Daniel Drew sold his stock in the Champlain Transportation Company, and in 1860 his nefarious local colleague, Oscar Burton, was removed from the helm.

The connections of the new president, Colonel Le Grand B. Cannon, were as imposing as his name: his brother-in-law controlled the Rensselaer and Saratoga Railroad. That line gradually purchased control both of the Transportation and Lake George Steamboat companies. When in 1870 the Delaware and Hudson leased the Rensselaer and Saratoga, the steamboat companies also passed under its aegis. This corporate network remained

78. LeGrand B. Cannon, Lake Champlain steamboat czar.

intact for over six decades. Without it the steamboats on the two lakes would
have passed into oblivion long before they did, for the D & H integrated them
with its summer train schedules between Montreal and Albany and with the
Hudson River Day and Night Lines to New York, providing one of the most
fashionable and, for the steamboat companies, lucrative inland water journeys
in the east.

The overlord of a baronial enclave at the crest of the bluff in Burlington and
a martinet in his insistence on safety, order, and neatness aboard his boats,
Colonel Cannon set as zealously to work drilling their crews as he did shoring
up the company's finances. Under his direction the Champlain steamers were
said to have become the first commercial vessels in the country to establish a
system of quarters.

Far removed from the tremors of the Civil War except as clandestine
carriers of fugitive slaves, of regiments of Vermont troops en route to the
front, and of the local militia during and after the Confederate raid from
Quebec on St. Albans in 1864, the *United States, Canada, America* (originally
the *R.W. Sherman*), and the *Montreal* steamed uneventfully through the Civil
War.

Since a wooden hull, however well braced with its "hog-frame" to support
heavy boilers and machinery, rarely lasted over 25 years, the company
proceeded to replace its older vessels with the 251-foot double-stackers *Adirondack* in 1867 and the 262-foot *Vermont II* in 1871. The joiner work of both

79. *Youthful* Adirondack *fell victim to the abandonment of the night line following the completion of the west-shore railroad, while the elegant* Vermont II *served over three decades.*

80. Size of paddlewheels becomes apparent in closeup view of ornate wheelhouse.

established new standards of opulence and comfort. With a stateroom hall 171 feet long fashioned in walnut, chestnut, and gilt; with 61 staterooms, president's and bridal rooms, a barber shop, and dining room for 150 people, the *Vermont II* acquired a reputation as one of the finest vessels in the country of her class.

In the fall of 1874 the *Adirondack* became the last line steamboat to clear

81. The Vermont II*'s stateroom hall surrounded stairs to main deck and vertical engine enclosure.*

the historic port of Whitehall, since the New York and Canada Railroad had built tracks north from there along the west shore to Ticonderoga. With trains now connecting Ticonderoga with Albany, boat service through the difficult Narrows was superfluous. Whitehall's loss to the forces of geography and economics became Ticonderoga's gain. Not that the village had dozed since the Revolution: waterwheels driven by the stream draining Lake George had

82. *Railroad trestle and steamboat landing on the west shore south of Fort Ticonderoga.*

enabled it to cut and ship lumber, build boats (some ten vessels a year after the opening of the canal), manufacture iron, and grind, card, and tan quantities of grain, wool, and hides.

A semicircular trestle at the foot of Mount Defiance now became the point of transfer between the trains, the Champlain steamboats, and those of Lake George at the upper end of town. The 1550-foot trestle, resting on 40-foot pilings, led out to a large platform 300 feet long and 100 wide, which supported the depot where the trains met the boats. It was also served by a 425-foot trestle roadway for the public. Stagecoaches rattled up and down the hill between the landings delivering streams of local or New York-bound passengers, who were now offered a water route to the south aboard the Lake George boats if they did not want to take the train to Whitehall and Albany. With the building in 1882 of a railroad spur from the south end of Lake George connecting with the Saratoga and Albany at Fort Edward, the water route was the one they chose. Like other landmarks in the changing transportation scene the Ticonderoga stagecoaches presently succumbed to another short-line railroad connecting the Champlain and Lake George piers.

At the same time Whitehall was abandoned and Ticonderoga adopted as the steamers' southern terminal, further developments were taking place to the north. No sooner had Rouses Point become well established as the northern junction of boats and trains than the railroad was extended south to Plattsburgh, and Rouses Point suffered the fate of St. Jean. In an epic achievement of track-laying along and through the rocky escarpments bordering the west shore, the long gap between Ticonderoga and Plattsburgh was at last closed in 1874 — a railroad milestone of such significance that the first train from Albany to Montreal, composed of seven Wagner Palace coaches, directors- and "hotel" cars and an open coach, carried such luminaries as President Chester A. Arthur, John Jacob Astor, Cornelius Vanderbilt, and J.P. Morgan.

For the boats the west shore line was a milestone of a different kind. Ending their monopoly of north-south travel, it forced the discontinuance of the night line. But the day boats still retained much of their patronage, for the Delaware and Hudson, which acquired the various west shore railroad lines, also controlled, as has been stated, the steamboat companies and continued to route its summer passengers from Plattsburgh to Albany by way of the Champlain and Lake George steamers.

83. Northern boat and rail terminal at Plattsburgh (hotel at top).

84. Former railroad ferry, converted to passenger packet Champlain, *was wrecked in 1875.*

After the departure of the British in 1814 Plattsburgh like Burlington, became a large forwarder of lumber, and of iron, wool, and other products over the Champlain Canal. And now trainloads of Montreal passengers arriving daily at its wharves transformed it into a lively port of entry and of transfer.

In 1874 the Transportation Company acquired from the railroads the *Oakes Ames,* a large ferry with two engines (one for each sidewheel) and two sets of tracks on the main deck. For six years it had carried thousands of railroad cars from Burlington to Plattsburgh by means of an ingenious device designed by its captain called a "self-adjusting railroad bridge" which, with the help of a steam engine on shore, could quickly transfer freight cars to the boat. Making four daily trips in each direction, the *Ames* had saved 18 miles over the shortest rail route between Boston and Montreal, and nearly 30 between Boston and Ogdensburg on the St. Lawrence. Because of the completion of the through line along the western shore the railroads no longer needed the big sidewheeler.

Renaming her *Champlain* (her previous namesake had become involved in the Credit Mobilier scandal), the Transportation Company ripped up her railroad tracks, converted her into a passenger steamer with appointments rivaling those of the *Adirondack* and *Vermont II,* and placed her on line-run between Ticonderoga, Burlington, and Plattsburgh. She had served a little over a year in this capacity when, after leaving Westport on a quiet July night in 1875, she suddenly rose up out of the water and shook from stem to stern in a crash so unaccountable that neither her captain, who had retired for the night, nor the pilot at her wheel knew what had happened. All was confusion in the darkness as the *Champlain* bent amidships and cracked, her stern settling into the water in the deepest part of the lake.

In a few minutes it was discovered that she had struck a rocky spur of Split Rock Mountain. But why? The night was good for navigation, the vessel was in perfect condition, and the pilot at the wheel, John Eldridge, had had 23 years' experience. Although the reason for the crash soon became apparent, the details have escaped public scrutiny for over a century.

To "sift the chaff and save every grain" the *Champlain*'s officers were directed to submit written testimony of what they did and saw others do, and to attend subsequent hearings. In his report Abijah North, the purser, wrote that the *Champlain* carried 47 crew, 60 passengers, and 45 tons of freight when she left Ticonderoga that fateful night. Seventeen passengers boarded her at Port Henry and 23 got off at Westport, leaving 54 and a few children—some of them going to the regatta at Burlington the next day.

North at first thought she had hit a canal boat, and was shoving it down in the water, "but the shock and vibrations were so powerful before she got still, I thought I must be mistaken. I closed the door and window and hurried to see what had happened — and there within 15 feet of the starboard quarters were the shore rocks. I immediately said out loud, 'The rudder chain must have broken,' as I could not believe it possible that such a thing should have happened *under the circumstances*, except through an accident of that nature.' . . ."

Captain George Rushlow testified that he too thought that the *Champlain* had run over some vessel. As he stepped from his stateroom he met the second pilot, Ell Rockwell, and asked him who was at the wheel, and he replied, "John Eldridge." (Rockwell had been relieved at Westport.)

"I noticed a slight escape of steam from the port boiler room," the Captain testified, "and also that the fires were being hauled on the starboard side, and gave orders to put out all the fires and blow the water from the boilers. As I went forward I met passengers coming aft, who said they had been ordered to do so. I told them to go forward. In the meantime a plank had been run on shore . . . and passengers and baggage (transferred) to the shore. The boats were lowered and men sent to intercept the steamer *Adirondack*, also to procure the assistance of a sail vessel nearby. I had lights burning on shore for the convenience of passengers, and ascertained by inquiry that no one was hurt. . . . The crew behaved well, the engineers remaining at the wreck for about one and one-half hours, when passengers and baggage were put on board her."

Captain Rushlow said that the *"Champlain's* back was broken, as we term it, but she kept settling and breaking afterwards. I considered her a wreck, and had part of her after-rooms dismantled to save the material." He could not account for the vessel's being run on shore, and stated he had not seen Pilot John Eldridge; he had gone off into the woods.

Pilot Ell Rockwell testified that he had been at the wheel until 12 o'clock, when Eldridge took over. When the crash came he went immediately to the pilot house and saw Eldridge standing at the wheel, dazed and astonished. "He asked me if I could account for the steamer being on the rocks. I said to him he must have been asleep. His reply was, "My God, how can it be, I was steering as I always steer, clear of the mountains. . . .""

Asked his opinion of Eldridge's skill as a pilot and of his personal habits, Rockwell said that he was a first-class pilot and was not known to drink, although there had been hearsay since the accident that he used drugs — but not to Rockwell's knowledge. At a renewal of his hearing on July 27 he reported, however, that Eldridge "will drop asleep often upon sitting down

85. *Large steamer was run full speed on to Steam Mill Point under mysterious circumstances.*

86. Ell Rockwell the oldest steamboat captain in the world.

87. Andrew Goodhue (left), father of Mrs. Calvin Coolidge, and George Rushlow, captain of the Champlain.

and while conversing, and his pipe drop from his mouth, upon which he would pick up the pipe and remark that he was not asleep. . . ." Rockwell said it was now his opinion that Eldridge was "stupefied by the use of drugs" when he drove the *Champlain* on Steam Mill Point.

Having returned from his erratic disappearance in the woods, Eldridge testified in his own defense that the *Champlain* was in good condition at the time of the accident, that he had not rung the bells to slow or stop his engines until after she struck, and that he could give no reason why she did, except that "Something came over me, but I had hold of the wheel when she struck." He declared he did not take morphine or opium, but admitted buying some for the use of his family.

But the *Champlain's* baggage master, Mr. T. Roberts, testified that he had purchased morphine for Eldridge "about one year ago. I purchased for him at Whitehall a bottle containing a white powder. Price $1. About two months after, I purchased for him at Whitehall, two bottles, same as the first. I looked at the paper he gave me, that is, the order to purchase, and saw marked on the same, two bottles of morphine. Mr. Eldridge told me he took the powder for a pain in his bowels and that part of the supply was for the coming winter. I never saw him take any."

The statement of a Rouses Point druggist to the steamboat inspectors was introduced as testimony. "When I was at the old store I used to sell Eldridge morphine occasionally. He said he used it for rheumatic pains. I have sold him about one bottle this year. I asked him if he used it now; he replied, 'a little.' It was about four or five weeks ago that I had sold him the bottle."

Subsequently three Burlington druggists declared they had sold Eldridge two or three bottles of morphine, one of them commenting that "he was in the habit of taking." A second said he had sold him morphine on the night after the wreck. A house painter who worked for Eldridge testified that he had "noticed him in a deep study sometimes with his eyes opened, and then appearing to rouse and awaken as if from unconsciousness. I noticed this perhaps a half dozen times. . . ."

In consequence of this testimony the inspectors of steam vessels determined that "inasmuch as the habits of Mr. Eldridge render him an unsafe person to act as pilot on steam vessels, we have revoked his license as such."

⁂

Although fire and human error claimed two steamers while under way, none succumbed to the greater hazards of fog and heavy winds. In contrast to vessels navigating vast open reaches of water in an ocean fog, those running compass courses on narrow lakes before the advent of navigational aids had to contend every few minutes with points, islands, and reefs, sometimes without benefit of visibility beyond their flagstaffs.

Under such conditions it was necessary to maintain a constant boiler pressure and engine speed, and therefore a given number of revolutions of the sidewheels per minute. The pilot could then calculate his position on his charted compass course, making appropriate turns at precisely indicated times and places. Sometimes Champlain navigators had to make their way through pea-soup fogs without seeing a single landmark until fog bells on the breakwaters announced their arrival.

Outlanders have often voiced astonishment at the size and destructiveness of Champlain's waves — not long swells, but the high sharp breakers storms raise in a few minutes. One such gale from the west heeled the *Adirondack* dangerously over on her port beam as she cleared Crab Island. In the absence of trimming tanks, the engineer was ordered to carry the water as low as he dared in the port boiler and as high as possible in the starboard. This stabilized her at least to a degree. Heavy seas were crashing over the Burlington breakwater and the pilots advised Captain Flagg not to enter it, but having never yet skipped a landing he put four men on the double steering wheel. As the *Adirondack* approached the wharf a giant wave drove her against the pilings, breaking them off like twigs, at the same time raising her guard over the dock and smashing her side. There she hung — the passengers were safely put ashore — until the wind abated and she could proceed to the shipyard for repairs.

A raging south wind once gave the *Vermont II* such a thrashing that her ponderous paddleshaft broke in two. Her large anchor was dropped but would not hold. Captain George Rushlow then ordered out the sea anchor, a large canvas buoy which at least slowed the rate she was drifting toward the Four Brothers Islands. In the nick of time the tug *J.G. Witherbee* steamed up and, passing her a hawser, succeeded in holding her off the rocks until the *Adirondack* arrived to tow her to the shipyard.

If a 262-foot vessel could receive such a mauling what of canal boats wallowing behind a tug? In his reminiscences of life on the lake Captain Frank Godfrey writes of a November gale in 1911 that struck the tug *Defender*, south-bound with 50 canal boats loaded with pulp wood and lumber. The captain managed to maneuver his tow into the lee of Providence Island.

That night the wind shifted and the captain proceeded south for Burlington. When nearly to Colchester Reef light, the wind hauled W.S.W., becoming a heavy gale with very heavy seas, and the tug could not even hold the tow. Captain Rockwell, with the *Robert H. Cook* was weather-bound with his own tow at Port Douglas, and on seeing the lights of the *Defender* and its tow, he put his wife on one of the boats in his tow and steamed to its assistance. After getting a hawser on the *Defender's* tow, which was no easy matter in seas of that kind, the two tugs headed

88. *Canal boats in tow and cargo-carrying windjammer headed north toward Rock Point.*

for Port Douglas. A short time later fourteen boats in the *Defender's* tow broke adrift. Captain Rockwell turned back and picked up the drifting boats and again headed for Port Douglas. But seven of the boats again broke loose, and because the sea made it impossible to turn back with his load, he proceeded to Port Douglas and then returned for the other seven boats.

He had only gone part way when the rudder on the *Robert H. Cook* unshipped and fouled the blade of the propeller so that she was completely disabled. The crew managed to get two heavy bow anchors down, though it was a miracle the way she was rolling and pitching. But the tug nearly brought up on Colchester Reef before the anchors held.

The captain of the *Defender* would not go back into the lake, but spent the night in the pilot house praying. During the night the seven drifting boats with women and children aboard drifted to Stave Island where all of them sank, and some became total losses. Fortunately none of those aboard was drowned, as the boats were loaded with lumber which kept the hulls afloat. Had it been a northbound tow of coal or iron ore there would have been a heavy loss of life.

On another such occasion John Montgomery, later a steamboat captain, approached the Burlington breakwater with his father on their 80-foot canal schooner, the *General Butler*, completely out of control in a northern gale. "We had come from Isle La Motte with six people aboard and right off we knew she was lost; she was at the mercy of the wind on the seaside of the breakwater. As she crashed we unloaded a couple of passengers by having them jump off. She crashed again and again and finally we got everybody off. The last time she hit the breakwater I jumped; she careened back about a hundred feet and went down in the sea."

Once in a great while even the steamboats did not venture out. But most of the time, even if the waves washed over their cross decks, they hewed to their schedules from the moment the ice broke up in April until it drove them into winter quarters in January.

The raid of the west shore railroad on through freight and passenger traffic and the loss of the *Champlain* reduced the Transportation Company's mid-Victorian fleet to the line boat *Vermont II* and two smaller boats, the *A. Williams* and *Maquam*. A fourth, the *Reindeer*, was built and always owned by the Central Vermont Railroad. Responding to the flourishing excursion business the Transportation Company launched in 1888 the handsome 205-foot *Chateaugay*, one of the sprightliest vessels of her class in the country. She had an iron hull and feathering wheels, which permitted her paddle buckets to work much more efficiently and quietly.

Having served 31 years, the longest of any wooden-hulled steamer, the *Vermont II* was retired in 1902, to be replaced by the third vessel to bear her

89. *Remarkable 19th-century photo of Burlington waterfront shows* Reindeer *at Central Vermont Railroad station pier. Sprightly* Chateaugay *traveled the lake for nearly five decades.*

90. *Palatial* Vermont III *heads toward Essex in 1923. Drawing by J. Henderson Barr.* Ticonderoga, *last of Champlain's sidewheelers, pauses for portrait with large load of excursionists.*

name, slightly larger but considerably more powerful than her predecessor — a floating chateau lighted throughout by electricity, with a capacity of 800 to 1000 passengers. Her white and gold stateroom hall was decorated with a blue Axminster carpet and mahogany furniture upholstered with plush. A hand-carved seal of the state of Vermont adorned the frame of the mirror at the head of the stateroom hall's ornate staircase, which descended to the purser's office, gift shop, newsstand, and barber shop (with pink marble sinks) in the recess. Her many-windowed dining room was placed, not in the hold as formerly, but aft of the recess on the main deck so that passengers could enjoy the scenery.

The crew of the *Vermont III* consisted of the captain, two pilots, two engineers, two oilers, six firemen, first and second mates, ten deckhands, two pursers, a freight clerk and a baggage man, a steward and two stewardesses, two hall and recess boys, a headwaiter and fifteen waiters, a dining room cashier, four cooks (main chef, salad, pastry, and short-order), two scullions, two bartenders, a barber, a newsstand operator, and a night watchman — a total of 62.

In a schedule similar to her predecessors' she laid over every night at Plattsburgh to receive passengers from the Montreal train, which reached her wharf at 8:30 p.m. The dining room gong rang as the steamer departed at 6:30 a.m. for Burlington. Breakfast was served until 10:30, to be followed almost immediately by lunch until she reached Ticonderoga, connecting with the train to Lake George at 12:25. Continuing south through the upper lake her passengers boarded the train for Albany at Lake George Village, and completed their trip to 42nd Street in New York on the Hudson River steamers. Receiving northbound passengers, the *Vermont III* returned to Plattsburgh (by way of Westport, Essex, and Burlington) to meet the evening train to Montreal.

In 1906 the Transportation Company replaced its last wooden-hulled steamer, the *Maquam,* with the steel-hulled *Ticonderoga,* 15 feet longer than

91. President Taft at Plattsburgh during lake's Tricentennial.

the *Chateaugay* but similar in design, with a stateroom hall of Vermont butternut and cherry. In 1909 the *Ticonderoga* interrupted her Westport-to-St. Albans schedule to serve as the flagship of the lake's tercentenary celebration, carrying from pageant to pageant and speech to speech President Taft, the British and French ambassadors, the premier of Quebec, and the governors of Vermont and New York. (The ceremonies resumed three years later when she returned to Crown Point for the dedication of a memorial wharf and tower, with a sculpture by Rodin depicting the spirit of France.)

Presidential appearances on the lake were the rule, not the exception during the Gilded Age. From the steamboat landing beneath towering Hotel Champlain at Bluff Point south of Plattsburgh — the summer White House in 1897 — William McKinley sallied forth on the *Maquam* to the Isle La Motte residence of Lt. Governor Nelson Fisk for a meeting of the Vermont Fish and

92. *Rambling Victorian hotel at Bluff Point, N.Y., the summer White House on several occasions, had its own steamboat landing, called Cliff Haven. Chateaugay is loading passengers there.*

93. Canal boat crew waits for a load above the reflections of the Maquam *and* Vermont II.

Game Club, the *nom de guerre* of the state's Republican apparatus. Theodore Roosevelt appeared there, too, in 1901 under the most ominous and portentous circumstances: just before the reception, word arrived that McKinley had been shot in Buffalo. Roosevelt departed immediately, not for Washington but for the west shore. When McKinley's condition turned for the worse the vice-president, strangely but perhaps typically, was to be found on top of Mount Marcy.

The Champlain Transportation Company acquired some remarkable national connections. The grandson of Captain Richard ("Dandy Dick") Sherman became vice president of the United States. The son of Henry Mayo, master of the steamer *Montreal*, commanded the Atlantic fleet during the first World War. From 1888 to 1920 the government inspector of steamboat boilers in the Burlington district was Andrew I. Goodhue, father of Mrs. Calvin Coolidge. In 1895 James Roosevelt, father of Franklin D., replaced LeGrand Cannon as president of the Transportation Company. Little is known of Roosevelt's six-year tenure other than such perfunctory statements at annual directors' meetings as:

". . . the year 1896 does not show as favorably as the year 1895, but in view of the fact of its being the year of a presidential election and of the generally depressed state of affairs all over the country, the falling off in our receipts is not greater than that of other railway and steamboat companies." Roosevelt enjoyed sitting on a camp stool in the steamers' boiler rooms talking French to the firemen, but was also reported by the late Captain A. A. Fisher as making the deckhands pay for their own sweaters.

He frequently brought with him his young son Franklin, who boasted of being one of two civilians (Vermont Congressman Plumley was the other) who could steer the *Maquam* through "The Gut" into St. Albans Bay (with Captain Hawley's help). In the White House, Franklin Roosevelt was heard to exclaim: "Who in Hell changed the name of Ram Island to Lazy Lady! Sounds like some New Yorker."

Among the local steamboat families whose reputations sprang from the isolated and closely knit community around the shipyard at Shelburne Point were the Whites: Robert, Andrew, LeVater, George, and Frank, all well known on the lake and some of them beyond. Captain George (son of LeVater, who planned the construction of the *Adirondack, Vermont II* and *Chateaugay*) became superintendent of the Van Sanfords' Hudson River Day Line in the opening years of the 20th century, overseeing the building of the kingly *Hendrick Hudson, Washington Irving,* and *Robert Fulton,* and ultimately heading the Passenger Carrying Lines Association, which encompassed the big steamboat fleets of the country. Daniel P. Loomis, son of the steamboat company's last general manager, became president of the Association of American Railroads.

The career of Captain George Rushlow began in 1844 aboard the schooners *Hornet* and *Melvina* and covered 60 years as mate, pilot, captain, chief engineer, general agent, and general manager. Captain Ell Rockwell, patriarch of a large boating family started out as a cabin boy on the schooner *Cynthia,* and in 1844 at the age of 14 helped handle the lines at the launching of the *Francis Saltus.* With the exception of six seasons he sailed the lake continuously from 1842 to 1928 — still master of the *Vermont III* at the age of 98, obviously the oldest steamboat captain on the globe.

During the first World War, when the Transportation Company was taken over by the federal government, the boats served as handmaidens to the Army Officers Training Corps at Plattsburgh, and of the cavalrymen and caissons of Fort Ethan Allen across the lake. It is an odd coincidence that Plattsburgh, so strategic in the Revolution and the War of 1812, should become the source of another war's largest contingent of civilian officers — the "ninety-day wonders" of Elihu Root's "Plattsburgh Idea," who nevertheless made the critical difference in France, just as Arnold and Macdonough had within gunshot of their barracks.

A post-war casualty, the first since the wreck of the *Champlain,* occurred in 1919 when the *Ticonderoga,* rounding the north end of Isle La Motte, struck

Point au Fer reef. As water poured through a large gash in her hull her fires were quickly drawn and her 300 passengers safely removed in lifeboats. Work began at once to apply a temporary patch to her hull and then to pump it out. But the patch came off as a tug dragged her off the reef. As it tried to push her ashore the rising water sloshing from side to side in her hull caused her to list so menacingly that she dipped into the lake almost up to the windows on the main deck. But the steam in the tool room's donkey boiler off the starboard companionway provided her engineer with a weapon. As the boat rolled to port he emptied the ballast tank of water on that side, at the same time filling the starboard tank with the submerged trimming engine in the hull — reversing the process as she rolled to the right. By this strategem the tug managed to beach her before she rolled over. Divers then installed a new patch on the inside of her hull so it could not be scraped off when she left the shore. Safely towed to the shipyard, the *Ticonderoga* was replaced for the rest of the season by the *Chateaugay*, which had been laid up since 1917 for want of business.

94. *Trestle between Larrabee's Point and Ticonderoga proved less than an unqualified success.*

95. *Engine No. 26 of the Rutland Railroad milk train navigates the "fill" from the mainland to South Hero. Westbound train (below) crosses Rouses Point trestle from Vermont to New York.*

During the preceding decades the grip of the railroads had become tighter than ever on traffic from all directions. The trestle that connected them at Rouses Point had for a time acquired a counterpart between Larrabee's Point and Ticonderoga which, however, spasmodically dumped locomotives and cars into the lake. The Rutland had provided the most serious new incursion with its ambitious stone causeway across the Mallett's Bay shallows to South Hero. Begun in 1898, the track-laying continued north to the border through the islands — the fourth railroad from the south and east to Montreal within a

96. *In the 1920's the* Chateaugay's *superstructure was chopped off for carrying automobiles.*

span of a hundred miles. The islands had previously depended upon the boats for the transport of their abundant harvests.

But the iron horse's final gallop was mild compared to the assault on the excursion business by the latest entry in the transportation sweepstakes — the automobile. The steamboat company's 100th birthday party in 1926, featuring a giant cake surmounted by a version in frosting of its first vessel, the *Franklin,* proved to be more of a wake. Already the *Chateaugay,* her superstructure chopped off fore and aft, had been reduced to ferrying automobiles between Burlington and Port Kent, the gateway to that perennial tourist mecca, Ausable Chasm.

Yet one more extraordinary occasion enabled the Company to return to its vaunted role as a monopoly: the November flood of 1927 which completely isolated northern Vermont. The destruction of dozens of railroad and highway bridges brought transport to a standstill, with no prospect of bringing in supplies from any direction for days or weeks.

The *Vermont* and *Ticonderoga* had been laid up for the season, but every available hand at the shipyard rallied to revive the *Chateaugay* in a few hours. It would be hard to devise a more melodramatic scenario than that of a 39-year-old sidewheeler in the midnight of her career steaming to the rescue of a paralyzed countryside. Hour in and hour out, day and night for two weeks her firemen fed her boilers as she ploughed through minefields of debris on the swollen lake between New York and Vermont — her decks so stacked with hospital supplies, meat, groceries, cement, lumber, express, and mail that her master, John Montgomery, said he couldn't put a chicken on her anywhere. "She was loaded down to the guards and plowing deep but for fifteen days and fourteen nights we never struck a thing."

The Great Depression added its depredations to those of the automobile. By 1931 the steamers were ploughing seas of red ink: $132,000 that year and $161,000 the next. Late in the summer of 1932 the stately *Vermont III* met her last train at Ticonderoga. That fall the old and honorable through line to New York City became history.

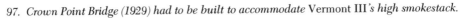

97. *Crown Point Bridge (1929) had to be built to accommodate* Vermont III*'s high smokestack.*

VIII

Reflections of an Inland Sea.

I NASMUCH as it is still possible to sail in almost a straight line from New York City to the St. Lawrence without setting foot on land, New England remains an island. It almost became more distinctly so. Were it not for the ice, for uncertain revenues, and the phenomenal cost of deepening the Barge and Chambly canals, the much debated Champlain Cut-Off or Seaway might have been built. Fortunately we have reached an era when such an undertaking rests upon considerations other than purely economic — when a wilderness of land or water is valued for its own sake.

If the modern channel had not straightened the old Elbow north of Whitehall, if there were no navigational buoys, and if an oil tanker or yacht did not happen along, an early nomad or Revolutionary sailor passing through the somber ledges and grassy marshes of the Champlain Narrows would be hard pressed to tell whether a millennium had passed, or just 200 years.

North beyond the Narrows in the bay at the foot of the waterfall from Lake St. Sacrement it would take more than a casual glance through the halyards to convince the Marquis of Montcalm that the walls of Fort Carillon are not the same as those he defended in 1758. But Professor Silliman of Yale who passed by in 1819 would become thoroughly confused, for in place of rubble and a solitary chimney, he would behold the spectre of an entire fort.

In 1820 William Ferris Pell, whose Loyalist father and grandfather had gone to Canada after the Revolution, received from Union College a deed to the garrison grounds of Ticonderoga. On business trips through the valley young Pell was disturbed by the removal from the fort of stone, beams, and planks for the building of settlers' homes. (The same thing was happening at Crown Point, as the grey stone Vermont dwellings on the road to Chimney Point across the narrow straight still testify.)

To preserve what was left of Ticonderoga, Pell bought up a number of squatters' rights, fenced the earthworks and redouts, and built a home close to the lake. Its destruction by fire failed to discourage him. In 1826, close by the *Jardin du Roi* that had been laid out by the French, he built the Pavilion, a much larger Georgian dwelling of wood, which still serves his descendants as a summer home. In 1838 tragedy struck when his son was killed in the explosion of a cannon he was firing to welcome his father home.

Upon the death of W.F. Pell his property was divided among ten children. None could afford to live in the Pavilion, but one of them, James Kent Pell, ran it for some years as a hotel and boarding house. (Upon his arrival one summer he unfortunately found that the stones from one of the redouts and a wall running from the fort to the lake had become a steamboat dock.)

When James Pell died his son, and then his grandson, John Howland Pell, managed the property. In 1909 Stephen Pell, John's son, bought the shares of seventeen relations and with the financial help of his wife and father-in-law, Robert M. Thompson, started to rebuild the fort and to collect anything that had ever belonged to it. In 1950 John H.G. Pell, Stephen's son, assumed the stewardship of what by then had become a thirteen-decade commitment to a homestead and celebrated historic site.

Year by year the stones that had fallen into the moat, and oak beams, rough-hewn from the Adirondacks, went up according to the original plans. Floor tiles made by French potters of the lakeshore's blue clay were faithfully reproduced. During the gradual course of reconstruction cannon, cannon balls, hand grenades, swivel balls and grapeshot, barrels, bullets and flints, hatchets, axes, hoes, bayonets, sword blades, keys, hinges, and locks were unearthed and placed on display along with innumerable gifts and bequests of a wide spectrum of benefactors. Among these is the blunderbuss carried by Ethan Allen during his capture of the fort. (He gave it to Benedict Arnold, who gave it to John Trumbull, from whose estate it was purchased by the Rhinelander family, who returned it to the fort.)

A cannon Henry Knox lost in the Mohawk River while hauling it over the snow to Boston. A silver bullet containing secret dispatches swallowed by a British messenger during the Burgoyne campaign. A thirteen-star flag from

98. Green Mountain Boys' descendants recaptured restored Fort Ticonderoga 200 years later.

General Schuyler's headquarters. A wool campaign blanket marked with the British broad arrow from the Hubbardton battlefield. Powder horns, paintings, maps, and prints.

Ultimately a restoration that must rank as the foremost of its kind in the country — one that could not conceivably have been accomplished other than by private philanthropy — was ready for the nourishment of the country's growing interest in its heritage. From dungeon and bakery to the pointed bastions and demi-lunes comprising the outer defenses, perhaps nothing more graphically signifies Ticonderoga's historical presence than a bronze plaque in the archway bearing the inscription: "Through this entrance to the Place

D'Armes of the Fort have passed: George Washington, Benjamin Franklin, Benedict Arnold, Horatio Gates, Anthony Wayne, Arthur St. Clair, Henry Knox, Philip Schuyler, Richard Montgomery, Ethan Allen, Seth Warner, Major Robert Rogers, the Marquis de Montcalm, the Duc de Levis, Sir Jeffery Amherst, Sir Guy Carleton, Major John Andre, Sir John Burgoyne, Thaddeus Kosciusko, and a host of other great men of our history. You who have tread in their footsteps, remember their glory."

In the presence of a Bicentennial assemblage on May 10, 1975, 200 years to the hour that the Green Mountain Boys captured the fort, their direct descendants crossed the lake and swept into the parade ground, again demanding the surrender of the fort in the name of the Great Jehovah and the Continental Congress.

Mount Independence across the water and Crown Point to the north cannot be counted as lucky. While the foundations of Fort St. Frederic are visible, and some of the walls of Fort Crown Point still stand, they were long subjected to the kind of neglect that arises when everyone's responsibility becomes no one's. However there is some aesthetic and historical value in ruins as such. Not having enough of them to suit their concept of a proper landscape, 19th-century Hudson River architects actually built their own new ruins.

There are very likely some good ones encased in the walls of the brick house standing on the site of the first French fort at Chimney Point, for at least one of its partitions is some three feet thick. Indeed, the late Millard Barnes, whose family owned the place for generations and carefully preserved the ancient taproom on the west side toward the lake, was convinced that some of the walls of the house date back to the French Fort de Pieux, if not to the English outpost built by Jacobus de Warm in 1690.

A lifelong historian with strongly voiced opinions, Barnes expressed contempt for a younger country's indifference toward its historical artifacts. His Van Dyke beard quivering as he paced his veranda, he would shake his fist alternately at Vermont and New York for not accepting the gift of the keel and stern piece of the *Congress,* which he had laboriously retrieved from the nearby bay where, in 1776, Benedict Arnold beached and burned it.

In Fort Blunder on the Canadian border Lake Champlain has another first-class ruin, although not so old. After the War of 1812 the government decided that the best place to prevent future invasions was Island Point, where the lake joins the Richelieu. In 1816 work began on a two-bastioned fort described by Benjamin Silliman as a great stone castle, like that on Governor's Island in New York. It had no sooner been completed than a survey of the 45th parallel revealed, to the consternation of the War Department, that its $200,000 fort was in Canada. After many conferences, much backing and filling, and shuffling of papers, the United States was successful in getting Canada to cede Fort Blunder and the land around it to the United States. But by that time it had fallen into such disrepair that the War Department decided to remove the remains and build another.

It was not until 1844 that work began on Fort Montgomery, named after the fallen general, an enormous medieval edifice built at Rouses Point of three-ton stones from Isle La Motte. Rising 48 feet from the water with five bastions, embrazures of wrought iron and cement, and spiral staircases of cut stone, the great pile was not finished until after the Civil War. But for what purpose? None whatever, as it turned out. In the absence of invasions or even threats from Canada except during the Confederate raid on St. Albans when the invaders came by land and not by sea, Fort Blunder the Second was abandoned to become a relic of outmoded warfare and government bungling — and a most imposing ruin.

In the broadening lake north of the bridge between Crown and Chimney Points a sense of timelessness returns to the north-bound traveler, as if a lake that had heaved and tossed for centuries were resting. This impression is enhanced by the villages on the western shore: Port Henry, shorn by competition of its iron works but in no greater hurry to find a new identity than Westport, a tranquil summer place bereft of the white hotel that dominated it for years.

Elsewhere the forests have returned to the phalanx of headlands guarding the ravines and coves all the way to Split Rock. The hills then retreat behind the wide bay that leads to Essex with its mellow Federal houses, four-square in the morning sun; and Willsboro, hidden behind its long point. Except for the occasional clearing of a farm, cottage or estate, the forests still prevail further north. Here the rising foothills of the Adirondack Park, and behind them the mountains rolling along the horizon like a giant parade of waves, seem almost primeval. Timelessness is no illusion in that deep refuge of the black bear and bobcat, fox and coyote, white-tailed deer, mink and beaver. Even where the narrow valleys and pungent pine forests give way to villages it is as if they were there on temporary leases.

The lake seems to partake of this wilderness. The Four Brothers islands might as well be a remote Pacific atoll, so completely have they been taken over by ring-billed gulls. In May and June they swarm in clouds over their crowded nests, filling the air with their cries. Elsewhere herring-gulls and terns claim other small islands, just as the waterfowl make Dead Creek on the east shore in Addison and the swamps of the Little Otter and the Missisquoi delta their own. The black and wood duck, mallard, canvasback, merganser, American goldeneye, and Canada goose have no intention of being diverted from their ancient flyway. While the passenger pigeon, slaughtered by the millions in the early days, has vanished along with the panther and wolf, most birds have survived, and most fish.

Although the Atlantic salmon no longer returns to the lake because of the dams on its tributaries, the landlocked salmon, trapped like the lowly smelt by the retreating glacier, has long forgotten his annual pilgrimage to the sea and is being vigorously cultivated. It is unlikely that fishermen will ever make much of a dent in the lake's huge population of small- and large-mouth bass, its northern pike, and its walleyes, although one wonders how enough of the latter managed to escape decades of wholesale seining in the Richelieu and Canadian bays. If there is a Champlain monster he might be the hulking 200-pound sturgeon which also must run the annual obstacle course on the Richelieu.

It is remarkable that so much wild-life has persisted in the presence of the Champlain Basin's nearly half-million people. Their depredations have been less harmful here than elsewhere only because there are fewer of them and they are so spread out. But so many live on tributaries affecting the lake's purity, that it has had to take considerable punishment through the years. Fortunately bond issues for sewage plants have fared well, and now the lake is at least holding its own, except in shallow bays where the discharge of phosphates has nourished thick beds of algae and weeds. This problem should find a near-term solution, since interest in the lake's welfare is strong and growing. At any given time, agencies, commissions and committees are at work — this one trying to resolve the sludge problem created by the International Paper Company at Ticonderoga, and that one considering the annual inundation of the flood plain on the Richelieu by the seasonal variation of eight feet in the level of the lake.

Aesthetic problems are harder to deal with, since their solution calls for such controls as zoning. Astonished at the lack of "development" while flying over the lake in 1966, President Lyndon Johnson told Senator George Aiken that things would really hum if Texas had it! Precisely. Americans are activists who think that something must be done about almost everything, when sometimes the best thing to do is nothing. The glory of Lake Champlain is not that it has changed but that it has remained largely the same. While parks occupy many miles of shoreline, as many or more large parcels remain in private hands, as they have for generations.

Sooner or later taxes, inflation, and real estate pressures will force the farms and estates, large and small, to be broken into small lots crowded with camps and trailers. That would be more democratic. But the price for the larger public would be the ruination of the shores. Considering the lake's location near very large metropolitan areas — Montreal to the north, Albany, Troy, and New York to the south, and Boston to the southeast — it is almost a miracle that the day of reckoning has not yet come.

⚜⚜⚜⚜⚜

Nature designed the terraces of the east shore's ancient sea bottom for grazing. After the Civil War the clouds of sheep covering these grasslands drifted on to the west, but the dairy cows and apple orchards that have replaced them seem secure. If they are not, it is because a farmer's temptation to sell to a developer rises with his expenses and the value of his land. In some places this has happened, and a cow would not recognize the quiet places where she used to come down to drink. But these are exceptions, not the rule.

Places inhabited for generations acquire overlays of human experience as conspicious in the mind's eye as the shoreline's visible features. While much of this experience has eroded away, some of it, such as what happened at a long-abandoned ferry crossing in Panton, erupts out of the past like an igneous column in a headland of clay.

The year was 1859. An audacious farmer on the slopes of the Adirondacks in North Elba — a man of "stern religious enthusiasm," a crazy fanatic or messiah, depending upon who in the nation was passing judgment — enlisted his three sons, a son-in-law, and other youths of North Elba in a desperate scheme to seize the Virginia arsenal at Harper's Ferry, to arm the slaves there, and then to withdraw to his mountain retreat to await the tide of liberty. Overpowered at the arsenal by the Maryland and Virginia militia (two of his sons, his son-in-law and his youthful conscripts from North Elba lay dead around him) he was delivered to the authorities for trial and execution.

His wife accompanied his coffin by train to New York, by boat up the Hudson, from Albany to Vergennes by rail (the Narrows were frozen and the steamboats were not running) and by team to Adams Landing. Early in December, over waters that had borne other visionaries, John Brown's body set sail for Barber Point. Loaded again on a wagon it at last reached North

Elba where, as almost everyone in the troubled Republic soon learned, it lay "moldering in the grave."

Adams Landing and Barber Point. Grog Harbor and Sloop Island. Time may have stripped many such places of all but their names, but the air is deep with vapors of the past.

North of Basin Harbor, where Thomas Macdonough found two aging vessels for his fleet, where the Winans steamboat family later lived, and where the lake's foremost resort has flourished in this century, the Otter Creek ends its placid wanderings through Vermont's western lowlands. The nomads of the early 19th century who stowed their belongings on packet boats at Vergennes and started west by way of the Champlain Canal and the Erie, would find little difference today in the river below the falls, except that trees along its banks, then cut down, have in many places returned. The "drowned" outlets of the Otter, Winooski, Lamoille, and Missisquoi reach far inland, their primeval swamps enlivened with the cries of heron, rail, and gallinule.

Just south of the Charlotte ferry, still shuttling to Essex after 17 decades, the verandas and gables of the long-lived summer colonies of Cedar Beach and Thompson's Point bathe in the afternoon sun. Several generations of a family have known the quartered-oak paneling and lingering smell of kerosene in some of these cottages, for their appeal is not subject to obsolescence.

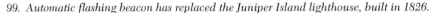

99. Automatic flashing beacon has replaced the Juniper Island lighthouse, built in 1826.

Like the tiny landings on Swiss lakes, both colonies were long served (until 1924) by steamboats, which picked up Burlington commuters every morning and returned them at night. The *Chateaugay* and *Ticonderoga* were the "alpha and omega of the Point day," Jessie Gibbs observes in her memoir. "The *Ti* left Westport at half past six. When you heard her tooting for the Point you knew it was breakfast time. In the late afternoon her friendly salute to Essex told you it was time to get the supper on the table. And that grand, roaring blast as she came by the bluff and prepared to make her wide and majestic circle of the reefs preparatory to the Point landing was the signal for the entire colony to rush for the dock."

On Saturday night every porch was trimmed with colored lanterns when the boat appeared for a moonlight sail to Westport, the music of its two itinerant musicians, one with a wooden leg and fiddle and the other with a harp, drifting across the water. Occasionally the *Ti* ran an all-day excursion to Port Kent and Ausable Chasm, attracting "the local swains in their buggies which they would leave in the woods near the Club House. This gave the Point juveniles a chance to change wheels on the buggies, and to use the horses during the day as cavalry mounts. The laments of the tired excursionists when they discovered the state of their equipment probably still haunt our North Shore woods."

When President Theodore Roosevelt arrived to visit Secretary of the Treasury Leslie M. Shaw, a resident of the Point, a torchlight procession formed at the dock. As it started for the Shaw cottage past a row of verandas decorated with Japanese lanterns and red, green, and blue kerosene lamps, a self-appointed marshal slightly in his cups, shouted: "Hooray for Cleveland!" A descendant of the creator of the headless horseman, Dick Irving, was the Point's most memorable resident — a raconteur and angler of such Falstaffian dimensions he had to be rolled into his fishing boat.

The Shelburne shoreline is occupied for miles, as it has been since 1888, by the descendants of Dr. and Mrs. William Seward Webb. After the death of her father, William H. Vanderbilt, they produced a manor with huge carriage houses, cavernous barns, and vast reaches of countryside that might be considered a northern outpost of Newport, Rhode Island, were it not even more extensive than the downcountry "cottages" her brothers and sisters competed with each other to build.

A north-bound sailor passing near the coast eventually arrives at the shale cliffs of Juniper Island, so directly in his way and so threatening at night that in 1826 the federal government built the first of a number of lighthouses there. Its white brick dwelling was attached to a tower and eventually fitted with a

French lens that projected its flame for 14 miles. Compared to the tenders of lights on reefs and craggy knolls, the Juniper Island keeper had ample elbow room with his hay field and garden to help him lay up supplies for the winter, although he could and did cross to the mainland on the ice. Climbing the circular staircase to light the lamp each night, he was also prepared to ring his fog bell housed under a separate roof, which he did by tripping a lever in a clock-like apparatus with a heavy spring.

Other similar lighthouses were stationed from south to north at Watch Point in the Narrows, Crown Point, Barber Point, Split Rock, Colchester Reef, Bluff Point, Cumberland Head, Gordon Landing, Point au Roche, Windmill Point and Isle La Motte — some with towers 50 feet high, and some still occupied, but not by keepers, who were eventually replaced by automatic flashing beacons. Many other locations from Whitehall to Rouses Point were and are served by towers without houses attached, by lanterns on piers, or portable beacons.

Colchester Reef, the worst on the lake, did not acquire its lighthouse until 1869. To make certain it would not blow away, its builders pegged it together, bolted it to eight-by-eight sills, and anchored it from top to bottom with iron rods embedded in three feet of stone. Twenty-five feet square with four bedrooms in its second story, and a kitchen and living room downstairs, it was inhabited for many years by two generations of a family whose children had no playground other than a few feet of rocks. To escape the stress and confusion of the outside world one of its bachelor tenders stayed 22 years and saved $28,000 by virtue of having nothing to spend it on.

The most hazardous night was one in April when the ice field was breaking up. Smashing the southwest corner of the first floor, it had started to wrench the entire building from its foundations when the wind happily changed directions and the ice subsided. Under a pressure that nothing short of a cliff of solid rock can withstand, the ice field has been known to pile up thirty feet high on a windward shore.

Outmoded by an automatic beacon in 1932 the Colchester Lighthouse gained an indefinite lease on life twenty years later. Dismantled piece by piece and moved ashore on a barge, it was rebuilt to display fresh and salt water art at the museum established by the J. Watson Webbs in Shelburne.

The long peninsula jutting into the lake on the west shore at Willsboro has an equivalent in Shelburne Point directly opposite on the Vermont side. The large bays they make are lakes in themselves.

If a landmark is to be defined as a place serving the same or similar purpose for two centuries, the shipyard in the sheltered cove inside the tip of

Shelburne Point must qualify. Even without facilities it must have served as a refuge during the Revolution. Commodore Macdonough armed and repaired some of his vessels at the harbor during the War of 1812, and from 1825 to 1906 thirteen steamboats were launched there. During World War II wooden subchasers, tugs, and barges began their careers on ways still used for overhaul and inspection by the lake's fleet of ferryboats. But the harbor has become principally a marina for native and visiting boats from Canada and the coastal waterways of the Atlantic. As evolution would have it, the sailing vessels that fell victim to the steamboats have returned in force, if not in size, to make the lake an unrivaled recreational resource.

The steamboats have disappeared — on the water at least. As the nation gradually recovered from the Great Depression the *Chateaugay* was returned to duty as a car ferry, and the *Ticonderoga* as an excursion boat. In 1940, after a career of over four decades on the lake, the *Chateaugay's* hull was sliced into sandwiches of iron and shipped to Lake Winnipesaukee, New Hampshire to be rebuilt as the diesel excursion boat *Mount Washington II*. The engines of the *Vermont III* were removed for scrap and her hull, stripped of her rotting superstructure, was prepared for further service as a diesel freight carrier on the Atlantic coast.

The *Ticonderoga* managed to survive intact until gasoline rationing during World War II happily allowed her to return to a regular schedule. Headed for the scrapheap in the spring of 1950, she was reprieved as an excursion and charter boat by a public fund-raising campaign conducted by the Burlington Junior Chamber of Commerce. Early the following winter she was purchased by the Shelburne Museum, and for three more years the deep blast of her whistle sounded from Montcalm Landing to St. Albans Bay.

By the fall of 1953 the federal boiler inspectors had become dubious about her boilers, then an unheard-of 48 years old. Licensed personnel for her pilot house, and particularly engineers who knew anything about her old-style engine had diminished to the vanishing point. In her youth the anthracite she burned cost four dollars a ton; by 1953 it had risen to twenty. Her fuel bill alone amounted that year to $10,000. After considering the ramifications of trying to keep an anachronism in service, the directors of the Shelburne Steamboat Company, a separate corporation formed by the Museum, decided to retire her. One hundred forty-four years of steamboat travel on Lake Champlain ended with her return to the shipyard that September.

But the end of the *Ticonderoga* was not yet. As the last survivor of the walking-beam sidewheel passenger packet, so familiar to generations of travelers on the lakes, sounds, and rivers of this country, and the last with a hand-made engine so beautiful that it deserved preservation under glass, she embodied a noble heritage. While she lay at the shipyard the trustees of the Museum, two miles inland as the crow flies from the head of Shelburne Bay, pondered how best to preserve her. A trolley line to bridge the harbor and the museum, a unique collection of the buildings and treasures of the New England past, was regarded as impractical. Isolated winter and summer from the grounds of the Museum, a maritime stepchild as it were, the boat would gradually sink into oblivion. The possibility of moving her overland was regarded as visonary, to say the least, since no such project had ever been undertaken. However, when a detailed study showed it could be done, the Museum trustees, particularly its president, Mrs. J. Watson Webb, decided that it would be done.

The first steps toward the portage of the boat were taken in the fall of 1954 at the southern end of Shelburne Bay, where soundings determined the depth and the amount of dredging necessary to tow the *Ticonderoga* up the mouth of the La Platte River. To get her out of the water and raise her 16 feet from the lake to the level of the terrain to start her overland cruise, plans called for digging out of the shoreline an immense lock-like basin 450 feet long and sufficiently wide to admit the boat.

On a cloudy morning in mid-September a land crane with a clamshell riding a string of steel pontoons began scooping muck out of the shallow river channel, while on shore four cranes and two bulldozers began digging 20,000 cubic yards of clay out of the proposed basin to a depth of eight feet below the level of the lake. When they struck hardpan and rock a squad of jackhammers and wagon drill and a fleet of trucks to haul away rock arrived at the scene.

Forty-three days after the digging started, the thin wall of clay separating the basin from the river was breached and water gushed into the proposed lock, around which an immense clay wall 24 feet high was being built. Twice as long as the *Ticonderoga*, the basin was divided into two equal sections, one at lake level into which the boat would be floated, and an adjoining section some 16 feet higher at terrain level. On the latter it was planned to construct a huge cradle resting on railroad trucks astride two sets of tracks. As soon as the boat was floated into the lower basin from the river and the 24-foot-high clay dike was filled in around her stern, it was calculated that by pumping in millions of gallons of water the boat could be floated up to terrain level and moved forward over her railroad cradle in the upper basin, then lowered on to it as the water was removed.

In late October a construction crew began laying ties and putting down the railroad tracks in the upper basin. In succeeding days 16 freight car trucks

Early stone warehouse overlooks marina and Salt Dock at the site where the port of Burlington originated in the 1780's. By Clyde H. Smith. Below: Charlotte ferry nears Essex. By R.N. Hill.

Although Vermont's largest city owes its origin and prosperity to the lake, it turned its back on its port until recently when large-scale urban redevelopment began in the area near the lake. The Green Mountains frame the eastern horizon. By Carolyn Bates. Right: Shipyard and marina at Shelburne Harbor, showing the old carpenter and machine shop next to the ways. Air view reveals the narrow neck of land separating the harbor from the broad lake. By Clyde H. Smith.

Mallett's Bay is a lake within a lake, like St. Albans Bay to the north. By R.N. Hill.
Overleaf: Lake Champlain sunset. By Clyde H. Smith.

with four wheels each were placed on the parallel sets of tracks, and the construction of the steel cradle began. In order to support the boat in two places, fore and aft amidships, and to allow it to follow the tracks and freight car trucks around curves, the cradle had to be designed in two sections, resting on a wooden platform coated first with a layer of wax, then grease. When assembled on top of the platform the cradle was pinned to it with a heavy rod in the center which would act as a pivot when, on its journey to the Museum, the boat approached a curve. Cold weather hampered construction of the cradle but by early November the dredging in the river had been completed and the lower basin was ready to receive the boat.

On the morning of the 6th two tugs arrived at the shipyard as a fascinated band of passengers boarded the old steamer for her last journey on the lake. Since the lower half of her ponderous paddlewheels, 18 feet across and as high as a two-story building, had been removed temporarily in order that she might be more easily admitted to the confining quarters of the basin, her engine was forlornly quiet and her main boilers were cold. But steam was up on her little auxilliary boiler so that the whistle might be blown en route to the basin; and her flags were flying.

At 10:10 a.m. the lines were cast off and the *Ticonderoga,* pulled by a tug, slowly backed away from the shipyard where she was built in 1906. Two long

100. Ticonderoga *was raised and positioned on railroad carriages by flooding a large basin.*

blasts of her whistle signalled goodbye. Presently, beneath a warm fall sun, she was under way against a moderate breeze. At 11:30 a.m. she entered the channel of the La Platte, and four hours later was successfully warped into the basin. As her whistle blew once more, the gangplank was run out on to the clay embankment, and the passengers trooped regretfully ashore.

Two days later workmen began filling in behind her stern the 24-foot dike, a task made no easier by its tendency to sink. Meanwhile a construction crew had begun to build a road as wide as a four-lane highway from the basin across the fields and through the woods to the Museum. The route selected was one with the least possible grades. Bulldozers leveled off the rises of ground, filled in the hollows, removed stumps in the wooded sections, and filled swampy areas. Even with its heavy surface of sand the roadbed could not possibly sustain the rails and their heavy cargo unless the ground was frozen. While the road could not be built after the ground froze, the steel rails with their heavy burden required a deep penetration of frost. The success of the portage thus depended upon the whims of the weather.

The flooding of the basin took place on December 30. At 4 a.m. in pouring rain workmen appeared to start the five large diesel pumps installed near the foot of the stern dike, with rubber hoses extending from the river up over the clay walls into the basin. Soon water began to pour into it at the rate of a million gallons an hour. At 6 a.m. the rain turned to sleet and by 8, to snow, but the *Ticonderoga* was gradually rising. When three small leaks appeared in the outer wall of the dike fear was expressed that the pressure of the immense volume of water, increasing hourly, might collapse the dike and spell disaster to the whole operation. At 11 o'clock water in the basin had reached a height within only two and one-half feet of the desired level. From a distance the *Ticonderoga* looked as if she were being supported by sky hooks.

At noon muddy gushers spurted from a dozen places in the dikes and were discharging so much water that four out of the five pumps were engaged merely in replacing the water leaking out, while a fifth pump was slowly gaining on the level in the basin. Forty-five minutes later the water had finally reached the six-foot mark over the cradle in the upper basin. Although the boat drew almost that, the engineers and surveyors now gave the signal to the bulldozers waiting in the field forward of the basin to tighten up on the lines that ran over the embankment to the bow of the boat. Since the railroad tracks and the cradle were now submerged under six feet of water in the upper basin, the problem was to float her forward over it, pin-point her exactly, and secure her with lines so that when the water was pumped out she would settle down securely on the now-invisible cradle.

101. Overland voyage was accomplished over frozen ground on double sets of railroad tracks.

As the surveyors signalled with flags the boat responded to the taut hawsers until, according to their calculations, she was on dead center over the cradle. As the roar of the diesels died away, lines from the boat to many points on the dike were tightly secured to prevent her from moving an inch in any direction. With leaks discharging thousands of gallons a minute, the water level began to drop rapidly and the hull gradually came into view. The boat was resting on her cradle, but how securely no one would know until most of the water was out of the upper basin. At 5 p.m. the entire hull was in view and the receding water had begun to reveal the cradle. An hour later the 892-ton steamer was checked by the surveyors in a rowboat and found to be within one-quarter of an inch of dead center! In another hour the water was all out of the upper basin.

The section of the dike in front of the boat now had to be removed so that the first sections of railroad tracks could be laid down and joined to those on which the boat rested. On the morning of the 31st it was 20 below zero. So congealed was the grease in the bearings of the 64 freight car wheels that it was necessary to hang cans of burning oil under the journal boxes, which gave the cradle and its strange cargo the appearance of a torchlight parade. Presently the carriage with its heavy burden responded to the pull of a heavy winch mounted on a truck. The wheels began to turn and the *Ticonderoga* was under way. The first day she traveled 150 feet to the edge of the highway, and the next move took her across the road through a gap in the power and telephone lines, which had been rerouted.

As she inched forward over her private highway, another large basin was being dug out to receive her at the Museum. There the frost had gone so deep that it was necessary to resort to the use of a one-ton drop ball. Sometimes, instead of the ground being broken up, the holding ring was torn out of the drop ball. In due course, however, 27,000 cubic yards of earth, even more than at the lakeside basin, were removed from the side of the hill at the Museum.

Obviously the digging, draining, and leveling off of this basin had to be

102. Portage nearly came to grief during a thaw in a swampy area just behind the barnyard.

completed well before the arrival of the boat, just as it was essential that the road construction crew keep well ahead of the movers. To avoid delays of weeks or months the entire route had to be traversed before the spring thaws. By March 3rd the boat had reached the half-way mark, 4,125 feet from her destination. Ahead lay three hazards as critical as the floating of the boat on to her cradle: first, the traversing of a brook and a second highway, then the climbing of a four percent grade, and finally the crossing of the tracks of the Rutland Railroad just west of the final berthing basin.

On the morning of the 9th the boat started forward over the ice-gripped marsh and brook, and across the macadam road into a barnyard where the cows, contentedly chewing their cuds, seemed oblivious to what was going on. By noon the next day the sun had turned the frozen swamp over which the boat had just passed into a pond that crept up to the level of the ties supporting the boat on the north side of the road. It was not possible to move her forward on to more solid ground because the previous day's move had used up the whole section of track. Time was necessary to remove it and lay a new 300-foot section ahead. By afternoon water had started to wash away the fill on one side of the tracks. As they began to sag the movers placed jacks at intervals under the hull to distribute its weight and to take some of it off the railroad carriages.

Word having spread of the dire possibility that the stern might sink or the boat capsize, the highway was choked with cars extending bumper to bumper for several miles. The news media, local and national, were present in force. Disaster was averted by cutting through the blacktop of the highway to relieve the damming of the brook. The water retreated but the ground was so saturated that it was not until the next hauling, bringing the boat 200 feet further south on solid ground, that the crisis passed.

Several more hauls brought the *Ticonderoga*, on March 29, to the four percent grade, which required more powerful winches and three systems of brakes to prevent her from rolling backward. When the hill was successfully conquered, only the last of the obstacles remained — the crossing of the railroad tracks. Just as a means had to be devised of moving the boat through the power lines without interrupting service, it was now necessary to cross, almost at right angles, the Rutland tracks during an interval between trains. Accordingly, on April 6, rails were laid up to the tracks of the Rutland, and beyond them into the berthing basin, so that after the passing of the noonday freight it would be necessary only to block up over the Rutland tracks with ties and fill in the missing segment of double tracks leading from the boat to the Museum.

103. Boat rests at Shelburne Museum next to the lighthouse moved from Colchester Reef.

Immediately after the 12:30 freight had passed, the boat's tracks went down over the railroad's and the winches started to turn. When the *Ticonderoga* reached a point about half-way across the main line, a local north-bound freight appeared from the south and was flagged to a stop. The boat, which had never waited for a train at a drawbridge because of maritime law giving ships precedence, did not have to do so now. When she cleared the tracks at 5:22 p.m. her rails and ties were quickly removed, and the Rutland freight, with a salute from its whistle, proceeded north. Soon thereafter the *Ticonderoga* was safe in her berthing basin, after a legendary journey of 65 days, 20 hours, and 28 minutes.

Shored up in her basin next to the Colchester lighthouse, which she used to pass every day, and refurbished from stem to stern, she proved to be a prime attraction at the Museum. Indeed, more people have boarded her there each summer than in any season she ever ran.

The blast of the steamboat whistle may have died away, but not the honk of the diesel ferry. That is more than can be said for abandoned Hudson River crossings all the way to New York. Since it is doubtful that more than the two present bridges will ever span the lake — it is elsewhere too wide or too deep — ferries will remain the indispensable carriers of several hundred thousand cars a year from Charlotte to Essex, Burlington to Port Kent, and Grand Isle to Cumberland Head.

There are few places in the country where within the compass of a very few miles a traveler can enter a thruway, board a passenger train, a large jet, an interstate bus, or a ferry boat, but that is true of the modern northern crossroads of greater Burlington. Having hung on as a ferry and oil-tanker terminal, its shrunken port is commanding new appreciation from a city that has long turned its back on its most precious asset — the view beyond the waterfront. The panorama that invades it from the south and west indeed is responsible in large measure for the complex of new buildings that have arisen from the once frowsy area northeast of the docks.

Five miles out, where the scenery is grandest, like a pipe organ with all its stops out, it is not easy to decide which view is more compelling — the blue sentinels of the Adirondacks, or opposite them the friendly shoulders of Mansfield and Camel's Hump. Here at its broadest, the moods of the lake in its various weathers dominate the senses. It can be as blue and serene as the eye of a hurricane, or as gray or black as the outside of one. It can hurl giant writhing columns of steam into the frigid air, or lie as flat, trackless and dazzlingly white as an arctic snowfield. In an early spring sunset it has been known to stage a pageant of great glistening multi-colored biscuits of ice. It can reward the sailor with the steadiest northwest breeze or, in a vile-tempered southern gale, all but strip him of his canvas. The lake presents those who savor its caprice with the key to a different kind of liberty — that of the spirit.

The so-called "broad lake" continues for miles to the north, until in the east it is divided by Grand Isle into the separate worlds of Mallett's and St. Albans bays. Applied to bodies of water whose distances dwarf their far shores, the word bay is a misnomer. The lake's northern bays are more like sounds, with far wider horizons than those of the main channel, passing to the west of the islands.

If the bays are separate worlds so are the Heroes and Isle La Motte with their occasional stone houses, orchards, and Yankee farms to remind us of one culture, but with evidence everywhere of their mingling with another. The French may have left in 1760, but as the names on the mail boxes of so many cottages and farms near the border testify, they have returned — as if after two centuries they were about to win that ambivalent area from the British after all. The schizophrenia that Vermont contracted from its mountains and northward-flowing lake still lingers: its eastern regions looking toward the Connecticut valley and Boston, its mid- and southwestern borders on the lake rather oriented toward New York, and the north absorbing the seepage across the border. As John S. Dickey has observed in his study of Canada and the American presence, geography and the "near misses" of history have lent "a slightly miraculous aura to today's outcome."

The New York shore proceeds northward with somewhat greater regularity

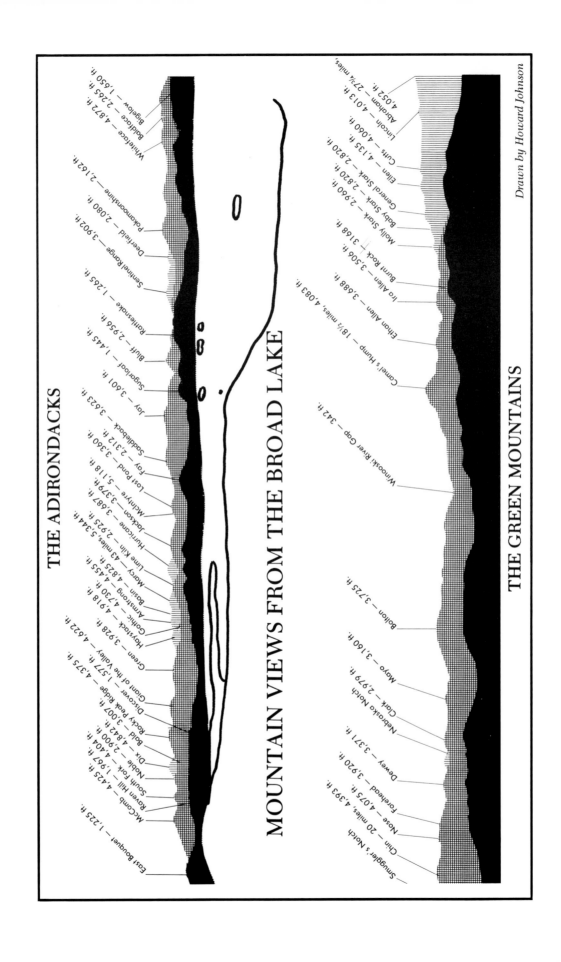

MOUNTAIN VIEWS FROM THE BROAD LAKE

THE ADIRONDACKS

Whiteface — 4,872 ft.
Baldface — 2,265 ft.
Bigelow — 1,650 ft.
Pokamoonshine — 2,162 ft.
Deerfield — 2,080 ft.
Sentinel Range — 3,902 ft.
Rattlesnake — 1,265 ft.
Bluff — 2,956 ft.
Sugarloaf — 1,445 ft.
Joy — 3,601 ft.
Saddleback — 3,623 ft.
Foy — 2,312 ft.
Lost pond — 3,360 ft.
McIntyre — 5,118 ft.
Jackson — 3,379 ft.
Hurricane — 3,687 ft.
Lime Kiln — 2,925 ft.
Marcy — 43 miles, 5,344 ft.
Armstrong basin — 4,825 ft.
Gothic — 4,730 ft.
Haystack — 4,918 ft.
Green — 3,928 ft.
Giant of the Valley — 4,622 ft.
Discover — 1,577 ft.
Rocky Peak Ridge — 4,375 ft.
Bald — 3,007 ft.
Dix — 4,842 ft.
Noble — 2,900 ft.
South Fork — 4,404 ft.
Raven Hill — 1,967 ft.
McComb — 4,425 ft.
East Bouquet — 1,225 ft.

THE GREEN MOUNTAINS

Lincoln — 4,013 ft.
Abraham — 27¾ miles, 4,052 ft.
Cutts — 4,060 ft.
Ellen — 4,135 ft.
General Stark — 2,820 ft.
Baby Stark — 2,820 ft.
Molly Stark — 2,960 ft.
Burnt Rock — 3,168 ft.
Ira Allen — 3,506 ft.
Ethan Allen — 3,688 ft.
Camel's Hump — 18½ miles, 4,083 ft.
Winooski River Gap — 342 ft.
Bolton — 3,725 ft.
Moyo — 3,160 ft.
Clark — 2,979 ft.
Nebraska Notch
Dewey — 3,371 ft.
Forehead — 3,920 ft.
Nose — 20 miles, 4,393 ft.
Chin — 4,075 ft.
Snuggler's Notch

Drawn by Howard Johnson

than Vermont's until it approaches Schuyler Island, and beyond it the island in the historical limelight — Valcour. Not much happened there after Benedict Arnold departed (except for the brief visitation in 1874 of a free-love colony called the Dawn Valcour Agricultural and Horticultural Association) until 1934, when a handsome yacht called the *Linwood* might be seen slowly passing back and forth between the island and the shore.

Having cruised the lake for years, its owner, Jacob Rupert Schalk, and its captain, L.F. Hagglund, a marine salvage expert, were fascinated by the lake's historical associations, particularly the whereabouts of the wreck of Arnold's flagship, *Royal Savage,* which had run aground and been burned on the southern tip of the island. Searching the bottom in a diving suit in 1932, Hagglund recovered some cannon balls. The wreck at first eluded him but while systematically crossing and recrossing the area in a rowboat his eye caught the outlines of a ship 150 feet off shore from the tip of the island, its upper end in less than 20 feet of water.

Returning two years later with the necessary salvage gear aboard the *Linwood,* and establishing a camp on the island, he and his crew finally identified his previous discovery as the *Royal Savage.* Some of her timbers lay in as little as 16 feet of water, while her stern, eight feet deeper, was partly covered with mud. Among the objects recovered were pewter buttons identified as belonging to Arnold's crews, a pewter spoon engraved "1776" and more cannon balls of the calibre of the *Royal Savage's* guns. By sinking drums and pumping them full of air the keel and ribs of the 52-foot schooner were floated, towed to shore, carefully marked, dismembered, and removed. However exhilarating this experience had been, Hagglund had found just a hull and his imagination was fired with the knowledge that Arnold's gondola *Philadelphia,* which the British had sunk intact in the channel, had to lie somewhere nearby in deeper water.

During the winter Schalk and Hagglund studied all the available American and British maps and sketches, and the following summer returned to Valcour on the *Linwood,* bringing with them an expert diver, William Lilja. The entries in the *Linwood's* log conveyed some of the tension that gripped every member of the crew on August 1 and 2 after many days of dragging with grapple irons. As darkness approached on the 1st it was decided to make one last run with a drag which had replaced the grapple irons. Suddenly the line tightened, bringing the *Linwood* to an abrupt stop. There was nothing unusual about this, for the drag had previously caught on rocks and waterlogged fishing shanties. By then it was too dark to send the diver down, but the spot was marked with buoys and the tired crew turned in for the night.

The next morning in the dim and eerie light 55 feet below the surface, Lilja was confronted with a startling sight — the ghostly mast of the *Philadelphia* rising 35 feet from her upright hull. One of her three nine-foot cannon still pointed from her bow, a bar shot half protruding from its muzzle, and her spars still lay across her decks, as they had for 159 years. In salt water the vessel long since would have disappeared, but wood, however waterlogged, lasts indefinitely in fresh water if not exposed to the air.

Abstracts from the log of the *Linwood* describe the excitement when Lilja emerged with the news he had found "a fish house with a stove," the code word for the *Philadelphia*, lest the news escape before his discovery was verified:

10:15 — With the entire crew assembled at the *Linwood* Rupe announced the finding of the *Philadelphia*. Some of the crew jumped overboard in their celebration. Diver made sketch of the wreck. This we all signed. We discussed the wreck and labor involved and I told them it meant three days' hard work to get the guns and a week to secure the hull. The decision was made to salvage vessel and guns for preservation. . . .

2:30 — Moored stern of *Linwood* and *Old Eli* over wreck. Sent outboard for barrels I had used to float the *Royal Savage* last year.

3:00-4:00 — Put diver down to secure barrels on one gun. Barrels were secured to gun that was wedged in and we could not budge it with boom on stern of *Linwood*. Broke boom stay trying.

Although the cannon were removed from the wreck during subsequent days the *Linwood's* hoist was not strong enough to raise them. They were left on the bottom outside the wreck while Lilja set to work with a high-pressure water jet washing away the mud in three places under the hull so that rope slings could be passed under it. In order to spread the weight and avoid the possibility of crushing the sides of the hull when it was raised, the slings, the ends of which were brought to the surface, were fastened to logs placed fore, aft, and amidships across the gunwales.

On August 9 a steam lighter arrived from Burlington and the cable of its derrick was rigged to a chain attached to the slings. In the absence of any kind of electronic communication between the diver and the lighter, Lilja had to signal to take up the slack by pulling a rope. When the strain on the lighter became such that it began to list, Lilja reappeared to explain that he was continuing to wash the mud away from the hull with the water jet so that the ship would respond more easily to the taut line of the lighter. Presently all was ready, and as the cable slid through the pulleys of the derrick, tension rose in proportion to the *Philadelphia's* distance from the bottom.

At 2:30 someone hollered: "There's the mast!" The spectators cheered. When it was six feet out of water the hoisting ceased while a young crewman plunged into the lake with a flag to pin to the mast. Finding it too slippery to climb he crawled up a plank extended from the lighter and the American stripes, if not the stars (the hand-made flag was authentic for the period) again fluttered from the *Philadelphia*.

When her bow appeared at the surface the hoist again stopped while a prayer was given. Then three volleys were fired, followed by the blowing of the lighter's whistle and the horns of spectators' boats. The lighter with its floating cargo now was towed to shallow water. Here the *Philadelphia* was allowed to rest temporarily in the sand while such preparations as wrapping a large piece of canvas around her hull could be made for her journey to Shelburne Harbor. Meanwhile the artifacts aboard her were removed and tabulated. Other than the cannon and cannon balls (including the one that sank her embedded in her hull) were human bones, teeth, leather soles, a wooden hour glass, hatchet heads, pewter buttons, even a spade with most of its wooden handle intact.

After careful examination on the marine railway at the Shelburne shipyard the 54-foot vessel and its contents went on a tour of the lake aboard a large barge. Failing to find a home for a number of years, it was covered over and berthed as an exhibit on the New York shore. Eventually it found the best

104. Grand Isle's separate world removes the main channel from Mallett's and St. Albans bays.

possible resting place, a special wing of the Smithsonian Institution in Washington, where the only such Revolutionary man-of-war has since awakened tens of millions of people to a lively interest in their past.

If these salutes to the preservation of the Ticonderogas — the fort and the steamboat — and of the *Philadelphia*, seem too vigorous, so be it. They are the tangible survivors of an area whose stock-in-trade is history. Places without history, like moonscapes, can be beautiful, but without footprints to follow, are all but meaningless. A present without a past is unthinkable. If we had not fathomed where we were we could not reckon where we are. Nor have the least inkling of where we are bound.

Beyond Valcour Island the north-bound voyager sights the promontory of Cumberland Head and presently arrives at Plattsburgh, whose harbor it protects. It has been a long time since the British sailed away, but as it happens this small city is still in the business of guarding the country — not by water but by air. The King's Highway has become the nuclear corridor for the eastern defense of the country, and Plattsburgh the rendezvous of the northeast's air flotilla, just as it was for Macdonough's fleet so many decades ago. As the geese fly and the ships sailed, so do the transcontinental jets and intercontinental missiles.

Champlain's thirty-six decades may be only a drop in the historical bucket, but so much has happened, technologically, since Benjamin Franklin established by way of the lake in 1788, the first postal service from Quebec to New York (when it took two weeks or so for a letter or traveler to make the trip) and so very much more has transpired even since the 1920's and 30's, when the rum-runners were streaking across the border in their mahogany Gar Wood speedboats, while overhead immense silver lighter-than-air ships like the *Macon* and *Akron* drifted majestically south toward the Hudson — that to predict the future of the gateway to the country is an exercise in fantasy.

Following the main channel beyond Cumberland Head to Point au Roche and Point au Fer, and Windmill Point on Alburg Tongue, the traveler finally reaches Rouses Point and passes through the railroad drawbridge. Beyond it he encounters Fort Montgomery and the Canadian border. There the Richelieu receives the lake's waters and carries them to the St. Lawrence, where they lose their identity in their long journey to the sea.

Epilogue

Treasures Beneath an Inland Sea.

THE greatest Lake Champlain revelation in the past twenty years is the discovery that it holds North America's most extraordinary collection of historic shipwrecks. If the lake were transparent, you would see literally hundreds of boats resting on its bottom, many of them in pristine condition—some with their masts still up, completely intact—because of the preserving effects of the cold, fresh water of Lake Champlain. The presence of this vast number of archaeological sites provides a new conduit into the historical record and, with proper study, potential for a better understanding of our past.

The study, interpretation, and management of this lake bottom preserve gave rise, in 1980, to the Champlain Maritime Society, a bi-state, citizen-based effort focused on the preservation of this special legacy. The success of the Champlain Maritime Society and increasing realization of just how significant and unexplored this underwater collection was, led, in 1986, to the establishment of the Lake Champlain Maritime Museum at historic Basin Harbor. Founded by Bob Beach Jr. and myself, the Museum is dedicated to preserving the heritage of the Champlain Valley and sharing it with the public. Over the past decade the museum has seen a remarkable rate of growth, a direct reflection of the lake's historical and archaeological significance.

105. This wheel of a nineteenth-century (c. 1862) schooner is
part of the lake's well-preserved collection of shipwrecks.
(John Butler)

The Lake Champlain Maritime Museum holds tangible evidence of Ralph's thesis that "Lake Champlain is the most historic body of water in the western hemisphere." We have begun to reveal that Lake Champlain may also contain the best preserved collection of submerged wooden watercraft in the western hemisphere! If you think about it for a minute it makes perfect sense: For centuries Lake Champlain's long, narrow, and navigable form gave rise to repeated episodes of military, naval, and commercial maritime activity. Each episode produced its own history, shoreline-related architecture (much of which is still present around the lake), and variety of period watercraft. We have come to realize that on any body of water where vessels exist, time and circumstance will take many of them to the bottom.

106. The schoolhouse (c. 1818) seen behind the block-and-tackle exhibit is the original building of the Lake Champlain Maritime Museum, a center dedicated to the special heritage of the Champlain Valley. (Lake Champlain Maritime Museum)

Over the past twenty years our team at the Lake Champlain Maritime Museum has been surveying the lake bottom, and, not surprisingly, has located dozens of shipwrecks. Several of these have been chosen for extensive documentation, not by removal, but through study underwater. This process of applying traditional archaeological techniques to shipwrecks is called "nautical archaeology," and we have come to formally characterize these shipwreck sites as "submerged cultural resources." This redefinition of terms better reflects our appreciation of the cultural value of these underwater sites and our approach to preserving them for future generations. To date, the submerged sites we have discovered represent just about every period of American history.

I have directed thousands of hours of fieldwork over the past two decades with my principal collaborator, Kevin Crisman, now of the Institute of Nautical Ar-

chaeology at Texas A&M University. Our underwater projects have documented
Native American dugout canoes, French and British naval ships (c. 1758–59),
American and British naval vessels from the Revolutionary War and the War of
1812, early steamboats, commercial sailing vessels, canal boats, and even a horse-
powered ferry (c. 1825). While the lake's cold water and variable depths and
visibility present a challenging working environment, they also create a relatively
stable world for these wooden time capsules. For this reason, the lake turns out
to be one of the best possible laboratories for training in archaeological documentation. The Lake Champlain Maritime Museum currently sponsors an annual nautical archaeology field school training program in conjunction with the
University of Vermont and Texas A&M University.

The situation at the other historic sites around the lake has also been extremely
dynamic. In his last chapter, "Reflections on an Inland Sea," Ralph gave an op-
timistic view of the future of Lake Champlain. Although he wrote over twenty
years ago, his predictions showed remarkable insight into the lake's future. Ralph
predicted many changes in the public's perception of the lake, and he actively
encouraged us to better appreciate this treasured place.

Ralph showed great appreciation to the custodians of the Fort Ticonderoga Museum for the preservation and reconstruction of one of America's
premier historic sites. That proud tradition has continued with the recent creation of the Thompson-Pell Research Library, providing the public with easy
access to the Fort's unparalleled historical materials. "Through these portals"
now pass over 100,000 visitors a year who get not only one of the most commanding views in the valley but also an orientation as to why, two centuries ago, that
view was so strategically important to French, British, and, later, American fortunes.

Ralph characterized the historic sites of Mount Independence, Crown Point,
and Chimney Point as "not so lucky" when he reflected on the public's apparent
lack of interest or appreciation for their historic contributions. I am pleased to
point out that times have changed for the better. In fact, it could be argued that
an indication of the public's renewed interest in the cultural legacy of Lake
Champlain is reflected in the great changes at all three of these historic sites. At
Crown Point, the largest British fort ever built in North America, the state of
New York has made steady progress in stabilizing the impressive ruins of French
Fort St. Frederic and British Crown Point. After extensive archaeological in-
vestigations an interpretive center has also been established to provide the public

107. A view of Crown Point State Historic Site with the interpretive center set between the ruins of French Fort St. Frederic in the foreground and British Crown Point behind. (John Butler)

with an impressive presentation about the French and British struggle to control strategic Lake Champlain.

On the Vermont side, Chimney Point, Millard Barnes' historic site, has been completely restored by the state. In the commanding brick building, witness to so many passing eras, a new museum focuses on the interpretation of Native American and early French settlement of the Champlain Valley. The visitor can see tools and weapons used by native peoples and gain an appreciation for how they lived in the valley for over 10,000 years before the arrival of Samuel de Champlain.

Perhaps the most neglected historic site, Mount Independence, is about to experience a momentous change. Vermont's Mount Independence is a sharp contrast to the other historic sites just reviewed. Occupied during the Revolutionary War between 1776 and 1777, it has an important story to tell even though its physical remains, which are primarily "archaeological," are at first glance less spectacular. Since the writing of *Lake Champlain*, efforts have been directed toward establishing a visitors center at Mount Independence. A renewed appreciation for the history of the site has recently been gained through archaeological investigations both on the land and in the water around the Mount. In the early 1980s Kevin and I led the first underwater survey near Fort Ticonder-

*109. A twelve-pound iron cannon being raised for conservation
from the waters around Mount Independence. (Lake Champlain
Maritime Museum)*

oga and Mount Independence and discovered a remarkable diversity of submerged cultural resources. We located three naval vessels from the French and
British lake squadrons of the late 1750s, as well as physical remains of the Revolutionary War Great Bridge (see the illustrations on pages 108 and 290). This fantastic structure consisted of twenty-two log cabin–style caissons, which provided
support for a 14-foot-wide floating bridge spanning the 1700-foot corridor.
Designed by American engineer Jeduthan Baldwin and built on the ice by troops
under his command during the winter of 1777, the bridge provided communication between Ticonderoga and the new fortification at Mount Independence.

Another significant discovery of this survey was a concentration of Revolutionary War artifacts located off the shore of Mount Independence. These objects, consisting primarily of a variety of iron cannon shot, were raised, identified,
and then returned to the bottom. A decision was made to collaborate with the
Fort Ticonderoga Museum on a study of the *Boscawen*, a British sloop-of-war
built in 1759 to provide the naval strength needed for General Jeffrey Amherst's
advance against the French. The Mount Independence artifact collection, we
reasoned in 1983, would be safe from disturbance because of the near-zero visibility of the water in this region of the lake. This management approach worked
until 1991.

On July 4th, 1991, a diver from Indiana was arrested for vandalizing this collection. During the diver's trial (he is the only diver ever prosecuted in Vermont) it was learned he had requested and received from state officials a copy of our 1983 survey report that detailed the location of what we had found. Around the same time a number of timbers from the caissons still resting on the lake bot-

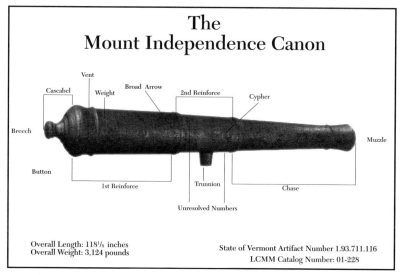

The Mount Independence Canon

Vent
Cascabel
Weight
Broad Arrow
2nd Reinforce
Cypher
Breech
Muzzle
Button
1st Reinforce
Trunnion
Chase
Unresolved Numbers

Overall Length: 118¹/₈ inches
Overall Weight: 3,124 pounds

State of Vermont Artifact Number 1.93.711.116
LCMM Catalog Number: 01-228

110. The Mount Independence cannon after conservation. Preliminary identifications of its markings suggest it was cast in Scotland in 1676. (Dan Nord)

tom had surfaced, raising concerns about the structural integrity of the Great Bridge. These two events galvanized public support, and the Lake Champlain Management Conference—a federally authorized program—commissioned the Lake Champlain Maritime Museum to execute a more systematic underwater survey of this region. This remote sensing and diver survey, undertaken in cooperation with Middlebury College in 1992, inventoried the cultural properties in a five-mile area of the lake and geologically mapped its bottom. During the survey a number of shipwrecks were located as well as two 300-foot-long railroad drawboats associated with the railroad trestle built across the lake in 1871 (see the photo on page 255) and four large, iron cauldrons of unknown origin. An in-depth structural evaluation was made of each of the twenty-two 218-year-old bridge caissons, and we completed a close archaeological study of the most intact caisson. We also focused a diver survey on the artifact-rich, submerged archaeological site surrounding Mount Independence, to determine its size, characteristics, and significance. This proved to be one of the richest concentrations of eighteenth-century artifacts ever located, and recognition of its quality and vulnerability led to an immediate recommendation for the conservation of such a unique and nationally significant collection.

This recommendation was implemented in 1993 through an appropriation by the Vermont Legislature. The project finished studying and documenting the bridge caissons and completed the artifact inventory, culminating in the removal of over 900 Revolutionary War objects. These materials, which new research suggests were thrown into the lake by retreating British forces following General Burgoyne's defeat at Saratoga in the fall of 1777, were transported to the Lake Champlain Maritime Museum where a conservation laboratory was established in collaboration with the Institute of Nautical Archaeology at Texas A&M University. While the public watched, each object was put through a variety of technical conservation treatments so that it might endure as part of a public

108. The ice provided a building platform for the massive caissons that anchored the floating bridge between Fort Ticonderoga and Mount Independence. (conjectural drawing by Joseph Cozzi)

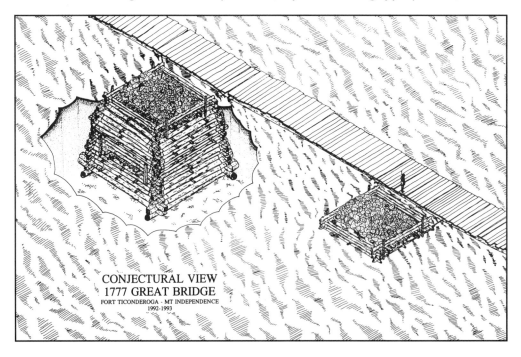

CONJECTURAL VIEW
1777 GREAT BRIDGE
FORT TICONDEROGA - MT INDEPENDENCE
1992-1993

collection forever. Once preserved, the artifacts were placed in storage by the Vermont Division for Historic Preservation, custodian of this public collection. The success of this project, along with several recent land archaeology projects at Mount Independence, generated strong grassroots support that led the 1995 Vermont Legislature to make an appropriation for construction of a permanent visitors center at Mount Independence.

Ships underwater are not the only historic vessels that need looking after. One of Ralph Hill's greatest accomplishments and one of which he was justly proud was his attempt to save the lake's last surviving steamboat, the *Ticonderoga.* The stories of the *Ticonderoga*'s last years as a working vessel and the Shelburne Museum's extraordinary effort to move her overland to her resting grounds are well chronicled in Ralph's last chapter. Since he wrote, however, the *Ticonderoga* has been threatened by new forces, and, for a time, was facing a cancerous death caused by rot and general deterioration.

Today, although on dry land, the *Ticonderoga* has the distinction of being the only surviving example of a passenger excursion steamboat with walking-beam engine. Built in 1906, she probably had an anticipated lifespan of twenty-five years as a working watercraft. By the time she was formally retired and moved to the Shelburne Museum, the *Ticonderoga* had already been in service close to fifty years. As a working vessel, the *Ticonderoga* was subject to the forces of nature in a fluid, freshwater sea. While these forces took their toll on her, there was always a crew devoted solely to her maintenance. Once installed on the grounds of the Shelburne Museum the *Ticonderoga*'s career changed, and her maintenance crew was replaced by a crew of interpreters. As the focal point of museum visitors the venerable steamboat could no longer change her position relative to the sun, and water that had rolled off her decks while she was afloat now worked itself into her woodwork. All this was occuring during a period when the vessel was boarded by more than a million people. Over the years the museum made several attempts to address the steamboat's increasing deterioration, but by the mid-1980s it began to look like the battle would be lost.

As the Shelburne Museum looked forward to 1997 and its 50th anniversary of public service, its board of directors identified restoration of the *Ticonderoga* as their top priority. Rising to this incredible challenge, Lois and J. Warren McClure, longtime supporters of the Shelburne Museum and a host of other community organizations, provided the financial support necessary to attack the problem. Responding to a marine survey by Captain Gifford "Giffy" Full, the

McClures donated a million dollars, $300,000 to be used immediately to hire a crew to focus on an intensive five-year effort to restore the *Ticonderoga*. Perhaps more importantly, $700,000 would be set aside in an endowment to provide for the *Ticonderoga*'s future maintenance. Upon his death in 1988, Ralph Hill bequeathed a generous gift to the Shelburne Museum, and this has been added to the endowment fund for the *Ticonderoga*, a decision that undoubtedly would have pleased Ralph very much.

This restoration effort, every bit as ambitious as moving the vessel overland, required the right director and the right plan. Fortuitously, as this is being written, the Shelburne Museum has been successful at addressing both issues. In 1992, Chip Stulen, a boatbuilder from the Great Lakes region, was recruited to head the restoration team. Although Chip has never faced a project this daunting before, his technical background and common sense approach to problem solving, coupled with an extremely dedicated crew, are proving to be the right combination.

After pondering the size and complexity of the project, the team began to move. It was obvious that the weight of the pilot house was causing stress to the deteriorating deck beams, so a decision was made to remove it and restore it in a new shop building set up just off the *Ticonderoga*'s aft starboard quarter. A temporary, movable shelter was erected over the vessel, which allowed the crew to work year-round on the project and repair the weather decks while protecting them from further damage.

Chip is quick to point out this is a restoration project—an effort to save as much of the vessel's original fabric as possible but also providing it with the stability to survive for another century. To that end, the decks exposed to the weather are getting replaced with the best modern materials available while their traditional appearance is being replicated. Rot in any structural member is being cut out and replaced, while soft areas found in nonstructural members may be "consolidated" with modern resins. Old fastenings which have been struggling to hold the old ship together are being replaced.

The project has generated tremendous support from the community, with businesses and individuals providing many of the materials needed in the restoration. An exhibit on view in the *Ticonderoga*'s former dining salon interprets the restoration for visitors, explaining the project and teaching valuable lessons about the preservation of big maritime properties. Three years into the five-year restoration effort there have been some setbacks and many unforeseen prob-

111. The Ticonderoga *pilothouse showing signs of age and weather. (Shelburne Museum)*

112. The pilothouse of the Ticon-deroga *being removed for restoration. (Shelburne Museum)*

113. The Ticonderoga *pilothouse after restoration. (Shelburne Museum)*

lems but generally steady progress toward getting the *Ticonderoga* ready not just for the Shelburne Museum's 50th Anniversary celebration in 1997, but for a new century of public service.

As you reflect on the problems experienced with the *Ticonderoga*, think about the problems of raising a wooden shipwreck intact from the waters of Lake

Champlain. When a vessel sinks below the surface and arrives on the lake bottom it is surrounded by cold, fresh water where the process of decay is significantly slowed. However, over the years, many submerged vessels have been raised from the lake and have suffered from rapid destabilization in air. One lucky survivor of that group is the *Philadelphia,* whose story Ralph told.

The *Philadelphia,* you may remember, was part of the fleet commanded by Benedict Arnold and sunk by British cannon fire at the Battle of Valcour Island on October 11, 1776. In 1935, Lorenzo Hagglund succeeded in locating and raising this historic vessel to the surface. For the next twenty-five years, Colonel Hagglund, an accomplished salvage engineer, exhibited the *Philadelphia* to the public, and because of his dedication the *Philadelphia* survived. Upon Hagglund's death the *Philadelphia* was bequeathed to the Smithsonian Institution where she is cared for and available to the nation's public. Unfortunately this is not the case with at least a dozen similarly historic shipwrecks, which were raised only to suffer destruction.

The Lake Champlain Maritime Museum is dedicated to finding new and innovative ways to share the rich history of the Champlain Valley with a broad audience. Through research, public education programs, and exhibits, the museum focuses on the nature and transitions of the significant periods of our past. At the same time, however, experience has led us to advocate keeping historic watercraft underwater. So as Vermont approached its Bicentennial in 1991, the Museum focused on creating a project which would combine both preservation and interpretation objectives. In hindsight we believe we struck on the perfect project: We would build, launch, and operate a full-sized working replica of the *Philadelphia!*

With a rare endorsement from the Smithsonian Institution, the first phase of the Philadelphia Project got under way in 1989. A shipyard materialized at the museum and work on the replica began. With the assistance of the Vermont Council on the Humanities, an interpretive exhibit reflecting on the life and times of the original *Philadelphia* and an eighteenth-century-style forge were incorporated into the new shipyard. Over the next three seasons professional boatbuilders joined with an army of dedicated volunteers from the community to push the project forward. A special educational curriculum entitled "1776" exposed thousands of regional schoolchildren to this important history, made in their own backyard. As new research shed increasing light on 200-year-old events, we found ourselves in a race to complete the new *Philadelphia* in time for the

114. The Philadelphia II *under construction at the Lake Champlain Maritime Museum. (Lake Champlain Maritime Museum)*

planned August 1991 launching. Launch time approached, and doubters whispered the boat could not be finished in time, while still others predicted once launched it would not float. On launch day storms threatened the crowd of over 4,000 people who had assembled to watch the historic event, but just as Senator Patrick Leahy's keynote remarks ended, the skies cleared and the crowd erupted into cheers as the *Philadelphia II* entered her historic home, Lake Champlain.

After undergoing "sea trials" in which much has been learned about the characteristics of this type of eighteenth-century craft, the *Philadelphia II* began her career as a floating reflection of Lake Champlain's rich past. For two years the *Philadelphia II* has traveled the lake from the birthplace of the original fleet at Whitehall (formerly Skenesboro), New York to St. Johns, Quebec, the place where the rival British squadron was constructed. She has visited the communities of Shoreham, Kingsland Bay, and Burlington, Vermont; and Ticonderoga, Crown Point, Westport, Essex, Plattsburgh, and Valcour, New York. In 1993, as a reflection of our shared history with Canada, the *Philadelphia II* ventured north to St. Johns and Isle Aux Noix. Now docked at North Harbor, a quiet bay at the Lake Champlain Maritime Museum, students and visitors seasonally board the vessel and find their thoughts transported back over 200 years to when the outcome of the struggle to create a new nation was still very uncertain.

While working in the present to appreciate and understand the lake's past, a glimpse of the future appears very exciting. Recognizing that the lake bottom contains perhaps hundreds of submerged cultural sites, we realize we have only just begun to explore this new frontier. So far, we have examined only a small percentage of the lake's bottomland. What makes this situation so exciting is that during the last decade the technology used to survey the lake has made quantum leaps. Recent improvements in sonar techniques and navigational control systems give us the capability to systematically examine and image the entire lake bottom and determine the number and variety of shipwrecks and other cultural sites located there.

The presence of a collection of shipwrecks scattered along the bottom of Lake Champlain gives us the potential to add greatly to the historical and archaeological record of the lake, yet also raises the important issue of resource management. How should these public resources be protected and enjoyed now and into the future? One interesting program that I assisted in developing with the Vermont Division for Historic Preservation in 1985 is the Underwater Historic Preserve. This innovative program selected several shipwreck sites and, through

115. *The* Philadelphia II *on its journey from Whitehall, New York to St. Johns, Quebec as a floating ambassador of the lake's history. (Lake Champlain Maritime Museum)*

the installation of Coast Guard–approved seasonal moorings, provided safe diver access. The underwater preserves are designed to provide divers with a museumlike interpretive experience while fostering among the diving community a protective rather than exploitive approach. As we begin to identify literally hundreds of submerged sites, keeping a management dialogue going will be critical to working out a thoughtful plan for the future.

Now, the presence of an unforeseen menace makes developing an accelerated lake survey and documentation program much more urgent. The dark cloud on the lake's horizon is in the form of a tiny zebra mussel. This non-native invader has been located in Lake Champlain, and if the experience in the Great Lakes is any indication of what's to come, this prolific nuisance will soon begin to impact water intake pipes as well the lake's shipwrecks.

The current interest in Lake Champlain embraces a wide appreciation for the entire interrelated ecosystem. The Lake Champlain basin, defined as the vast watershed that ultimately culminates in the lake, has been recognized by the United Nations as one of the world's special environments. The basin has also been selected as a federal "Special Designation" program, which has focused an intensive research and planning effort on the lake. This five-year Lake Champlain Basin Program is examining all of the region's resources in an attempt to map out a blueprint for protecting the health and vibrancy of this special place for future generations.

Ralph's book appeared at time of relatively low interest in and awareness of the lake's special nature. His enthusiastic writing and steady advocacy changed all that and helped trigger profound changes in the public's perception of historic Lake Champlain. We who currently labor to study, document, and share this legacy with the public are grateful that we can build on the efforts of Ralph Nading Hill and others who have recognized that Lake Champlain is the most historic body of water in the western hemisphere.

—Arthur B. Cohn

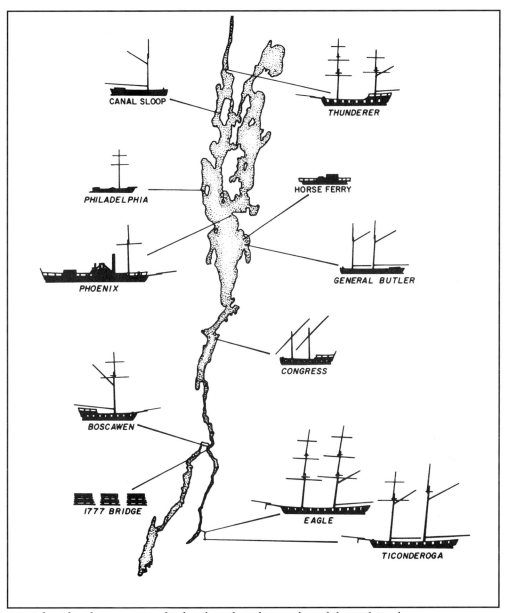

116. *Selected underwater sites of Lake Champlain shipwrecks and their relative locations.*

A List of Museums, Historic Sites and Preservation Programs.

Adirondack Center Museum
Route 9, PO Box 428, Elizabethtown, NY 12932 (518) 873-6466
Regional history—pioneer settlements, mining, transportation, gardens

Adirondack Museum
Box 99, Blue Mountain Lake, NY 12812 (518) 352-7311
Regional history—logging, mining, transportation, tourism

Ausable Chasm
Route 9, Ausable, NY 12911 (518) 834-7454
Geological history—walking trails, boat tour

Bennington Battle Monument
15 Monument Circle, Old Bennington, VT 05201 (802) 447-0550
Military history—commemorates 1777 battle

Chimney Point State Historic Site
RD #3, Box 3546, Vergennes, VT 05491 (802) 759-2412
Regional history—Vermont, Native American, and French heritage

Crown Point State Historic Site
RD #1, Box 219, Crown Point, NY 12928 (518) 597-3666
Military history—fortifications, French & Indian War, Revolutionary War

Ethan Allen Homestead
Winooski Valley Park District, Burlington, VT 05401 (802) 865-4556
Regional history—restored 1787 farmhouse

Fort Chambly National Historic Site
2 Richelieu Street, Chambley, Quebec, J3L 4B9
Military history—fortifications

Fort Lennox National Historic Site
161 Avenue St. Paul, Isle Aux Noix, Quebec J0J 1G0
Military history—fortifications

Fort Ticonderoga
Route 74, Box 390, Fort Ticonderoga, NY 12883 (518) 585-2821
Military history—fortifications, French & Indian War, Revolutionary War

Lake Champlain Basin Program
54 West Shore Road, Grand Isle, VT 05458 (800) 468-5227
Ecological

Lake Champlain Basin Science Center
411 Main Street, Burlington, VT 05401
Ecological

Lake Champlain Committee
14 South Williams Street, Burlington, VT 05401 (802) 658-1414
Ecological

Lake Champlain Maritime Museum at Basin Harbor, Inc.
RR #3, Box 4092, Vergennes, VT 05491 (802) 475-2022
Regional history—nautical archaeology, maritime exhibits, Revolutionary War gunboat replica

Lake Champlain Transportation Company
King Street Dock, Burlington, VT 05402 (802) 864-9804
Ferry boats

Mount Independence
RD #3, Box 3546, Vergennes, VT 05491 (802) 759-2412
Military history, walking trails

Penfield Homestead
Ironville Historic District, Crown Point, NY 12928 (518) 597-3804
Regional history—19th-century life, iron industry, Civil War, farming, transportation

Robert Hill Fleming Museum
University of Vermont, 61 Colchester Avenue, Burlington, VT 05405 (802) 656-2090
Art and anthropological collections

Rokeby Museum
Route 7, Ferrisburgh, VT 05456 (802) 877-3406
Regional history—underground railroad, farming industry

Saratoga Battlefield
PO Box W, Saratoga Springs, NY 12866-0327
Regional history—Revolutionary War

Shelburne Farms
Harbor Road, Shelburne, VT 05482 (802) 985-8686
Regional history—farming industry

Shelburne Museum
Route 7, PO Box 10, Shelburne, VT 05482 (802) 985-3346
American folk art in period homes, historic buildings, steamer Ticonderoga

Sheldon Museum
1 Park Street, Middlebury, VT 05753 (802) 388-2117
Regional history—collection, gallery, gardens

Skenesboro Museum
6 Williams Street, Box 238, Whitehall, NY 12887 (518) 499-0716
Local history—navy, railroad, canal

St. Albans Historical Museum
Church & Bishop Streets, St. Albans, VT 05478 (802) 527-7933
Local history

Ticonderoga Heritage Museum
Montcalm Street, Ticonderoga, NY 12883 (518) 585-2696
Regional history—paper and pencil industry, waterpower

Vermont Division for Historic Preservation
135 State Street, Montpelier, VT 05633 (802) 828-3226

Vermont Folklife Center
Painter House, 2 Court Street, PO Box 442, Middlebury, VT 05753
(802) 388-4964
Regional history—folk art and rural traditions

Vermont Historical Society
109 State Street, Montpelier, VT 05609-0901 (802) 828-2291
Regional history—changing exhibits on Vermont history and people

Acknowledgments

A mere list of the people who have helped with this book seems wholly inadequate. I would prefer to tell what each of them did, since more than most books this has been a joint endeavor. I hope the following people will accept, individually and collectively, my lasting appreciation: Urban Bergeron, Edith Boldosser, Reed Byrum, Connell Gallagher, Philip Hastings, William Haviland, Frank Heinrich, Peter Jennison, Rik Jesse, Howard Johnson, Jane Lape, Donald Lefebvre, Kathy Letour, Christopher Lloyd, Gordon Mills, H.N. Muller, Nancy Muller, Linda Dean Paradee, Moore Payette, John Pell, Stuart Perry, Penelope Pillsbury, Armand Poulin, Roland Poulin, John Read, Frederick Reed, Tim Rivers, Clyde H. Smith, Albert Spaulding, Gerrie Tucker, Laura Twitchell, Philip Wagner, Winston Whitney, Jim Wilson, and John Wood. Alfred A. Knopf, Inc., New York, has kindly given permission to quote from *Champlain: The Life of Fortitude* by Morris Bishop, copyright 1949.

— R.N.H.

Grateful acknowledgment is made to the following for permission and use of the illustrations listed below by caption number.

American Heritage Publishing Co. Reprinted by permission from the *American Heritage Atlas* (copyright 1966): 4, 27, 36

Archives of the Provence of Quebec, redrawn by Armand Poulin: 20

Bennington Museum (Bennington, Vt.): 49

Gordon Cutler: 94

Fort Ticonderoga: 15, 22, 23, 24, 25, 26, 28, 29, 30, 31, 33, 34, 35, 38, 46, 47, 48, 50, 53, 66

Philip R. Hastings: 95

Joseph Dixon Crucible Co. (makers of Ticonderoga pencils): 37

Jane Lape: 82

Stuart Perry: 1, 3, 52

Neva H. Piermont: 86

Plattsburgh State University, Northcountry Collection: 80, 81, 91, 92 lower

William Rowe, III: 59, 60, 73.

Shelburne Museum (Shelburne, Vt.): 55, 56, 57, 61, 62, 100, 101, 102, 103

John Smith: 5

The Frick Collection, New York (copyright): 45

University of Vermont — Department of Anthropology: 5, 6, 7, 8, 9. Fleming Museum: 10, 11. Special Collections, Bailey Library: 13, 44, 63, 64, 74, 75, 79, (after a painting by James Bard) 84, 87, 88, 89, 96, 97, 99

Vermont Historical Society: 19, 51, 54

Vermont Travel Division: 98, 104

Jim Wilson: 6, 7, 8, 9, 11

ALSO

Dover Publications, Inc., New York, *1800 Woodcuts by Thomas Bewick and His School* (copyright 1962) for uncaptioned illustrations in Chapter V

Mountain Views From the Broad Lake, p 278, was re-created from a drawing by Clarence Cowles.

National Aeronautics and Space Administration for picture opposite page 24

Sources

Allen, Ethan. *A Narrative of Colonel Ethan Allen's Captivity* . . . Walpole, N.H.: Thomas and Thomas, 1807.

American Heritage Book of the Revolution. The editors of *American Heritage*. New York: American Heritage Publishing Co., 1958.

American Heritage Pictorial Atlas of United States History. The editors of *American Heritage*. New York: American Heritage Publishing Co., 1966.

Anburey, Thomas. *Travels through the Interior Parts of America*. New York: Houghton, 1923.

Bailey, John H. "Archaeology in Vermont." *The Vermont Alumnus*, February 1939.

Bassett, T.D. Seymour (ed.). Francois Dollier de Casson: "A Terrible Winter on Isle La Motte." Nathaniel Hawthorne: "An Inland Port, 1835." *Outsiders Inside Vermont*. Brattleboro, Vt.: The Stephen Greene Press, 1967.

Bishop, Morris. *Champlain: The Life of Fortitude*. New York: A.A. Knopf, 1949.

Blow, David J. "Lake Champlain's First Steamboat." *Vermont History*, vol. XXXIV, no. 2, 1966.

Bourne, Annie Nettleton (translator). *The Voyages and Explorations of Samuel de Champlain, 1604-1616, Narrated by Himself*. Vol. I. New York: Allerton Book Co., 1922.

Bredenburgh, Oscar R. "The Royal Savage." *The Bulletin of the Fort Ticonderoga Museum*, vol. XII, no. 2, 1966.

Bulletin of the Fort Ticonderoga Museum, vol. I, no. 1, 1927 to vol. XIII, no. 4, 1973.

"Burton, Oscar A. Typescript." Champlain Transportation Co. records. Special Collections, Bailey Library, University of Vermont.

Bush, Martin H. *Revolutionary Enigma: a Reappraisal of General Philip Schuyler of New York*. Port Washington, N.Y., 1969.

Canfield, Thomas H. "Discovery, Navigation and Navigators of Lake Champlain." *Vermont Historical Gazetteer*, edited by Abby Maria Hemenway, vol. I. Burlington, Vt., 1868.

Chambers, Capt. William. *Book of Directions*. Edited with introduction and notes by Edward G. Bourne. New York: Barnes, 1906.

Charlevoix, Pierre Francois Xavier. *History and General Description of New France*. (vols. II-V) Chicago: Loyola University Press, 1962.

Cone, Gertrude. "Studies in the Development of Transportation in the Champlain Valley to 1876." Unpublished thesis. University of Vermont, 1945.

Coolidge, Guy Omeron. "The French Occupation of the Champlain Valley from 1609 to 1759." *Proceedings of the Vermont Historical Society*, New Series, vol. VI, no. 3, 1938.

Crockett, Walter Hill. *Vermont: The Green Mountain State* (4 vols.) New York: The Century History Co., 1921.

——. *A History of Lake Champlain*. Burlington: Hobart J. Shanley, 1909.

Cuneo, John R. *Robert Rogers of the Rangers*. New York: Oxford University Press, 1959.

Day, Gordon H. "The Eastern Boundary of the Iroquois." *Man in the Northeast*, no. 1, 1971.

Dickens, Charles. *American Notes*. London: Chapman and Hall, 1842.

Dickey, John S. and Shepardson, Whitney H. *Canada and the American Presence*. New York: New York University Press, 1975.

Dutcher, L.L. "The Black Snake." *Vermont Historical Gazetteer*, vol. II, (St. Albans). Burlington, Vt., 1868.

Everest, Allan S. (ed.). *Recollections of Clinton County and the Battle of Plattsburgh, 1800-1840*. Plattsburgh, N.Y.: Clinton County Historical Assn., 1964.

——. *The Journal of Charles Carroll of Carrollton*. Fort Ticonderoga, N.Y.: Champlain-Upper Hudson Bicentennial Committee, 1976.

Flexner, James Thomas. *The Traitor and the Spy*. New York: Harcourt Brace and Co., 1953.

Forbes, Charles S. "President McKinley in Vermont." *The Vermonter*, vol. II, no. 10, 1902.

Furcom, Thomas B. "Mount Independence, 1776-1777." *The Bulletin of the Fort Ticonderoga Museum*. Vol. XI, no. 4, 1954.

Gerlach, Don R. "Philip Schuyler and 'the Road to Glory'; a Question of Loyalty and Competence." *New York Historical Society Quarterly*, vol. XLIX, 1965.

Gibbs, Jessie. *Thompson's Point: A Few Facts and Fancies about a Favorite Summer Resort*. Burlington, Vt.

Godfrey, Frank H. "Recollections of the Champlain and Erie Canals." Typescript. Rome, N.Y.

——. *The Godfrey Letters*. Syracuse, N.Y.: The Canal Society of New York State, 1973.

Gove, William G. "Burlington, the Former Lumber Capital." *The Northern Logger*, vol. XIX, no. 11, 1971.

Hall, Basil. *Travels in North America in the years 1827 and 1828*. London: Simpkin and Marshall, 1830.

Hall, Francis. *Travels in Canada and the United States, 1816-17*. London: Longman, Hurst, Rees . . ., 1818.

Hamilton, Edward P. *Fort Ticonderoga, Key to a Continent*. Boston: Little Brown, 1964.

——. "The French Colonial Forts at Crown Point Strait." *The Bulletin of the Fort Ticonderoga Museum*, vol. XII, no. 6, 1970.

Haviland, William A. "Archaeological Sites of the Champlain Valley." *Lake Champlain Basin Studies*, no. 8. Department of Resource Economics, University of Vermont, 1970.

——. "Man Hunted in Vermont in 6000 B.C." *Vermont Life*, vol. XXIV, no. 2, 1969.

——. *Vermont Indians and Prehistory for Schools: A Selected Annotated List of Sources for Teachers*. Montpelier, Vt.: Vermont Historical Society, 1975.

Heinrichs, Waldo H. "The Battle of Plattsburg, 1814: the Losers." *American Neptune*, January, 1961.

Hemenway, Abby Maria. *Vermont Historical Gazetteer*. Vol. I (Addison, Burlington, Charlotte, Colchester, Ferrisburgh, Milton, Shelburne, Shoreham, Panton, Vergennes). Vol. II (Alburg, Georgia, Grand Isle, Highgate, Grand Isle, Isle La Motte, North Hero, St. Albans). Vol. IV (Swanton). Burlington, Vt., 1868.

Hill, Henry Wayland. *The Champlain Tercentenary; Report of the Champlain Tercentenary Commission*. Albany: J.B. Lyon Co., 1911.

Hill, Ralph Nading. "Champlain Ferries." *Vermont Life*, vol. XVI, no. 4, 1962.

——. *Sidewheeler Saga*. New York: Rinehart and Co., 1953.

——. *The Story of the Ticonderoga*. Shelburne, Vt.: The Shelburne Museum, 1957.

——. *Yankee Kingdom: Vermont and New Hampshire*. New York: Harper and Brothers, 1960.

Hubbard, Timothy William. "Battle at Valcour Island: Benedict Arnold as a Hero." *American Heritage*, vol. XVII, no. 6, 1966.

Huden, John C. *Archaeology in Vermont; some reviews supplemented by materials from New England and New York*. Rutland, Vt.: Charles E. Tuttle Co., 1971.

——. "Indian Legacy." *Vermont Life*, vol. XIII, no. 4, 1959.

——. *Some Early Maps depicting the Lake Champlain Area, 1542-1792*. Burlington, Vt., 1959.

"Investigation into the wreck of the *Champlain* (1875)." Champlain Transportation Co. records. Special Collections, Bailey Library, University of Vermont.

Jellison, Charles A. *Ethan Allen: Frontier Rebel*. Syracuse, N.Y.: Syracuse University Press, 1969.

Kalm, Peter. *Travels in North America*. (2 vols.) London: Wilson-Erickson, 1937.

Kenton, Edith. *Black Gown and Redskins.* London and New York: Longmans, Green, 1956.

"Lake Champlain: 350 years." *Vermont Life,* vol. XIII, no. 4, 1959.

Lamb, Wallace E. *The Lake Champlain and Lake George Valleys.* (Vol. I) New York: The American Historical Co., 1940.

Lape, Jane. *Ticonderoga: Patches and Patterns from Its Past.* Ticonderoga, N.Y.: Ticonderoga Historical Society, 1969.

Lathrop, Gideon. "Diary." *The Bulletin,* Columbia County Historical Society(Kinderhook, N.Y.), no. 52, 1941.

Macdonough, Rodney. *Life of Commodore Macdonough.* Boston: Fort Hill Press, 1909.

Mahan, A.T. "Commodore Macdonough at Plattsburgh." *The North American Review,* 1914.

——. *The Major Operations of the Navies in the War of American Independence.* London: Simpson, Low, Marston & Co., 1913.

Muller, H.N., III. "The Commercial History of the Champlain-Richelieu River Route, 1760-1815." Unpublished Ph.D. thesis. University of Rochester, 1968.

Murray, Eleanor. "The Burgoyne Campaign." *The Bulletin of the Fort Ticonderoga Museum,* vol. VIII, no. 1, 1948.

Nickerson, Hoffman. *The Turning Point of the Revolution.* Boston: Houghton Mifflin Co., 1928.

O'Callaghan, E.B. *The Documentary History of the State of New York* ... Albany: Weed, Parsons, 1850-51.

Palmer, Peter S. *History of Lake Champlain.* Albany, N.Y.: J. Munsell, 1866.

Parkman, Francis. *France and England in North America.* Boston: Little Brown and Co., 1883.

Pell, John H.G. *Ethan Allen.* Boston and New York: Houghton Mifflin Co., 1929.

——. "French Village at Fort St. Frederic, Fact or Fallacy." *The Bulletin of the Fort Ticonderoga Museum,* vol. XII, no. 1, 1966.

Pell, Stephen H.P. "Fort Ticonderoga: Its Salvation, Preservation and Restoration." *The Bulletin of the Fort Ticonderoga Museum,* vol. VII, no. 1, 1945.

——. *Fort Ticonderoga, A Short History.* The Fort Ticonderoga Museum, 1968.

Perkins, George Henry. "Aboriginal Remains in the Champlain Valley." *American Anthropologist,* 1909-1912.

——. Archaeological papers relating to Vermont. In the *Proceedings of the American Association for the Advancement of Science,* and other journals. Special Collections, Bailey Library, University of Vermont.

"*Philadelphia:* The Continental Gondola Raised from the Depths after 158 years." Special edition, the *Burlington Daily News,* 1935.

Power, Tyrone. *Impressions of America During the Years 1833, 1834, and 1835.* (2 vols.) London: Richard Bentley, 1836.

Ritchie, William A. *The Archaeology of New York State.* Natural History Press, 1965.

——. and Don W. Dragoo. *The Eastern Dispersal of Adena.* New York State Museum and Science Service (Albany), bulletin no. 379, 1960.

Rogers, Robert. *Journals of Robert Rogers* ... Albany: Joel Munsell's Sons, 1883.

Roosevelt, Theodore. *The Naval War of 1812* ... New York and London: G.P. Putnam's Sons, 1903.

Ross, Ogden J. *The Steamboats of Lake Champlain, 1809-1930.* Albany: Press of the Delaware and Hudson Railroad, 1930.

Royce, Caroline H. *Bessboro.* Westport, N.Y., 1902.

Sergeant, Frederic O. and Gilbert, Alphonse H., and Gratton, Yvonne. "Archaeological Sites of the Champlain Valley." In "Lake Champlain Basin Studies." Typescript. Burlington, Vt, 1972.

Shaughnessy, Jim. *The Rutland Road.* Berkeley, Cal.: Howell-North Books, 1964.

Silliman, Benjamin. *Remarks made on a short tour between Hartford and Quebec in 1819.* New Haven: S. Converse, 1820.

Taylor, D.T. "The Shores of Champlain: Fort Blunder." Newspaper series. In G.M. Miller scrapbook. Special Collections, Bailey Library, University of Vermont.

"Twin Stamps for the U.S. Bicentennial." *Canada Weekly*, Department of External Affairs, vol. IX, no. 20, 1976.

Wallace, Willard M. *Traitorous Hero; the Life and Fortunes of Benedict Arnold*. New York: Harper and Brothers, 1954.

Warner, C.B. and C. Eleanor Hall. *History of Port Henry, N.Y.* Rutland, Vt.: Tuttle Co., 1931.

Watson, Winslow C. *Pioneer History of the Champlain Valley* . . . Albany, N.Y.: J. Munsell, 1863.

———. *The Military and Naval History of the County of Essex, New York*. Albany, N.Y.: J. Munsell, 1869.

Weld, Isaac. *Travels in North America*. London: John Stockdall, 1799.

Wilbur, James B. *Ira Allen, Founder of Vermont*. (2 vols.) Cambridge: The Riverside Press, 1928.

Index